Praise for *Virtual U*

"Surreally funny . . . Mr. Seife is an adept consolidator of information, and he has a choosy shopper's knack for selecting fresh anecdotes and examples." —Dwight Garner, *The New York Times Daily Book Review*

"Persuasive and thus disconcerting and frightening . . . Mr. Seife . . . is a meticulous writer, and he quickly won me over—unfortunately."
—Howard Schneider, *The Wall Street Journal*

"A cogent, balanced, quietly impassioned call for Internet skepticism."
—*Nature*

"Informed, nimble, endlessly quotable, and timely . . . An indispensable guide to almost everything sinister about the Internet."
—*The Christian Science Monitor*

"An ingenious overview of a wildly unreliable Internet."
—*Kirkus Reviews* (starred review)

"Seife demonstrates how easy it is for fallacies to become accepted truths online. But rather than writing a Luddite screed, he aims to 'act as a guide for the skeptic, a handbook for those who wish to understand how digital information is affecting us.'" —*Scientific American*

"Intense and incisive, Seife's exposé of potent tricks on the mesmerizing, overpowering Internet makes us very wary about anything that cannot be verified with our own eyes." —*Publishers Weekly*

"Author Charles Seife spots the falsehoods and fakes that make their way onto the information superhighway."
—*Science Friday*, PRI (NPR)

ABOUT THE AUTHOR

Charles Seife is the author of five previous books, including *Proofiness* and *Zero*, which won the PEN/Martha Albrand Award for first nonfiction and was a *New York Times* notable book. He has written for a wide variety of publications including the *New York Times*, *Wired*, *New Scientist*, *Science*, *Scientific American*, and *The Economist*. He is a professor of journalism at NYU and lives in New York City.

VIRTUAL UNREALITY

The New Era of Digital Deception

CHARLES SEIFE

PENGUIN BOOKS

PENGUIN BOOKS
An imprint of Penguin Random House LLC
375 Hudson Street
New York, New York 10014
penguin.com

First published in the United States of America by Viking Penguin,
an imprint of Penguin Random House LLC, 2014
Published in Penguin Books 2015

THE LIBRARY OF CONGRESS HAS CATALOGED THE
HARDCOVER EDITION AS FOLLOWS:
Seife, Charles.
Virtual unreality : just because the Internet told you, how do you know it's true? /
Charles Seife.
pages cm
Includes bibliographical references and index.
ISBN 978-0-670-02608-1 (hc.)
ISBN 978-0-14-312767-3 (pbk.)
1. Computer network resources—Evaluation.   2. Internet—Safety measures.
3. Internet fraud—Prevention.   4. Internet literacy.   5. Electronic information
resource literacy.   I. Title.
ZA4201.S44 2014
025.04—dc23
2013047849

Printed in the United States of America
10 9 8 7 6 5 4 3 2 1

Set in Minion Pro with Print
Designed by Daniel Lagin

CONTENTS

INTRODUCTION:
VIRTUAL UNREALITY

> The new environment shaped by electric technology is a can-
> nibalistic one that eats people. To survive one must study the
> habits of cannibals.
>
> —MARSHALL MCLUHAN

On October 5, 2001, the world learned what evil can lurk in the heart of a Muppet.

He was first spotted in Bangladesh, in Dhaka, at an anti-American rally. He was in the background, almost hidden from view, but there was no question: it was his unmistakable visage, jaundiced and unibrowed, glowering angrily over the right shoulder of enemy number one. The next sighting was in Djakarta, Indonesia. Again, he was hard to pick out at first—cameramen from Reuters and the Associated Press didn't even notice him in their photographs for a few days—but there he was, directly behind the figure of Osama bin Laden. It was Bert, pointy-headed resident of Sesame Street, roommate of Ernie, pigeon fancier—and apparently right-hand man to the most important and most violent terrorist of modern times.

The image was everywhere. Furious mobs, chanting and shouting, bore the photograph of bin Laden and his fuzzy yellow henchman on posters and placards. "Do the global terror links reach even as far as Sesame Street? Is Bert the Muppet a henchman of terrorist mastermind Usama bin Laden?" asked an astonished reporter for Fox News. The evidence was solid; several different photographers had taken pictures clearly showing Bert alongside Osama. Claims of a hoax were quickly dismissed by the news agencies responsible for the snapshots. "This is a legitimate photograph," Reuters spokeswoman Felicia Cosby insisted, brushing off any insinuations that the photos might have been doctored. So did Jack Stokes of the Associated Press. "We haven't changed the photo at all," he said. "We have very strict editing guidelines."

Bert's corporate masters were furious about Bert's appearance at pro–Al Qaeda rallies. "Sesame Street has always stood for mutual respect and understanding. We're outraged that our characters would be used in this unfortunate and distasteful manner. This is not humorous," Sesame Workshop producers told a CNN reporter. "The people responsible for this should be ashamed of themselves."*

The man most responsible, Dino Ignacio, wasn't ashamed. He was terrified.

Since the late 1990s, Ignacio, a California-based artist, had run Bert Is Evil, a mildly amusing surrealist website of the kind that proliferated in the early years of the internet.† The site portrayed the ill-tempered Muppet as a malevolent Forrest Gump, quietly present in the background at darker moments in human history. Ignacio digitally altered photographs to create a photographic record of his evil influence, such as a black-and-white shot of the Muppet sitting casually beside Adolf Hitler; a fuzzy Zapruder still where, barely visible, he

----

* That's right. Participants at a violent mob rally celebrating the September 11 attacks and lionizing the mastermind behind them ought to be ashamed . . . of misappropriating the image of a puppet.

† Witness, for example, such websites as "Mr. T Ate My Balls," "Hampster Dance," and "Mahir." Nowadays, they seem as funny as a punch to the solar plexus, but back in the day, they were comedy gold.

lurks in the crowd; mugging for the camera along with O. J. Simpson. As Bert Is Evil grew a small cult following, fans created reams more photographic evidence. Bert squatting next to Pol Pot, Bert handing out Kool-Aid at Jonestown, Bert with Slobodan Milosevic, Bert with Joseph Stalin, with Saddam Hussein, with Robert Mugabe, with Ayatollah Khomeini.

And with Osama bin Laden. In the photo, Bert wears a ribbed white turtleneck and a windbreaker, and stares at the camera from a place of pride directly behind Osama bin Laden. Brows knitted, he grins evilly. The Muppet is clearly in his element.

Then September 11 happened. Bin Laden and Al Qaeda became symbols of resistance to the United States. Anti-American protesters around the world displayed his face on placards. And when a Bangladeshi print shop sought bin Laden photos for their (suddenly very profitable) protest-placard business, they found the one with Bert. Apparently, nobody seemed to think it odd that the terrorist mastermind had a Muppet henchman, so they slapped it on their latest placard design. From there, it was only a matter of hours before the photo was everywhere, in the hands of angry demonstrators seeking to glorify the name of Osama bin Laden.

The news shot round the world in an instant. Bert really was in the company of terrorists. It was as if Ignacio's imagination had suddenly transformed itself from fantasy to reality. Bert really was now the most evil puppet on the face of the planet. "Yesterday a lot of you alerted me to a picture of a Taliban propaganda poster with Bert," Ignacio wrote on his website shortly after finding out about the poster. "Reality is imitating the Web! I am honestly freaked out! Holy shit!" He took the site down immediately. "I am doing this because I feel this has gotten too close to reality and I choose to be responsible enough to stop it right here."

Of course, he couldn't. Nobody could. The photograph had gone global, and no power on earth could possibly remove it from circulation, unpublishing what had been published. And this was part of what spooked Ignacio. It was a queasy feeling that he had subtly altered the fabric of reality. There it was in the newspapers: Bert, grinning, his portrait carried by a crowd vowing to destroy America. It started off as a joke, a whimsical idea—and somehow pure thought had crystallized and become real.

Digital information is different.

The switch to digital information is a revolution as important as the advent of the printing press. On one level, there's no difference in content between a printed book and an e-book, a handwritten sheet of paper and a scanned PDF, an old photograph and a digital image, an old celluloid copy of *Casablanca* and one on DVD. The information contained in those different media assaults our senses in roughly the same way; if done well, the digital is all but indistinguishable from the analog. But there's still a difference.

Digital information is a break from everything we've known before because it has a combination of physical properties shared by no other form of information. It can move around the world at the speed of light. It can be stored in virtually no space at all without fear of decay or degradation. It can be copied with perfect fidelity at almost no cost. All media, be it print, visual, audio, or something else, can be processed by a computer sophisticated enough and can be stored in essentially identical devices. At first glance, these properties might not seem that important, much less revolutionary. But by looking at the field of epidemiology, we can see that these very properties make digital information a superbug of the mind, something that spreads unbelievably rapidly, infects all corners of society, and becomes all but impossible to control. When we learned to turn all of our information into bits and bytes, we unleashed an entirely new creature upon the world, one whose powers—and dangers—we only dimly understand. The digital medium is changing the way we interact with the world.

In some ways, it is akin to the birth of genetic engineering. In the past three decades, we've designed tools that allow us to remove, insert, and delete bits of code from the genomes of living organisms. By exploiting some of the peculiar and seemingly contradictory properties of DNA and RNA—such as their ability to replicate over and over nearly error free while, at the same time, being extremely susceptible to errors inserted by lab technicians—we've learned to alter our very biology. For better or for worse, we've become genetic engineers.

In roughly the same period in which we began altering the genome, we learned how to insert bits and pieces into our reality and delete them as well. We've created new tools that allow us to exploit some peculiar and seemingly contradictory properties of information; we've learned to alter our very perception of truth. We have become reality engineers.

It used to take the entire resources of a totalitarian state—one that controlled the media, one that had absolute control of the information consumed by its citizens—to construct an alternate reality for its populace. Now, thanks to the new tools at our disposal, a single person can do it on a small scale. Big organizations are learning how to do it in a deliberate and systematic way. The digital revolution has dramatically changed not just how we gather information about the world but also how we can tamper with the information that others are gathering.

What's more, digital information is changing our perception of identity and reshaping our society. We're altering our behavior toward one another because of the influence of the online world—we humans are deeply social animals, and the online world is reshaping how we make and maintain social bonds. In so doing, it's altering the way we interact with one another, changing the nature of public discourse, and driving us to ever more extreme beliefs.

The parallel with biology is deeper than it might seem at first. Just as organisms are engaged in a constant genetic struggle, attempting to defeat one another in the battleground of natural selection, so too is there a silent war in the realm of information. Underneath the headlines, imperceptible until you know where to look, there's an ever-escalating evolutionary arms race, waged by robots and corporations as well as by humans. There are feints and thrusts, attacks and counterattacks, as different parties vie for supremacy. Media outlets are rising and falling based upon how well they adapt to the ever-changing digital landscape. And it is all a war over who gets the ability to affect your reality, to shape your social interactions, to manipulate your beliefs and control your behavior.

It's a frightening picture, to be sure, but don't think that this book is a Luddite screed about the evils of the internet. Far from it. Gone are the days of scanning periodical indices so that you can figure out which scratched-up microfilm might contain a scrap of useful information. Gone are the days of trying to figure out where someone lives by using a pile of white-pages directories. Anyone who cares about knowledge and information on a small scale—not to mention someone who needs to use a database to sort through hundreds of thousands of pieces of data—knows that the digital revolution is a wonderful thing. It has banished a zillion tedious tasks from our lives and made possible countless things that could never have been contemplated before. We were once confined to our village, and then to our telephone network. We are now interconnected so that each of us has the ability to communicate with billions of other people on the planet—the world has become a very small place. Digital devices are becoming a part of our sensorium, shoveling information into our brains and, in its way, becoming as indispensible to us as our eyes and ears. Digital information is a superlatively powerful tool.

But because of that power, you must try to understand not just how digital information can be used, but how it can be misused. And once you learn to see the signs, you can see how (and why) people are using the properties of digital information to try to alter your perception of reality. Just as important, you can figure out how to see through digital manipulations and thus how to counter them.

That's the point of this book—not to rail against the internet, but to act as a guide for the skeptic, a handbook for those who wish to understand how digital information is affecting us. For many of the things we perceive—or don't perceive—are altered by the digital medium through which we all now interact with the world.

We now live in a world where the real and the virtual can no longer be completely disentangled. At times, there is little distinction between what is real and what is unreal. This is virtual unreality, and, as Dino Ignacio knows, the results can be very uncomfortable.

Even though Ignacio took down his website as soon as he found out about the protest in Bangladesh, he was unable to stop the association of Bert the Muppet with Osama the terrorist. A faked photo had linked the two in a way that could not be undone. Not even death would sever the relationship.

On May 2, 2011, nearly a decade after Ignacio deleted his website, two specially modified Black Hawk helicopters flew low over the Pakistani countryside. The Navy SEAL team inside made their last-minute preparations for the raid. In case their radio traffic was being monitored, the team had assigned code names to everybody who might be in the compound.

As the SEALs forced their way into the house, the target popped his head out of the bedroom and then quickly retreated, slamming the door behind him. The team had found their prey. It was the United States' public enemy number one. It was Osama bin Laden.

Like everyone else in the compound, bin Laden had been assigned a code name. To SEAL Team Six, their target was "Bert." Two shots rang out. One to the chest and one to the skull.

Bert was dead.

CHAPTER 1
CATCHING THE
STUPID BUG

A lie will go round the world while truth is pulling its boots on.

—CHARLES SPURGEON

I n terms of sheer gruesomeness, it's hard to beat the disease now known as "Corrupted Blood."

When the syndrome takes hold, a victim periodically spews blood from every pore, creating a fine mist. Quite naturally, anyone caught nearby is likely to be covered—and infected, making Corrupted Blood a hugely contagious disease. And exquisitely deadly, as scientists discovered in late 2005.

Within a few short hours of the first case of the disease, the plague was already spreading out of control. Despite every effort to quarantine the region of the outbreak, the contagion moved quickly into populated areas, "turning the capital cities into death traps," according to epidemiologists Nina Fefferman and Eric Lofgren. On YouTube, you can find dozens of videos of the early part of the pandemic, when the chaos began. The scenes are all the same: people run willy-nilly, unsure of how to react. Then panic sets in. The mob rushes in all directions, trying to get away from the infected. Soon the air is filled with gut-wrenching "squick" sounds of victims spurting blood, punctuated only by the screams of the dying.

Within a few hours of the initial outbreak, even major cities like Ironforge and Orgrimmar were uninhabitable. Dead bodies lay everywhere, unburied and unmourned. And the entire world was in peril.

There was a solution, but it was drastic: complete annihilation. In other words, reboot. Humans, dwarves, orcs—all the characters in the *World of Warcraft* universe—popped briefly out of existence as engineers worked to rid the system of the plague that had ruined their artificial cosmos.

Corrupted Blood was a virtual disease in a fantasy world; it was not a physical organism, but a collection of bits and bytes that resided on computers. However, when the *World of Warcraft* programmers introduced it—intending it to be a challenge to high-level players fighting in a particular dungeon—it escaped. The digital plague behaved so much like a real disease that epidemiologists like Fefferman and Lofgren used it as a model for how a real-life pathogen spreads through a population. At the same time, the Corrupted Blood plague can be used to demonstrate exactly the reverse: the spread of bits and bytes—information—through a population is very much like a disease outbreak.

Yet there are some very important differences between a real, physical disease and a virtual, digital idea. It is these differences that make digital information so much more powerful than anything we've ever encountered before. For the special properties of the internet turn digital information into the most virulent, most contagious pathogen that humanity has ever encountered.

In a very real sense, a biological disease is information warfare. It's an attempt to co-opt the information at the core of our existence and turn our own cells against us.

A virus really is nothing more than information—a message encoded in DNA or RNA—stuffed into an envelope made of proteins. It's not really alive; it doesn't eat, it doesn't breathe, it doesn't reproduce on its own. If left alone, it will sit, inert, indefinitely. But when it encounters a living cell, like the ones in our bodies, the virus recognizes that it has an opportunity to reproduce, to produce more of its kind. So it springs into action, and the battle begins.

The first step is to find a target, a vulnerable cell, and stick to it. When a virus attaches to, say, a white blood cell, the virus's envelope breaks open and injects the viral information into the cell's protoplasm. From there, the information—a set of instructions encoded in a long chain of chemicals—works its way to the cell's information-processing centers.

Our cells really are, fundamentally, information-processing machines: they read out the instructions, the genetic code, written in our DNA and take actions based upon that code, building proteins, turning chemical switches on or off, or even making changes to the cell's instruction set. When viral information enters the cell, it takes over the information-processing machinery. Instead of manufacturing proteins and other compounds that the cell needs to function properly, the cell begins to synthesize proteins that make up the viral envelope—and to make copy after copy after copy of the viral instructions that have hijacked the cell's machinery. The cell is no longer functioning as it should, processing and obeying the genetic code passed down from generation to generation of humans; it has become a slave to the viral information. Depending on the virus's nature, the end can take different forms. Often the cell simply disintegrates, falling apart into fragments, which, full of viral instructions, assemble themselves into new viruses. The cell becomes the birth mother of a whole new generation of viruses, each primed to take over a new host with its only weapon: information.

No matter whether a disease is caused by a virus, a bacterium, or a parasite, the illness is caused by information warfare taking place in our bodies. This is true even of cancer: a cancer cell is, fundamentally, a cell that's learned to ignore certain instructions that are designed to limit its spread throughout the body. Freed from such constraints, it attempts to replicate itself and spread its information as widely as possible, completely oblivious to the fact that if it's successful, it will kill the organism in which it resides.

Epidemiologists have a standard measure for how contagious a disease is: a number known as R_0, the basic reproductive number of the disease. In an ideal situation, R_0 represents how many people, on average, get infected by a single person who comes down with the disease. That is, imagine that a disease has an R_0 of 2. This means that if one person catches the bug, he'll infect two people. Each of these two people will infect two more—a total of four new infections. Each of the four patients infects two more, causing eight new cases. And so forth. Naturally, the higher the R_0 is, the faster the disease will spread through a population.

There are three big factors that affect R_0: transmissibility, persistence, and interconnectedness. Transmissibility is a measure of how easy it is for a disease to jump from person to person. A high transmissibility means that the disease will spread easily (think influenza), whereas a low transmissibility means that it's relatively difficult for the virus or bacterium to infect a new host (as with HIV or tuberculosis). Persistence tells you how long a person carrying the disease is infectious; with the flu, a person will stop spreading the disease after a few days, while with HIV or tuberculosis, the person can be a source of new infections for years and years. The more persistent the disease, the more new cases a given patient is likely to cause. Finally, interconnectedness tells you how many people a patient is likely to come into contact with in such a way that it spreads the disease. This depends a bit on the nature of the disease, but also on the patient's social habits—and the structure of his society. In a highly social setting, patients are more likely to come into contact with lots of people in a short amount of time and spread the disease more widely.

Every time a whooping-cough patient coughs, for example, he spews bacteria into the air around him—bacteria that's extremely well adapted for invading our bodies. It's an extremely contagious disease. It's also infectious for a relatively long time—for several weeks after the bacterium first takes hold; it resides in the body, safe from our immune defenses, happily spreading its information into the world unhindered. And whooping cough is infectious even at the very beginning of the ailment, when the symptoms are relatively mild, so the patient will be able to walk around and spread the disease in the community before he even realizes he's come down with a serious disease. Thus, whooping cough has high transmissibility, high persistence, and a relatively high contact rate in a postindustrial society. Scientists estimate that it has an R_0 of 12 or more; that is, in an unvaccinated population, every case of whooping cough will lead to twelve new cases. And those twelve lead to 144. And those 144 lead to 1,728, and so forth and so forth. Very rapidly, even a single case of whooping cough can lead to a major outbreak.

Corrupted Blood made whooping cough look benign. Lofgren and Fefferman estimated that its R_0 was in the hundreds—per hour. It was spread every time a character came into contact with an infected character's blood. Since the disease made blood ooze out of a character's every pore, it was likely that every avatar near an infected player would catch the disease as well. The transmissibility was incredibly high just from that alone. Even more interesting: the disease would rapidly kill its weaker victims, which would ordinarily limit the persistence of the disease. (After all, it's harder for a dead person to spread an ailment.) However, there were a number of "reservoirs" where the disease would hide, waiting for the opportunity to infect new victims.

Players in *World of Warcraft* could have pets. Pets could get sick, too—and they wound up being a major reservoir of the disease. Even when a character had recovered from the disease, he would reunite with his sick pet and get reinfected, starting the ailment over again. Worse yet, there were extremely powerful "non-player characters" like shopkeepers and blacksmiths who also got sick but wouldn't be killed by the virus. Like virtual versions of Typhoid Mary, they would harbor the disease and pass it on to other characters. There was no digital antibiotic or other cure that could clean out the reservoirs, so there the disease remained, waiting for fresh victims. Thus, its persistence was incredibly high, too.

But what put Corrupted Blood over the top was the third factor: interconnectedness. In the digital universe of *World of Warcraft,* interconnectedness went far beyond anything that could be realized in real life. Characters had the ability to teleport from city to city in an instant, spreading the disease far more quickly and widely than a real flesh-and-blood human ever could. In a virtual world, a character could be anywhere and everywhere in the blink of an eye, and with him came the disease. As a consequence, Corrupted Blood was unstoppable in a way no earthly disease could be. As Lofgren and Fefferman wrote:

> In an effort to control the outbreak, Blizzard Entertainment employees imposed quarantine measures, isolating infected players from as-yet uninfected areas. These strategies failed because of the highly contagious nature of the disease, an inability to seal off a section of the game world effectively, and more than likely player resistance to the notion. The game's developers did, however, have an option that remains unavailable to public-health officials: resetting the computers. When the servers ravaged by the epidemic were reset and the effect removed, the outbreak came to a halt.

The disease was so powerful that the gods had to intervene, reset the world, and start anew.

Computer diseases, like physical diseases, are at heart a competition around the spread of information; the invading organism attempts to get its own bits and bytes copied and spread around, even as the host attempts to stop the invasion.

Even though Corrupted Blood was merely a flow of information in a virtual universe, Lofgren and Fefferman were able to pick out some interesting consequences of ultra-high-transmissibility diseases—and one could easily imagine that if there happened to be a super-infectious outbreak of a real disease, the same consequences would apply in real life. For example, they noted that the outbreak was made worse by people who came to the aid of the first victims of the disease. *World of Warcraft* characters that were able to heal others quickly swarmed into the cities, only to catch the disease themselves and help it to spread. Just as bad, their healing powers kept infected characters alive longer, allowing them to spread the disease more effectively. When a disease with huge transmissibility and long persistence strikes a society with huge interconnectedness, the traditional ways of stopping the spread might be worse than useless—they might do more harm than good.

In other words, once your transmissibility, interconnectedness, and persistence increase beyond a certain point, the old rules break down.

Transmissibility, persistence, and connectedness govern how diseases spread in a population. They also dictate how information flows in a society. The great revolutions in the way humans have learned to communicate all are, fundamentally, discoveries that have changed the nature of these three properties.

Humans have been around for hundreds of thousands of years; primitive societies have been around for at least several tens of thousands. Yet we have very little insight into what these societies were like or what those early citizens believed. All we have are fragments: a shard of pottery, a well-worn tool, an unmarked grave, a rustic figurine. All else is lost to time; the memories and thoughts of those primordial peoples are entirely gone, except for perhaps a few ghostly whispers that echo in our earliest myths and in the ancient roots of our languages.

Over countless generations, human civilization advanced. We mastered fire. We learned to tame animals and till the soil. We created art and crafted religions. We extracted gold and other precious materials from the bowels of the earth and learned to smelt copper. And all of this happened in the dark, amorphous ages of early humanity. Then, five millennia ago, a new invention first blazed, lighting our way out of the undifferentiated murk of ancient time. The written word.

In prehistoric times, humans could certainly communicate with one another, transmitting information. We would speak, shout, gesture. We could remember what we had been told and what we had seen and tell it to our friends and family. But this communication method was inherently limited.

The information had to be communicated from person to person. This meant that the information wasn't very transmissible; one person could spread the news to only a handful of people at a time. And this meant that it could travel only as far and as fast as people could travel. Interconnectedness was low.

More important, the medium in which that information was stored was the human brain, which meant that the information was stored and recalled imperfectly, with a chance of losing fidelity each time it was used or transmitted. Information passed on in this way is likely to be distorted and then even lost entirely after just a few retellings. Even though information can be kept relatively pristine for decades or even generations, especially through the use of trained storytellers or griots, most information has no hope of surviving intact as century after century slips by. Persistence was low; the information was as perishable and fallible as the brains it was stored in. And this is why we have so little information from the earliest civilizations.

Then, five thousand years ago or so, we humans figured out how to preserve information by setting it down in an external, physical form that could survive long after the demise of the flesh from whence it sprang. Our ideas finally began to transcend time. The printed word (or the chiseled one)—in clay, in stone, upon papyrus—made our thoughts persistent enough to survive hundreds or even thousands of years. The birth of the written word was, quite literally, the dawn of history.

From an epidemiologist's point of view, the great revolution of writing was fundamentally one of persistence. It improved transmissibility somewhat: an inscription on a monument or a scroll in a library could reach more people than a single orator could—though this was tempered by the fact that it took much longer to inscribe a copy by longhand than it did for a speaker to relay the same information. And the interconnectedness was mostly unchanged; the information could spread only as far and as fast as people could carry the word abroad. But the newfound *persistence* of written language transformed civilization.

The persistence afforded by writing was amazing; we can read inscriptions about monarchs and temples and property transactions that would have been forgotten four millennia ago but for the fact that someone thought to set the information down in writing. However, that persistence is flawed. It's dependent not only on the creation of a written record, but also the physical survival of that record despite the weathering of centuries. Ancient books are littered with references to volumes that have submerged back under the sea of time, never again to resurface. All we have left are cryptic references. In the book of Joshua, for example, the description of the famous battle at Jericho says that "the sun stood still, and the moon stayed, until the people had avenged themselves upon their enemies. Is not this written in the book of Jasher?" We know little about what the Book of Jasher was, or what it contained—but there are not one but two references to it in the Bible. (The second reference, in 2 Samuel, involves the Israelite army's learning to use the bow in warfare.) So, too, have we lost the Book of the Wars of the Lord, the Book of the Chronicles of the Kings of Israel, the Book of the Chronicles of the Kings of Judah, and many more.

Most of the knowledge accumulated in the ancient world is gone for good, because even relatively permanent media can be destroyed. A fire can destroy papyrus; a conqueror can smash stone and clay. A document's survival depends not only upon the medium it's written on, but also upon how widely disseminated it has become—the more copies there are, the harder it is to lose that document for eternity. Unfortunately, writing was labor-intensive and expensive. Copying had to be done by hand, and thus copies of even the most popular works of ancient times were incredibly rare by today's standards. A single catastrophic event, like the destruction of the Library of Alexandria, could (and did) extirpate large sections of our collective memory.

When a book was important enough for scribes to make large numbers of copies, the very fact that it had to be copied by hand threatened the information the book contained, because the act of copying would create disparate versions of the original. If we're lucky enough to have several copies of an ancient manuscript, it's the norm for these copies to differ, often in significant ways. Copyists would make errors or, even worse, edit the work, inserting or deleting elements of the text if the whim struck them. Even in the best-case scenario—when there's a deep prohibition against altering the text or introducing errors—mistakes creep in. With the Torah, for example, copyists are enjoined to copy not just every letter but every character faithfully; failing to do so, even in the slightest respect, renders the scroll unusable. Yet even so, you can see errors that have crept in over the years: enlarged or shrunken characters, backward and upside-down letters, even a "broken" version of a vowel. These anomalies, likely introduced initially by scribes' errors, are now copied faithfully—any Torah must contain these now deliberate mistakes in order to be considered kosher. The very act of copying the manuscript degraded the information it contained at the very same time that it enhanced its persistence.

So things stood until the invention of the printing press. In the West, the age of print began in the fifteenth century, with Johannes Gutenberg.* By putting interchangeable, easily fabricated metal letters into a frame, Gutenberg was able to churn out huge numbers of nearly error-free copies of the same manuscript cheaply and quickly. Not only did this increase persistence by virtue of the existence of many, many more copies of important works than ever before; it also revolutionized transmissibility.

Back when information had to be copied by hand, a single storyteller could reach thousands of people in the time it took to write out just a single copy of a manuscript longhand. Even though the written copy was hardier—and it could survive for much longer than a

---

* In Asia, printing, including printing with movable type, was invented centuries earlier.

storyteller would—mere writing didn't herald a dramatic change in how easy it was for ideas to spread from person to person. It was still a slow and difficult process, limited by the small number of copies of the information. But after the invention of the printing press, it became possible to print hundreds or thousands of copies of a document, which meant that transmitting information had become as easy as handing out one copy of a mass-produced pamphlet. Information, even complex information that takes pages and pages to set down, could spread more quickly, more easily, and more widely than ever before. Our voices had suddenly become amplified. The information had become much more transmissible.

Nevertheless, the spread of that information was limited by the time it took to physically transport a book or a pamphlet from place to place. The printing press made information easy to spread through a society, but it couldn't change the speed at which that information would travel. It would take weeks and even months for messages to cross the Atlantic from Britain to North America, for example. This is why the Battle of New Orleans was fought after the formal end of the War of 1812—it took more than a month before the warriors on the American continent would discover that the hostilities were supposed to have ended. So, while information was more transmissible, the interconnectedness of people was more or less the same as it was in ancient times. News could spread only as far and as fast as people could carry it on their backs. As a result, there were always people in a society who had zero chance of encountering a new piece of information for days and weeks and months after it had first emerged.

This didn't change for centuries. Information could travel only as fast as post-horse. But in the mid-nineteenth century, the telegraph made it possible to send messages across the world in an instant. It took only seconds for the phrase "What hath God wrought?" to fly from Washington, D.C., to Baltimore, a trip that would have taken hours even by train. With that message, information was liberated. It was no longer shackled to the movements of people. And then, with the invention of wireless, the sender and receiver didn't even have to be connected in any physical manner. Information could simply wing its way through the air at the speed of light, leaving its flesh-bound creators far behind.

This was a revolution in interconnectedness. Parts of the world that were previously isolated from one another, information-wise, had suddenly been brought into direct contact. It used to be that after leaving port and sailing away from the shore, a passenger on a ship was totally cut off from the rest of the world. But by the early twentieth century, even that had ceased to be true, as the infamous Hawley Crippen discovered.

In 1910, Dr. Crippen murdered his wife and, along with his lover, fled England aboard a cruise liner bound for Canada. After setting sail, the captain recognized the fugitives and sent a message via wireless to the mainland: "HAVE STRONG SUSPICION THAT CRIPPEN . . . AND ACCOMPLICE ARE AMONG SALOON PASSENGERS." A Scotland Yard agent boarded a faster ship, beat the doctor to Canada, and slapped the manacles on the murderer before he could set foot in the New World. Even a ship in the middle of the ocean was no longer isolated from the rest of society.

Telegraphy both wired and wireless, telephony, radio, television, satellite communications—all of these inventions allow communication of various kinds at the speed of light, linking us all together more tightly and thoroughly. It is now possible to find out what is happening on the opposite end of the globe with little more effort than it takes to find out what's going on a few miles away. Physical distance has ceased to be a barrier to information.

Even as these inventions increased interconnectedness, in some sense they decreased persistence: a telephone conversation or a radio transmission was, by its very lack of physicality, evanescent. It had to be: information needed to be captured, transformed into something that could be moved around at the speed of light, then transformed again into a form that we could view and understand. The information couldn't be inscribed in a medium as immutable as a stone tablet, because the very act of high-speed transmission required that the information be able to change. It took extra effort (and often new inventions) to take that protean light-speed information and chain it to a fixed medium. It wasn't easy to preserve the information in a television broadcast so that it could be replayed over and over again. But these barriers to fixing broadcast information in a permanent medium could be overcome, however imperfectly, with ticker tape or magnetic tape or fax paper—it was possible to create a lasting physical record of information that had flown across the world in a fraction of a second.*

Then came the internet.

And with it came what may be the ultimate information revolution. Digital information—information stored in bits and bytes—combined all the attributes of the previous revolutions. Digital information is incredibly persistent. Not only does a single copy, stored correctly, last longer than a book; it also costs almost nothing to store data—and the storage takes up almost no space at all. Digital information can be copied with perfect fidelity in a tiny fraction of a second, dwarfing the abilities of even the best printing press. And anywhere there's power and an internet connection, or even a cell-phone signal or a decent view of the sky, it's possible to hook into the internet and access vast stores of digital information in the far corners of the

----

* At first, these storage media were analog. Analog recording is an attempt to store a signal directly in a medium. For example, an LP would store sound waves by inscribing grooves in a disk; the texture of the groove was directly related to the pressure of the air hitting the recording device. Digital media, on the other hand, convert the signal into numbers—which then act as instructions for a machine to reconstruct the signal. If analog recording is like putting a piano sonata on an LP or a cassette tape, digital recording is like storing the sonata on a rolled, punched tape so a player piano can play it back later. There's necessarily some loss in quality due to the conversion, but if you've got a player piano that's sophisticated and versatile enough, its playback can match—and surpass—the quality of the analog recording. (And since the raised-pin instructions that control music-box-like automatic musical instruments go back at least as far as the ninth century, one could argue that digital information was puttering around for more than a thousand years before such devices became practical.)

globe. Persistence, transmissibility, and interconnectedness were all increased dramatically as the whole world came online. From an epidemiological point of view, the R_0 of information had just gone through the roof.

For good and for ill, digital information is now the most contagious thing on the planet.

At its core, your brain is an information-processing machine. It takes information from the outside world through its sense organs, extracts the important stuff, churns on it, and digests it. Then, based upon that new information as well as information it already has stored up, it decides how to behave.

Bad information is a disease that attacks the brain. It messes with your head, making you do things that you shouldn't, causing you to make wrong decisions. Just as a potent virus co-opts your cells' machinery, bad information can co-opt your behavior. It can alter the way you interact with the world and, as a result, it can change the world.

At noon on May 16, 2007, the technology website Engadget posted a scoop about Apple. Thanks to a leaked internal memo, the Engadget crew had gotten wind that there was going to be a several-month delay in the release of the new iPhone. It was bad news for Apple, which had been banking on huge sales from the new device. Within seconds the stock was plunging, and it quickly lost more than 2 percent of its value. Hundreds upon hundreds of people had lost—and others had gained—millions of dollars.

Within a few minutes, an Apple representative called the website with an important piece of information: the memo was a fake. Someone had crafted a fraudulent but convincing-looking internal memo and e-mailed it to various people; by using a spoofed e-mail address, the hoaxer made it look as if the e-mail had come from Apple itself. So what Engadget had considered a reliable source was anything but—it was somebody who had wanted to mess with Apple by spreading bad information.

In less than half an hour, the stock had climbed back almost to its previous value—but not before a lot of money changed hands. A bit of bad information had, in a few minutes, changed people's perception of the value of a company; and almost as quickly, the misperception disappeared. A worthless piece of information, conjured out of thin air and disguised in just the right way, wound up echoing around the world, had a real financial impact on individual portfolios, and affected the fortunes of a major company.

The market has always fluttered at the slightest rumors. What is new about digital information is the volume of information that flies back and forth between so many people so quickly and so effectively and with so little verification of the facts contained within. But the speed at which a rumor takes hold and, consequently, the dramatic effects that bad information can have are almost unthinkable. Witness the "flash crash" of 2010. In less than five minutes, the Dow Jones dropped fully six hundred points as traders around the world sold stocks. One trillion dollars had simply evaporated. The trillion dollars was back fifteen minutes later. And stock traders from Bombay to Kalamazoo were all experiencing the same heart palpitations.*

Digital information has an unbelievably high R_0, and this means that it's hard to stop once it emerges. It spreads from person to person—even those at a great distance—incredibly quickly, thanks to its high transmissibility and the high interconnectedness of digital society. Once it escapes into the wild, it's all but impossible to stop its spread. This is wonderful, so long as the information is correct and useful. But if it's wrong, if it alters our brains for the worse, if it makes us make mistakes and think incorrect things, it's a scourge.

Bad information is a disease that affects all of us—a disease that has become unbelievably potent thanks to the digital revolution. And there's no vaccine.

----

* See chapter 9 for more on the flash crash.

CHAPTER 2
APPEAL TO AUTHORITY

Hierarchy is there for a reason, my friend.

—STEPHEN COLBERT

People who root for the Cyprus-based soccer team AC Omonia Nicosia have a reputation for being a little odd. A few years ago, on the occasion of a match against a well-known Manchester-based team, the *Daily Mirror* casually mentioned one of the many quirks of Omonia's fans (known as "the Zany Ones"): the fans wear hats made out of shoes. It sounds bizarre, but if you went to Wikipedia you'd be able to confirm the story—and find out a whole lot more. The Zany Ones often sing a song about a little potato and traditionally store their season tickets in the oven to keep them safe. In 1995, the most famous player on the team was film star Jean-Claude Van Damme, and the athletic club competes not only in soccer but also in volleyball, basketball, and hitlerball.

Anyone who read the Omonia article carefully would instantly see that it was chock-full of nonsense. (Van Damme playing soccer instead of acting? Hitlerball?) The team's Wikipedia page had been "enhanced" by denizens of a British website called B3ta as part of their running joke of making the media print their in-jokes without realizing it.* And Wikipedia is the perfect tool to help them in their game.

Chances are that you've used Wikipedia; after all, by most measures it's one of the most visited websites in the world (usually hovering around number five or number six). With some four million articles about obscure soccer teams, pop stars, arcane mathematical theories, historical figures, world cultures, and everything in between, Wikipedia has become one of the leading repositories of eclectic knowledge in the English-speaking world. One of its most important features is that it is not written by a select group of experts and editors; it's written by volunteers—ordinary people like you and me who happen to have a computer, an internet connection, and a little spare time on their hands. And sometimes an agenda.

"What we're doing is bringing democracy to knowledge," said Comedy Central's Stephen Colbert in 2006. What's more democratic than giving citizens the ability to alter our collective perception of reality—or, as Colbert dubs it, our "Wikiality." And to show the power of that new democratic ideal, Colbert exhorted his fans to alter Wikipedia to state that the population of African elephants had tripled in just a few months. "Together, we can create a reality that we all agree on—the reality we just agreed on."

It was a silly exercise—one that Wikipedia contributors such as "EvilBrak," "Wiki Wikardo," and "Spockguy" quickly carried out (and whose edits were just as quickly deleted by other contributors)— but the deeper point was valid. The internet is a great democratizer, even when it comes to knowledge. It's not just universally accessible; it's universally changeable—anyone can manipulate it. Yet knowledge is inherently anti-democratic. It's elitist. It's not subject to the will of the majority, much less to the whims of the mob. Facts are no less true

----

* For example, they ran a (successful!) campaign to get a goatse-inspired graphic into a newspaper. If you don't know what goatse is, consider yourself very, very lucky.

if they're unpopular—and it's often the facts that the majority refuse to accept that are the most important.

Yet as we rely more and more upon Wikipedia and other internet outlets for our information, we are forcing knowledge to conform to internet democracy. This process is having a profound effect on our perception of the world.

Unlike traditional encyclopedias, which until recently were written on dead, pulped trees, Wikipedia doesn't come in clearly delineated or labeled editions; it isn't published on a schedule. It's drafted and edited at all hours of the day and night by volunteers around the world. Every single word in Wikipedia is at risk of being changed at any moment.

This property makes Wikipedia the best example of one of the paradoxes of digital information: it's more persistent than any other kind of information, but, at the same time, it's incredibly labile. Even though Wikipedia articles are all but impossible to erase entirely—the traces of long-ago-deleted pages still rattle around through the ether—there's no canonical form, no "final" copy, nothing that gives any one version more authority than another. The information is constantly changing. Indeed, Wikipedia was designed so that it was easy for anyone to make a change, to alter the collective information accumulated in the digital data banks of the Wikiverse. Those changes are instantly broadcast to the entire world, giving any individual the power to affect a tremendous number of people's perception of reality. This is Wikipedia's source of power—and its weakness.

Because of the ease of editing or even creating a Wikipedia page, it's almost trivial to perpetrate a Wikipedia hoax. T. Mills Kelly, a professor of history at George Mason University, teaches his students how to do it. In his course "Lying About the Past," Kelly instructs his students to "make up our own hoaxes and turn them loose on the Internet to see if we can fool anyone." The first time he ran the course, he and his students fabricated the tale of Edward Owens, the "Last American Pirate." Owens, a failed oysterman, ostensibly plundered vessels along the East Coast of the United States in the 1870s, before retiring a few years later. Bolstered by a Wikipedia page and a blog that seemed to provide evidence of Owens's career, the story got a bit of coverage in the press, including at a *USA Today* blog. But Owens never existed. He was created all in the name of fun—and learning. As was a hoax perpetrated by a Dublin University student when Maurice Jarre, the famed composer of film scores, died, in 2009. The student, Shane Fitzgerald, inserted a sappy phrase supposedly uttered by Jarre—"One could say my life itself has been one long soundtrack"—and watched as newspaper after newspaper used the quotation in their obituaries of Jarre. "I am 100 percent convinced that if I hadn't come forward," Fitzgerald told the Associated Press, "that quote would have gone down in history as something Maurice Jarre said, instead of something I made up."

It's quite possible. Though the Owens and Jarre hoaxes were cleared up within weeks, there are plenty of deliberately false Wikipedia entries that have lasted years—and no doubt there are many that have not yet been discovered. As I was writing this book, Wikipedians suspected that a Harvard student—on the occasion of his writing a paper about the limitations of Wikipedia—planted a fake article that stated he had been elected mayor of Yinchuan, in China. Editors at Wikipedia became suspicious after seeing the entry used as an example in a Harvard guide about proper and improper use of sources, so they deleted the article. It had taken more than seven years to find it. In another instance, it took a little less time—five and a half years—to discover that there had never been a small seventeenth-century war between two Indian states known as the Bicholim Conflict.

Sometimes falsehoods are never expunged. By virtue of their having been published on Wikipedia, the falsehoods can alter the truth. Take the case of Mike Trout, an up-and-coming outfielder for the Los Angeles Angels. On June 28, 2012, an anonymous Wikipedia contributor from Massachusetts made a subtle edit to Trout's Wikipedia page, giving the player a nickname: the Millville Meteor. (Trout grew up in Millville, New Jersey.) Nobody noticed that the nickname was totally made up—a joke by goons who hang out on the prankster-frequented website *Something Awful*. Within two weeks the nickname was in the press. "Trout was nicknamed the Millville Meteor, and his meteoric rise continued as he went 2 for 4," read a piece in the July 13 issue of *Newsday*. With that act, the fake nickname became real. When asked about it, Trout reportedly said, "I don't know where they got that," but he apparently now signs baseballs inscribed with the Millville Meteor nickname.

Now Mike Trout's Wikipedia page cites the *Newsday* article as independent, external confirmation of his Meteor moniker. This is a particularly insidious kind of circular proof. Wikipedia uses *Newsday* uses Wikipedia, and a bogus fact has sprung seemingly from nowhere and achieved verified status.

If Wikipedia were an analog, print encyclopedia, it would have been nigh impossible for this to happen. The bogus fact would have a clear origin; editors couldn't alter already printed copies of the book to change the sourcing of a statement. But because Wikipedia is digital, and in constant flux, circular proof happens all the time. People knock out citations and replace them with fresher or more authoritative ones, and it becomes extremely difficult to find the true origin of a particular factoid. So once an external source parrots a dubious Wikipedia fact, a Wikipedia editor can wipe out the initial citation and replace it with one from that source—an independent site—giving the lie extra credibility. And if anyone tried to trace the source of the fact, it would seem to lead back to the gullible journalist or writer who first believed the lie. Like a cuckoo, the Wikipedia prankster deposits his creation and departs, leaving others to help the lie grow— completely ignorant of its true parentage. The mere statement of a phony fact in Wikipedia means that it has the potential to be "confirmed" via circular proof within hours or days.

It's a troubling state of affairs, threatening the whole concept of verifiability. The evanescent yet permanent nature of the digital universe forces someone to ask not only where a fact originated, but when. And those whens are often obscured, or even destroyed, as new pages and new information clobber the old. To its credit, Wikipedia keeps an extensive list of edits to its pages—who did what to the pages and when—but it is difficult to sort through, not very accessible to search engines, and all but useless unless you know exactly what you're searching for. Even worse are other sites that tend not to archive old, outdated pages. Often, the creation of a false fact is lost to time. No doubt Wikipedia is home to scores of dubious statements, their origins buried behind a constant cascade of change and their veracity unchallenged, thanks to "external" sources that are anything but.

Wikipedia doesn't have a monopoly on false information—far from it. Indeed, by some measures, one can argue that Wikipedia is roughly as accurate as its paper-and-ink competitors. A 2005 study in *Nature* compared the accuracy of Wikipedia's science articles with those in *Encyclopaedia Britannica* and found that the venerable *Britannica* fared only slightly better. And, of course, a Wikipedia entry is less likely to be outdated, by virtue of its round-the-clock publishing schedule. But there's a difference between the kind of error one would find in Wikipedia and what one would find in *Britannica* or *Collier's* or even in the now-defunct Microsoft Encarta encyclopedia. The Bicholim Conflict, the Owens story, and indeed the majority of hoaxes on Wikipedia could never have appeared in the old-fashioned encyclopedias. For this kind of false information is a by-product of the digital revolution.

It's trivial to become a Wikipedia editor. Find an article that you would like to alter. Near the top of a page, there's a little tab marked "Edit." Click on it and type away. You don't even have to have a Wikipedia account or user name to manipulate the entries; anyone with a smartphone or a computer is able to make changes to the text. The moment you hit the "Save page" button, your changes will instantly become visible to everybody in the world.

When Wikipedia gave everyone in the world the ability to create and to edit encyclopedia pages, it was not merely an act of democratization; it was also an act of anarchy. At least at first, everyone had the same access to the information at the heart of the encyclopedia; nobody had any special privilege or power to force other contributors to agree with their version of reality. Just as you could eradicate and replace someone else's words, the next contributor could eradicate and replace yours.

There was no pride of place given to those who knew the subject better or those who were more able writers or those who had particular knowledge that others didn't—everyone's words were equally evanescent. Every person's contributions were distributed equally widely across the globe, with no accounting for expertise. In short, Wikipedia's most dramatic step was a rejection of the concept of authority. Even a Nobel-winning physicist's treatise on the Higgs boson could be modified or eradicated by any random thirteen-year-old sitting at his computer.

Perhaps the clearest illustration of just how radical that idea is sits on the Wikipedia page about Philip Roth's novel *The Human Stain*. The protagonist of the book, Coleman Silk, is a professor whose career falls apart after he's accused of racism. It's revealed in the novel that Silk was actually a light-skinned African American who had passed as white. On October 17, 2004, an anonymous editor from Vancouver added a few sentences at the end of the page, stating that "Coleman Silk is partially based on the deceased *New York Times* literary critic Anatole Broyard, a 'black' man who passed as a 'white man' for many decades."* That assertion remained mostly untouched (one editor added an "at least" before "partially based") for about four years. It disappeared briefly in early 2008 as the page underwent major revisions, then reemerged—this time alluding to a piece by a literary critic who suggested the connection between Broyard and Silk. And so it remained for another four years, until another Wikipedian removed it: Roth's biographer.

Broyard was not any sort of inspiration for the character; according to Roth, the character was based upon Mel Tumin, a sociology professor at Princeton. "I have removed the reference to Anatole Broyard, at Philip Roth's insistence," wrote Blake Bailey. "I am Roth's biographer, and have removed it at his request." It took just one minute before a Wikipedian, "Jprg1966," wiped out Bailey's revisions and restored the passage. Half

----

* The editor cited an essay by Henry Louis Gates Jr. on the death of Broyard, seemingly as support for this statement. However, that essay was written several years before *The Human Stain* was published and mentions neither Roth nor any of his writing. The citation soon disappeared.

an hour later, Bailey tried once again to correct the article. "Once again, I removed the reference to Anatole Broyard. It is wholly inaccurate and therefore pointless," Bailey wrote. "I am Roth's biographer, and have removed it at his request." This time, the revisions lasted a full five minutes before another Wikipedian, "Parkwells," undid Bailey's edits—and doubled down, adding extra information on Anatole Broyard to make the parallels between Silk and Broyard more clear, as well as a citation from *New York Times* literary critic Michiko Kakutani. Unlike Bailey's edits, Parkwells's went unchallenged for weeks.

Fed up, Bailey approached the Wikipedia administrators about setting the record straight. The result was less than satisfactory, as Roth made plain in an open letter to Wikipedia that he published in *The New Yorker* in September 2012: "My interlocutor [Bailey] was told by the 'English Wikipedia Administrator'—in a letter dated August 25 and addressed to my interlocutor—that I, Roth, was not a credible source: 'I understand your point that the author is the greatest authority on their own work,' writes the Wikipedia Administrator—'but we require secondary sources.'"

Before Roth went public, he couldn't get his own assertions about the inspiration for *The Human Stain* to stick to a Wikipedia page for more than five minutes before it was wiped out by another editor—one with just as much power to shape the public record on what was inside Roth's head as the author's biographer and the author himself. Now, there are plenty of reasons for not letting an author dictate his literary legacy (including the problem of spin), but to so firmly reject an author's statements about his own opus in favor of semi- and fully anonymous editors with no pretense of expertise—that's radical. That's a doctrine of intellectual Levellers. And it's a consequence of the peculiar properties of digital information.*

----

* The Wikipedia page for *The Human Stain* now has a section devoted to the controversy about the Wikipedia page for *The Human Stain*. Like the mythical oozlum bird, Wikipedia seems to have the ability to fly around in ever-decreasing circles until it flies right up its own rectum.

A Wikipedia page is persistent; its information can influence people for years and years.* And it is freely accessible to anyone with an internet connection. Yet it's also infinitely malleable: anyone can shape its information and have those changes broadcast around the world. This combination of properties could never have coexisted before the advent of computers. There was no way to have a universal collaboration, no way to give every human a say in crafting the record of our collective knowledge, no means of assuring that the information accessible to a household in Cheyenne, Wyoming, could be affected almost instantly by a few computer keystrokes in Melbourne, Australia. The medium has allowed Wikipedians—and countless others—to tear down to the foundations the way in which we collect knowledge. Out the window went not just verifiability but also our traditional ideas of authority. This is the root cause of Wikipedia hoaxes; if there are no distinctions made among contributors, then any practical jokester's edits are considered just as seriously as the most established historical scholar's. And this leaves Wikipedia wide open to the influence of manipulation—of spin. And here, again, the problem of authority raises its head.

In March 2006, a minor "edit war" about orcas erupted on Wikipedia. An anonymous Wikipedian changed references to "orcas" in the SeaWorld entry—SeaWorld shows often feature orcas—into "killer whales," writing that "'Orca' is an inappropriate shorthand of the animal's [Latin] species name: orcinus orca. The common name is 'killer whale.'" What the Wikipedian didn't explain was why he deleted a passage in which conservationist and painter Richard Ellis questions the ethics of using killer whales in SeaWorld shows. The anonymous editor wiped out Ellis's criticism, leaving behind only a single

----

* This influence can persist even after the page is deleted, thanks to the influence that Wikipedia has upon other sources. Google "Chen Fang Yinchuan" and you'll see multiple sources confirming that Chen is the former mayor of the town, even though the Wikipedia source of that information was long ago exposed as a hoax.

sentence: "SeaWorld has been criticized by animal rights activists for keeping killer whales in captivity." After a heated back-and-forth about whether the passage should remain and whether it's better to call the creatures orcas or killer whales, the anonymous Wikipedian admitted that he was the communications director—chief spin doctor—for Busch Entertainment, the company that owns SeaWorld. "I did delete some, but certainly not all, of the criticism of marine mammal captivity, primarily because it belongs in an article devoted to that subject," he wrote. "I mention earlier that I do not shy from a debate over captivity, but way too many people who argue the points you make trade in half-truths or outright falsehoods. For every scientist like Ellis, by the way, there are 10 who hold precisely the opposite opinion. Their voices should be heard too." And though the word "orca" was restored throughout the article, in 2011 a Wikipedian with the name "Jnemo412" once again changed all "orcas" back to "killer whales"* and added a statement that the average life span of a killer whale had been extended due to better care. Is Jnemo412 a SeaWorld flack? It's hard to tell for sure, but my money would be on it.†

A few years ago, an enterprising computer science graduate student at the University of Alabama, Virgil Griffith, wrote a computer program that allowed users to link Wikipedia edits back to the corporations that were making them. There were oodles of examples. PepsiCo, ExxonMobil, Wal-Mart, Diebold, and plenty of other corporations were repeatedly editing their Wikipedia pages, busily burnishing their public images by altering the language on Wikipedia. Politicians, too, have learned that it's much easier to craft one's image by altering words on a webpage than by trying to affect public opinion in other ways. In

----

* It's unclear why pro-SeaWorld types would prefer the term "killer whale" to "orca." The SeaWorld websites almost exclusively use the former term and eschew the latter. It's almost certainly a subject extensively studied by Sea-World's marketing team.

† At the very least, Jnemo412 has an abnormal affinity for SeaWorld-promoted videos on YouTube.

2006, a Massachusetts paper showed that the staff of House Democrat Marty Meehan had "wiped out references to his broken term-limits pledge as well as information about his huge campaign war chest" in his Wikipedia biography. And, it seems, the same group of staffers saw fit to write in Republican Eric Cantor's biography that he "smells of cow dung." These edits were just the tip of the iceberg; dozens upon dozens of edits to Wikipedia biographies were apparently altered by congressional staffers to boost the reputations of their bosses and allies and to smear their enemies.

What's so disturbing about these incidents is not that the people who wrote the articles didn't have any authority to write about the subject; after all, a SeaWorld employee probably knows more about killer whales than the average Joe, and Marty Meehan's staffers certainly know more about their boss's life than almost anyone else. The problem here is that the editors approached Wikipedia by deliberately hiding their authority—and their biases. By masquerading as common people, the spin doctors' edits were thought to be the same as anyone else's, when in fact they were very different in nature and intent.*

By refusing to examine the authority of its editors to contribute to its articles, Wikipedia created two big problems that undermine its credibility. On one hand, people with genuine insight into subjects are marginalized, while, on the other, those with an agenda are granted equal access to alter the information at Wikipedia's heart. It's a wonder that Wikipedia's pages are as valuable as they are.

Wikipedia is useful because it is not quite as anarchic as a pure antiauthoritarian movement would have to be. There's a system for resolving disputes, as well as an informal hierarchy that provides a little bit of structure. Once Philip Roth publicly embarrassed Wikipedia, the author's opinion of his own inspirations took pride of place on the Wikipedia page devoted to *The Human Stain*. When Marty

----

* Such masquerades are quite common; chapter 3 discusses how digital technology allows one to blur one's persona online.

Meehan's shenanigans came to light, they were promptly altered. If there weren't at least a rudimentary system to prevent ExxonMobil and Wal-Mart from tarting up their Wikipedia pages, each company's page would quickly become nothing more than a free advertisement. To prevent this from happening, there has to be at least some semblance of authority within the teeming masses of contributors. There have to be individuals who can resolve disputes and prevent gross abuse of the Wikipedia pages.

Since 2004, Wikipedia has had a mediation committee and an arbitration committee, which, according to the website, are peopled by trusted, seasoned, and experienced editors. But the nature of this trust—and what counts as experience—in the Wikisphere is very different from what it is in traditional publishing or academia. It's not through scholarly achievements that one gains authority in the world of Wikipedia. It's by acquiring authority from fellow Wikipedians through your devotion to the cause and through your service to the encyclopedia. External credentials, factual knowledge, expertise, and training are all secondary. Social credentials are much more important. And, in fact, this is where the authority in Wikipedia resides.

In 2006, when *New Yorker* writer Stacy Schiff sought to explain the Wikipedia phenomenon, she approached the site's management team for suggestions about Wikipedians to interview. They suggested "Essjay," a respected member of the community, no doubt in part because he "holds a Ph.D. in theology and a degree in canon law" and is a "tenured professor of religion at a private university"—one who somehow found time to edit or write some sixteen thousand Wikipedia entries. Essjay's position near the top of the Wikipedia hierarchy was a beautiful illustration that, even in the chaotic, anti-authoritarian environment of Wikipedia, ivory-tower-quality intellectuals would rise and flourish. Essjay was the poster boy of the new way of gathering knowledge; he was evidence that, as Schiff put it, "working collaboratively, [Wikipedians] can produce an encyclopedia that is as good as any written by experts, and with an unprecedented range." Or, as Wikipedia founder Jimmy Wales told *The New York Times*, "it was important that the general public not think that Wikipedia is 'written by a bunch of 12-year-olds.'"

Essjay wasn't twelve—he was twenty-four. And he wasn't a professor and didn't hold any advanced degrees. What's most interesting about the incident, though, is that the fabricated credentials didn't faze Jimmy Wales at all. A company Wales co-founded, Wikia, had recently hired Essjay, and Wales stuck up for his employee even after Essjay's lies were exposed. He told *The New Yorker* that he regarded the invented credentials as "a pseudonym and I don't really have a problem with it."* It's hard to imagine a more graphic demonstration of how little such external credentials mean to the Wikipedia community. Yet, at the same time, it shows that loyalty and hard work for Wikipedia earn one an authority that transcends anything that mere subject-matter expertise can give you.

And this authority, like any other, can be abused. Jimmy Wales himself has been accused of manipulating Wikipedia entries for his own ends. One of his ex-girlfriends, Canadian pundit Rachel Marsden, released a transcript purported to be from an online chat in which he appears to be throwing his weight around to get her Wikipedia page cleaned up. (Wales denied any wrongdoing: "I care deeply about the integrity of Wikipedia. . . . I would never knowingly do anything to compromise that trust," he wrote.) Just a few weeks later, a former Novell computer scientist claimed that, in exchange for a $5,000 donation to the Wikimedia Foundation, Wales had edited his webpage to make it more favorable. (According to the BBC, Wales called the claim "nonsense.") And this wasn't the first—or last—accusation of pay-for-play on Wikipedia, despite the public assertion that Wikipedia would never accept any offer of money for an editorial massage by high-ranking Wikipedians. As I was writing this book, in September 2012, another scandal erupted. A

----

* Once it became apparent that the Essjay fiasco was robbing Wikipedia of its credibility, Wales promptly reversed himself. "I misjudged the issue," he wrote. "It was not OK for Mr. Jordan, or Essjay, to lie to a reporter, even to protect his identity." He then asked Essjay to resign.

trustee of Wikimedia UK, a foundation with ties to Wikipedia, and a "Wikipedian in Residence" stand accused of manipulating their clients' Wikipedia pages and helping those pages get prominent placement. (Wales said that, if true, such activities were "wildly inappropriate.")

Wikipedia is perhaps the most influential and popular example of how authority is being redefined in the digital age, but it's far from the only one. With the democratizing power of the internet—the fact that everyone can, in theory, be seen and heard by everyone else on the planet—it's natural that we reexamine how we decide whom we believe: whom we accept as authorities we listen to and whom we don't.

The change in the nature of authority is hitting other sources of information as well. It's one of the big issues at the heart of my own profession: journalism.

For most people, journalists are sensory organs that tell them what's going on in the world around them. But unlike our biological sensory information, journalistic information has a worldwide reach; it can give you inklings of events that are happening thousands of miles away. And unlike sensory information, journalistic information can be stored in a permanent medium so that it can be recalled long after the events have passed from people's memories. There's good reason why journalism is often called the first draft of history.

But journalists aren't trained as historians. There isn't any special credential that makes one a journalist. Many journalists have never even gone to a journalism school, much less acquired a higher degree. Yet in the pages (online or otherwise) of a journalistic publication, you'll see a bewildering array of highly specialized subjects being covered by these nonexperts: nitty-gritty details about the functioning of federal, state, and local governments (not to mention foreign governments), subtle arguments about interpreting laws and regulations, arcane financial-sector dealings, nuances of foreign policy and military strategy, minutiae about new technology and advances in medical knowledge, arguments about scientific theories, and much, much more besides. Journalists aren't doing a perfect job, to be sure, but most of the time good ones are able to get you to trust their work despite (typically) having no special training in the subject they're informing you about. Journalists face the same problem that Wikipedia faces: How can you convince the public to take you seriously when you're not an expert? And journalists had a working solution.

When I went through journalism school, the traditional answer was, in part, a clever passing of the buck. If we wanted to express an opinion in a news story, we would seldom do it ourselves. We would instead get a credentialed expert to express that opinion for us, usually with a direct quotation that supports the opinion.*

For example, instead of simply saying:

> Pope Benedict's decision to step down was one of the most dramatic acts in the history of the papacy

The New York Times's story on the papal resignation read:

> Some said that Benedict's decision to step down was one of the most dramatic acts in the history of the papacy. "This decision has been the only great reform of Benedict, and at the same time it is a revolutionary step for the Catholic Church," said Marco Politi, a Vatican expert and author of a book on Benedict's papacy.

This way, it's not a *New York Times* reporter who is expressing her opinion, but an expert on Vatican affairs. The statement is believable because it comes from a genuine authority, not a journalist. (Never

----

* Different eras of journalism had different standards. At various times, it wasn't that unusual for journalists to stand on a soapbox or even to make stuff up to attract an audience. In the mid-nineteenth century, for example, the *New York Sun* thought nothing of printing ludicrous hoaxes to boost circulation. The most famous was a six-article series, published in 1835, about astronomer John Herschel's discovery of lunar man-bats and other odd creatures living on the moon.

mind that the authority doesn't *quite* make the same assertion that *The New York Times* reporters are trying to support. The fact that it's in the ballpark is good enough.)

This is a subtle switch in emphasis. As a reporter, you don't write about your belief that the pope's resignation is a big deal; instead you relay the fact that some people believe that the pope's resignation is a big deal. The former is an opinion, the latter is a fact, and by sticking to other people's statements, you never have to write anything that's not factually correct.

Of course, this is a bit disingenuous. It's a disguise: the reporter appears to be merely the vessel for other people's ideas, rather than the originator of them. Naturally, journalists have opinions about what they write about. A reporter's job is to spend time gathering facts and talking to experts to learn about their opinions. If, at the end of the process, a reporter doesn't have any opinions of his own about the matter—well, let's just say that it's not a hallmark of great intelligence to be so untouched by information flowing into your brain. Nevertheless, we journalists are supposed to suppress our own opinions, at least to some extent.

It's ludicrous to pretend that reporters are completely neutral and objective observers, but this approach has a big advantage. By being as transparent as possible about sources and about reasons for making assertions, the reporter is doing little more than putting a bunch of facts on the table in an easily read format. The reader can examine those facts and decide whether or not to come to the same conclusion. No longer does a skeptical reader wonder whether the reporter knows what he or she is doing as much as try to grapple with an independent interpretation of the same facts.* And it checks a reporter whose

----

* For example, if the *Times* had merely said that Pope Benedict's resignation was one of the most dramatic acts in the history of the papacy, a knowledgeable reader might wonder whether the reporters were hyping the issue or were just ignorant. After all, the papacy is littered with stories of sex scandals, poisonings, heresy, schism, and war. But by having an expert say that the move was a "revolutionary step," the reader wonders instead how revolutionary the step really is.

opinions are outside the mainstream. If he can't find someone else worth listening to who shares his views, his ability to share that with the world is limited—at least outside the opinion pages.

The media outlets that attempt to ensure that their reporters cleave to this practice tend to be trusted by readers, although if you look carefully enough, you'll see that the rules get bent when convenient, even at the most august institutions. (*The New York Times*, for example, regularly ignores its own standards for using anonymous sources, which, by design, are precisely the opposite of transparent.) But, generally speaking, the standard practice is to borrow the authority of credentialed people—or, at the very least, people in the position to answer a question—rather than have the reporter assert his own authority.

The advent of digital information is eroding this practice in two major ways. The first has to do with interconnectedness. As the speed of information transfer in society approached the speed of light, it became harder and harder to bring something genuinely new to one's readers. It used to be that every local paper could break the same national story; people in Chicago learned whether Dewey defeated Truman from the *Tribune* on their doorstep, just as people in Philadelphia learned it from the *Inquirer* and people in Houston learned it from the *Chronicle*. The papers seldom competed directly; each one could break news to its audience regardless of what the others did simply by virtue of being more accessible. That's no longer true. If the *Sydney Morning Herald* breaks a story, it breaks the story worldwide. Everyone can instantly read it on their iPads and smartphones. The *Trib*, *Inky*, and *Chronicle* are all instantly behind the curve.* And every second they wait to publish their own story is a second that other outlets are using to get their stories up—and to push your outlet further and further into irrelevancy.

The internet has put immense time pressure on media outlets. And what's beginning to fail under the pressure is reporting. For the

---

* Unless they resort to digital skulduggery. More on this in chapter 7.

majority of serious news stories, the bottleneck is the reporting. It takes time to find people—eyewitnesses, academics, and other authorities—and to get them to talk to you. Some won't return your phone call; others will slam the door in your face. It takes only a few minutes to bang out a 300- or 450-word news item once you've got the material in hand; it's the gathering that's the hard part. And, as a result, that's the part of the newswriting process that's getting squeezed the hardest. Which means that reporters are under increasing pressures to find authorities quicker and quicker, no matter their quality—or to make do with less external comment or authentication.

The second way digital information has changed the way reporters deal with authority is through the democratizing influence of the internet. Everyone has a louder voice; everyone has a platform from which their words echo around the world. Combine that with the fact that everyone has the ability to pose, convincingly, as an authority on something—a phenomenon that's the subject of chapter 5—and you've got problems. Democracy means, on some level, that everybody is equal. But the whole concept of authority is rooted in the fact that some people are better than others. Some are more knowledgeable, more insightful, more thoughtful, at least in certain narrow areas. Authority is inherently elitist; it's something that can't be doled out in equal measure to everyone. Yet the line between the haves and the have-nots is getting harder to see, at least if you're not looking carefully.

"Appeal to authority" is a classic fallacy. Since ancient times, orators have tried to convince crowds that something is true by attributing the argument to someone trusted and respected—yet it's a rhetorical trick, not a valid way of reasoning. Authorities are fallible, after all.

However, on some level, authority underlies everything we believe—at least everything we haven't verified with our own eyes. Figuring out what to accept and what to reject is largely a process of weighing authorities against each other. You listen to what trustworthy people say about a subject. You read books and articles and devour other media on the matter, which are themselves authorities of a different sort. You might even look at primary documents or eyewitness accounts. And then, at the end, you take all of that information, gauge how far each source is to be trusted, and modify your thinking accordingly. In a very real way, the quality of your thinking depends on your ability to tell good authorities from bad.

Sadly, digital information is making that task more difficult than ever before. It's even getting harder to tell whether an authority is a real person or just a simulacrum.

CHAPTER 3
AN ARMY OF ONE

Most people are other people.

—OSCAR WILDE, *DE PROFUNDIS*

Amina Arraf was kidnapped on a Monday evening. But it would be a few more days before she truly disappeared.

Arraf was a thirty-five-year-old Syrian American—Virginia-born and living in Damascus—who had become a prominent blogger. Her blog, *Gay Girl in Damascus,* described life in Syria during the beginning of the uprising against Bashar al-Assad. Liberal and lesbian, she was in a precarious position as a protester in a conservative and unstable society. Just how precarious became clear when police came to arrest her in April 2011. It was a dramatic scene—her father heroically stood up to the police, shaming them into beating a retreat—and it garnered her blog a large following. Despite the ever-present threat of arrest, she continued to write, and in May *The Guardian* dubbed her "an unlikely hero of revolt in a conservative country." Yet her situation rapidly deteriorated when government forces sought once more to silence her.

In the early evening of Monday, June 6, 2011, she was walking to meet a friend in downtown Damascus when three young men grabbed her. One put his hand over her mouth as they wrestled her into a red minivan, which screeched off into the dusk. Arraf's cousin posted details to Amina's blog. The outcry was immediate—loud enough to echo around the world. *The Guardian* reported the kidnapping immediately, and so did *The New York Times*, Fox News, Al Jazeera, the *Daily Mail*, *Gawker*, CNN, *The Huffington Post*, the Associated Press, and a number of other news organizations. The *International Business Times* asked how the United States should respond to the abduction, and "Free Amina" websites and posters began to spring up on the internet.

Within a few hours, though, Andy Carvin, an NPR journalist, noted that none of the people who had ever interviewed Arraf had met her or even spoken to her over the phone. "It's just odd that I can't find anyone who has actually met her in person," he tweeted. And once someone began to question Arraf's identity, the illusion quickly shattered. By the morning of June 8, the *Wall Street Journal* had discovered that photos purportedly of Arraf were, in fact, snapshots of a woman living in London. Shortly thereafter, a website in communication with Arraf was able to show that her computer was in Scotland, not in Syria, as she had claimed. Soon it became clear that Arraf wasn't a "she" at all. She was the creation of Tom MacMaster, a Ph.D. student at the University of Edinburgh. Everything about Arraf was completely made up—her repeated run-ins with Syrian police, her brave father's intervention to save her from arrest, her sexuality—the totality of her existence was a fabrication. MacMaster had created Arraf's Facebook page, her Twitter account, her e-mail address—and had conducted interviews with numerous journalists in her name.

Why? It was a matter of authority. MacMaster had some very strong views on Middle Eastern affairs, and he felt that his ideas weren't taken seriously:

> I was involved with numerous online science-fiction/
> alternate-history discussion lists and, as a part of that process,

I saw lots of incredibly ignorant and stupid positions repeated on the Middle East. I noticed that when I, a person with a distinctly Anglo name, made comments on the Middle East, the facts I might present were ignored and I found myself accused of hating America, Jews, etc. I wondered idly whether the same ideas presented by someone with a distinctly Arab and female identity would have the same reaction.

It wasn't an idle thought for long. MacMaster created Amina Arraf to give his ideas credibility. By putting his words in the mouth of a homosexual Syrian woman, he was trying to cloak them in an authority that they wouldn't otherwise be granted. And he was right. A random alternate-history fan from Edinburgh wouldn't likely be able to attract worldwide attention to his views on what's going on in Syria. But a lesbian woman who's actually involved in the protests— and blogging, at grave risk to herself—that's another story.

This is the power of the sockpuppet.

Sockpuppetry—the use of a false identity for the purpose of deception— is not a new phenomenon. Indeed, several centuries ago, it made possible what is perhaps the best practical joke in all of recorded history.

In February 1708, a halfpenny pamphlet entitled "Predictions for the Year 1708" began circulating on the streets of London. Written by one Isaac Bickerstaff, the pamphlet made a number of astrological predictions for the future:

> I have begun to calculate from the time that the sun enters into Aries. And this I take to be properly the beginning of the natural year. I pursue them to the time that he enters Libra, or somewhat more, which is the busy period of the year. The remainder I have not yet adjusted, upon account of several impediments needless here to mention. . . .
>
> My first prediction is but a trifle, yet I will mention it, to show how ignorant those sottish pretenders to astrology are in

their own concerns. It relates to Partridge, the almanack-maker. I have consulted the stars of his nativity by my own rules, and find he will infallibly die upon the 29th of March next, about eleven at night, of a raging fever; therefore I advise him to consider of it, and settle his affairs in time.

John Partridge was an esteemed astrologer who made his living by publishing annual almanacs that predicted events that would take place the coming year. Bickerstaff's unusually specific forecast not only set a precise time and date for Partridge's death, but also mocked the almanac maker for not foreseeing his own demise. Partridge was, quite naturally, flustered and incensed by what the villainous "sham-prophet" had published. But that was just a taste of what was to come.

On March 30, copies of a letter spread across London with incredible speed: an eyewitness account of the death of John Partridge. Written by an unnamed civil servant, it told of how the astrologer had died by fever:

> After half an hour's conversation I took my leave, being half stifled by the closeness of the room. I imagined he could not hold out long, and therefore withdrew to a little coffee-house hard by, leaving a servant at the house with orders to come immediately and tell me, as nearly as he could, the minute when Partridge should expire, which was not above two hours after, when, looking upon my watch, I found it to be above five minutes after seven; by which it is clear that Mr. Bickerstaff was mistaken almost four hours in his calculation. In the other circumstances he was exact enough.

At the same time, an anonymous poet circulated an elegy for the death of Partridge, along with an epitaph:

Here, five Foot deep, lies on his Back,
A Cobler, Starmonger, and Quack;

Who to the Stars in pure Good-will,
Does to his best look upward still.
Weep all you Customers that use
His Pills, his Almanacks, or Shoes. . . .

All of London was abuzz with the news, and after it became clear that Partridge was still alive, the esteemed astrologer became a laughingstock. By his own account, Partridge couldn't leave his house without someone making a crack about his death:

> I could not stir out of doors for the space of three months after this, but presently one comes up to me in the street; Mr Partridge, that coffin you was last buried in I have not been yet paid for: Doctor, cries another dog, How d'ye think people can live by making of graves for nothing?

Someone even bought Partridge a marble headstone:

> My nameless old persecutor had provided me a monument at the stone-cutter's, and would have erected it in the parish-church; and this piece of notorious and expensive villainy had actually succeeded, had I not used my utmost interest with the vestry, where it was carried at last but by two voices, that I am still alive. That stratagem failing, out comes a long sable elegy, bedecked with hour-glasses, mattocks, sculls, spades, and skeletons, with an epitaph as confidently written to abuse me, and my profession, as if I had been under ground these twenty years.

What made this hoax so effective was sockpuppetry. Bickerstaff, the civil servant, and the poet were all the invention of Jonathan Swift, the rascally author of *Gulliver's Travels*. Swift had created a small cadre of personalities, each playing a different role, to carry out the plan—the personalities even contradicted one another slightly to help build the illusion that they were independent people. The fabricated personalities gave the hoax a short-lived boost of credibility that Swift could never have achieved had the pamphlets seemed to come from the same source. The interlocking pamphlets and poems assured that the story of Partridge's phony death gathered a tremendous amount of momentum in a short period of time. The whole affair soon became a grand joke shared by all literate Londoners, leaving Partridge humiliated. Swift, the puppet master, had his puppets drive Partridge to distraction.

Though sockpuppetry is centuries old at the very least, the advent of the digital web made it tremendously easier than ever before to create and maintain sockpuppets and, as a consequence, has increased our susceptibility to being manipulated by fake people. That's in part because we have all become used to interacting with disembodied quasi-fictional personae online.

Before the internet, it was fairly rare to encounter a stranger in any way other than in person; other than starting a correspondence based upon an unsolicited letter, there would be few ways in which to interact for any length of time with someone whose identity was a mystery. This would greatly limit one's ability to create a false persona. The situation changed once we started living in a digital world, because the extreme interconnectedness of the internet makes this sort of nebulous faux personality a necessity. We can't meet most of the people we interact with on the internet physically; we're trapped in "meatspace" and can't travel at the speed of light. So, by necessity, we create online avatars who represent us in the online world, avatars who can travel at the speed of light and represent us in countries we've never set foot in.* If you go to any forum on the internet, most likely it's filled with people with names like "EvilBrak" and "Spockguy"—complete strangers who control, at least to some extent, what you know about them. If someone claims to be forty years old or a blond female, most of the time you've got to take her word for it, because you

---

* If you want to get philosophical, you could argue that this means we're all puppet masters. The personae we craft online are designed—at least on some level, conscious or subconscious—to shape others' ideas about who we really are.

generally have no means of verifying it for yourself. You can get into a heated discussion—or even have an online relationship of sorts—with "Furious George" or "Navel Gazer" without ever knowing a single thing about who the person is in real life. Indeed, you'll occasionally see online people talk about who they are "IRL"—in real life—making it clear that the online personality is not necessarily the same as that of the person who's typing at the keyboard. Indeed, it's natural for us to create avatars that represent what we want to be rather than what we are. And it's only a short step from there to manipulating others' perceptions of us to give ourselves an advantage of some sort, to deceive. To become puppet masters.

Tom MacMaster's creation of Amina Arraf, along with a small cast of supporting characters to help bolster her story, was an elaborate and high-profile deception. However, it's fairly typical of one kind of false persona: what I call "Type 1" sockpuppetry. In Type 1 sockpuppetry, the puppet master fabricates a phony persona who has a specific attribute or experience that the puppet master himself lacks—an attribute or experience that gives the puppet master extra authority in a conversation or extra ability to generate a reaction from others. MacMaster couldn't get people to take his views on Syria seriously, so he created a Syrian sockpuppet to give him authority when talking about Syrian matters—and it worked beyond his wildest dreams. A Type 1 puppet master might masquerade as a woman to get a leg up on a conversation about feminism, or as a doctor to lend credence to certain views about a disease, or as someone of a particular ethnic heritage to give weight to someone's ideas about racism. The possibilities are almost endless; there are Type 1 puppet masters pretending to suffer from various diseases, or to be veterans, or to be victims of various crimes. And in all cases, the point seems to be to seek either authority, attention, or profit.*

----

* One infamous example of a profiteer is Laura Albert, who took on the persona of a male ex-prostitute—JT Leroy—to write fiction about (what else?) prostitutes and drug addicts.

Debbie Swenson, it appears, was after attention when she created a Type 1 sockpuppet, a fictitious teenage daughter named Kaycee Nicole. Around 1999, Kaycee started appearing on the internet, and she soon revealed the attribute that would allow her to get a great deal of attention and sympathy: she was fighting leukemia. In a weblog she called *Living Colours*, she described in great detail the ups and downs of her battle—the remissions and the setbacks. On May 14, 2001, Kaycee Nicole lost her struggle, dying of an aneurysm.

In the two years she was blogging, Kaycee had attracted a large number of fans, and when she finally died, the outpouring of grief was real and palpable. Denizen after denizen of the popular website MetaFilter expressed heartbreak. "Rest in peace kind, bright, wonderful soul. . . . I'm in tears and wishing I could offer you more," wrote one user. "My mind is kinda blurry now. I've smiled today. I've cried uncontrollably. I'm sad and relieved. I said my final goodbye to her a few weeks ago," wrote another user, who had been in correspondence with her for several years. Kaycee's death was a cloud that hung over the site for several days. Then, on May 19, the user "acridrabbit" posted a simple question: "Is it possible that Kaycee did not exist?"

Not only were there some inconsistencies in Kaycee's story—some odd-sounding descriptions of how the doctors talked about leukemia, some strange contradictions in the timing of various events, the difficulty people were having in finding an address for flowers and cards—but it also appeared that nobody had ever met Kaycee in person. Immediately, some MetaFilter sleuths started picking apart the story, even as Kaycee believers, like "bwg," who had hosted her weblog, appeared to suffer genuine anguish because of the cynicism:

> STOP! STOP!! STOP!!! this is deplorable. it's making me sick to my stomach! i have spoken to kaycee on the phone, as well as her mother, numerous times. i can assure you kaycee was quite real. . . . it's not bad enough that i have lost someone so close and so dear to me, but now you are asking me to prove it? as far as i am concerned, all the cynics can go to hell.

But the truth was that Kaycee simply didn't exist. Debbie Swenson admitted the next day that Kaycee had been a fabrication.

Stories like Kaycee's are surprisingly common, to the point that psychiatrists and psychologists started noticing a pattern—a syndrome that's now called "virtual factitious disorder" or, more snappily, "Munchausen by internet." In the syndrome, a person creates an online persona who suffers a progressive and deadly disease, a disabling condition, or some other kind of personal tragedy and milks the resulting outpouring of sympathy and concern. As psychiatrist Marc Feldman puts it:

> Online, one can quickly acquire an education, find a discussion group or some other online forum dealing with the phenomenon, and be accepted instantly. That's the explicit purpose of these groups: not to question. They receive real care, concern, even love. There's a sense of power, and if it goes badly at any point, there's instant escape.

Create a sockpuppet or two, give it a tragic problem that will garner sympathy, and then commit "pseuicide." It's almost guaranteed to cause a big stir, so it becomes almost irresistible to the extreme attention seeker. Any sufficiently large online community will encounter one of these sooner or later.

More common than Type 1 sockpuppetry is Type 2 sockpuppetry, in which the attributes of the puppet are mostly irrelevant. There's only one thing that matters for a Type 2 sockpuppet: the fictional personality must be someone other than the puppet master. It doesn't really matter who that fake person is—a man or a woman, an old person or a young one—so long as it's someone supposedly unconnected to the puppet master himself.

Type 2 sockpuppets are often deployed as reinforcements in an online feud. Because these sockpuppets are meant to seem independent of the puppet master, these false personae give the impression of a group of online people who agree with and bolster the puppet master's position—or attack his enemies. It might seem petty and unnecessary to have fake people agreeing with your arguments and fighting your adversaries alongside you, but it's everywhere.

John Lott, a gun researcher, created a fake student who defended his writing online and gave him a positive review on Amazon.com. Amazon reviews are a common leitmotif:* mystery writer R. J. Ellory used a brigade of sockpuppets not only to give his own books glowing reviews, but also to depress his rivals' ratings. Professor Orlando Figes, an esteemed British historian, lost much of that esteem by doing precisely the same thing, and in a legal settlement Figes apologized and agreed to pay his rivals' legal bills.

Type 2 sockpuppets can be fun if only for the schadenfreude they cause when the puppet master is exposed. More than once, some thin-skinned pseudo-celebrity has become a laughingstock as his sockpuppets were revealed. Scott Adams, the creator of the comic strip *Dilbert*, deployed a sockpuppet when one of his essays was getting savaged on MetaFilter. His sockpuppet's defense was so hamhanded ("he has a certified genius I.Q., and that's hard to hide...") that the very next comment was "Welcome to Metafilter, Scott!" and Adams was savagely mocked from coast to coast. Sockpuppet exposures can also be damaging to people's careers. Journalists like *The New Republic*'s Lee Siegel and the *Los Angeles Times*'s Michael Hiltzik were disciplined by their companies because they were caught sockpuppeteering.

The Type 2 sockpuppet is an easy weapon for an online skirmisher with a fragile ego. It's also a great sales booster for a company that wants to tinker with its online reviews. But don't make the mistake of thinking that these are the only people who deploy sockpuppets. In fact, sockpuppets are now being used for intelligence and for defense.

----

* Bing Liu, a computer scientist at the University of Illinois who studied Amazon reviews, told *The New York Times* that approximately a third of reviews on the internet were likely fake. These are either created by sockpuppets or purchased wholesale.

In a very real sense, our borders are now being patrolled by an army of sockpuppets—and they could be watching you, too.

Anthony Weiner was a rising star in the Democratic Party. Political commentators forecast a bright future for the young New York City congressman. Perhaps a mayoral run, and then perhaps higher office. But all those hopes were dashed* in mid-2011 when Weiner used Twitter to send a sexually charged photo to a college student. Even though Weiner deleted the tweet quickly, Republican operatives instantly got hold of the photo and sent it to a right-wing website. After some vigorous denials, Weiner was forced to admit that he had sent the photo (and several others to different women) and resigned.

Nothing on Twitter is truly secret, even if it's deleted quickly, but in the wake of the scandal, it became clear that Weiner was under enemy surveillance. According to *The New York Times*, "one or more people created two false identities on Twitter in order to collect information to use against [Weiner]."

"Nikki Reid" was purportedly a sixteen-year-old fan of Weiner's who campaigned online to get Congressman Weiner to be her prom date. She eventually got Weiner to "follow" her, allowing her to send and receive "private" messages to the congressman. But Nikki Reid didn't really exist; she was a fiction dreamed up by a conservative operative. Working from the inside, she was attempting to get Weiner to do something stupid—or to get a trusting soul to share dirt that she could use. It's unclear precisely what role "Nikki" played in the scandal, but it's fairly clear that the sockpuppet was being used to gather information and maybe even to act as a provocateur.†

A number of social media sites reveal more information about you

----

* Except for the hopes of the mayoral run—which he attempted in 2013, despite the photo scandal.
† People are particularly vulnerable to fakes when they're looking for romantic involvement. See chapter 8 for more on dating sites, fake identities, and robot scammers.

to your "friends" or "followers" than they do to the general public. This means that people who have an interest in knowing something about you—people who want to learn your preferences, your habits, your purchases, or something else—have a vested interest in trying to get you to invite them into your inner circle. This is not mere paranoia.

In 2012, Raymond Kelly, commissioner of the New York City Police Department, declared that officers could create false identities—and use laptops that can't be traced back to the NYPD—to hang out on social media sites in hopes of spotting crime. Police have been using similar tricks for years—impersonating underage children on the internet, for example, in hopes of catching pedophiles—but the ease of creating a large number of sockpuppets on the internet for the express purpose of infiltrating social media sites is making civil libertarians nervous.

A number of us have been staked out already. Witness Nicole Bally, an attractive and fit blond woman from New York. In a few years, she managed to become the online friend of a number of very influential and powerful people: media personalities like Arianna Huffington, Jeffrey Toobin, David Carr, Howard Kurtz, and Dana Milbank; technology types like Vint Cerf, Steve Case, Chris Anderson, and Douglas Rushkoff; venture capitalists and economists like Nouriel Roubini, Henry Blodget, Teymour Boutros-Ghali, and Tim Draper; left and centrist political types like Joe Trippi, Markos Moulitsas, and Wesley Clark; and many, many more besides. Her friends list, some seven hundred strong, is like a who's who of technology, journalism, and venture capital. But Bally is (or was) a fake—her profile disappeared after it was exposed in 2011 by a blogger who ventured a guess as to the hidden people behind the sockpuppet:

> it seems likely that our conversations are being spied on, recorded and analyzed, either by folks from China or by corporate sleuths hiding behind seductive masks to track and influence conversations about their clients, customers and competitors.

Paranoid? Maybe . . . but maybe not. In March 2012, unknown parties repeatedly tried to get sensitive information about NATO's supreme allied commander in Europe, Admiral James Stavridis, by impersonating him on Facebook and insinuating themselves into his circle of friends and colleagues. NATO sources said they didn't know who was responsible, but other experts suggested that the culprit may have been China.

China has acquired a reputation—probably justly—for gathering information on its enemies and rivals through sockpuppeteering and other underhanded internet tricks. But it's not the only state in the sockpuppet game. The U.S. is, too.

In late 2010 or early 2011, the United States Central Command (Centcom)—the branch of the military responsible for operations in Iran, Iraq, Afghanistan, Pakistan, and the Middle East—signed a $2.76 million contract with Ntrepid, a California company, to provide the ultimate sockpuppeteering software. According to the original contract proposal, Centcom was looking for a software suite that would allow fifty users to create ten sockpuppets each, "replete with background, history, supporting details, and cyber presences that are technically, culturally and geographacilly [*sic*] consistent. Individual applications will enable an operator to exercise a number of different online persons from the same workstation and without fear of being discovered by sophisticated adversaries."

The internet has become a battlefield for virtual personalities—sockpuppets all attempting to gather information and using that information to help their causes and hurt their enemies. It's a war without bystanders, for we're all caught up in the fighting, whether we're aware of it or not.

CHAPTER 3½
TELLING FAKE
PEOPLE FROM REAL

Most of the people you interact with online are not real, at least on some level. They're virtual personae. Each one may be a reflection of a real person, or it might be a complete fabrication. Most of the time, this should make little difference to you. Sometimes, however, it does. When you interact online—if you're sending money, or forming strong social bonds—it's a good idea to establish whether the person is who he says he is. This is true even for people you know personally.

Not so long ago, I got an e-mail ostensibly from my colleague Bill, bearing alarming news:

Sorry to bother, But I had a sudden trip out of the country to Belgium to see my ill cousin, she is suffering from Kidney disease and must undergo Kidney transplant to save her life. The surgery is very expensive here, so I want to transfer her back home to have the surgery implemented. I really need to take care of this now but my credit card can't work here. I traveled with little money due to the short time I had to prepare for this trip and never expected things to be this way right now. I need a loan of $1,500 from you and I'll reimburse you at my

return. I will really appreciate whatever amount you can come
up with if not all, get back to me I'll advise on how to transfer it.

This sort of thing is a fairly common scam nowadays—a fraudster gets
hold of someone's e-mail address book and sends out letters requesting help in hopes of making a quick buck.

I knew instantly that this didn't come from Bill (he's a stickler for
AP style and wouldn't capitalize "Kidney" or abuse commas the way
this writer did). But any doubt evaporated when I pulled up the IP address of the sender. The message wasn't coming from Belgium; the
e-mail had originated in the United States.

An IP address is something like a set of coordinates for every
computer that's sending or receiving data on the internet. It's a set of
four numbers* that tells internet machinery where to send the data
you're requesting. And it can tell you, at least in rough terms, where a
message originated. For example, you'd be able to tell that a computer
using the IP address 128.122.118.245 was not only in the New York
region but part of New York University's network of computers. Every
e-mail you receive is stamped with IP addresses indicating not only
where the message came from, but also some of the computers it's
passed through on its way to your e-mail account.

E-mail readers don't display those IP addresses by default—they
are messy and hard to parse, and clutter up the screen. But you can
generally force your e-mail program, whether on the web or on your
computer, to display those addresses. (It's usually a command hidden
on a menu somewhere with a name like "Show Headers" or "View
Source" or the like.) Look for the IP address with the earliest time-
stamp, and that will give you the computer closest to the origin of the
e-mail. And then plop that number into an IP lookup website† and you
can often figure out where the message came from. Unfortunately, the

----

* This is the IPv4 protocol, which is slowly going out of style in favor of IPv6—
which looks slightly different but has the same function.
† Such as WhoIs.net or IP-Lookup.net.

method isn't foolproof, as there are addresses—particularly those associated with mobile devices—that are hard to trace.

If you don't have an IP address to work with—as you probably won't with your run-of-the-mill blogger or web personality—your job is a bit harder. What you've got to try to do is assemble facts that paint a portrait of the person. The most valuable are attributes that can't change or change only slowly—just as a tattoo can help you identify a person, a fragment of information that sticks to someone and can't rub off can give you a little handhold that helps you pinpoint the character. And then you look for contradictions.

For example, a few years ago, a professor called me about a potential problem with a student journalist. The student had submitted a piece about HIV in New York City that quoted several interesting people, such as Gene Laroche, a physician working in the HIV Counseling Department of Presbyterian Hospital, in New York,* but the professor had a suspicion that something wasn't quite right—her BS detector had gone off. The question soon became: Does Gene Laroche exist?

We had a few bits of information that should have stuck to Mr. Laroche: we knew where he worked (Presbyterian Hospital, in New York City), which implied that he lived nearby as well— probably in New York, New Jersey, or Connecticut. We also knew that he was a physician specializing in HIV counseling. These are the kinds of concrete facts that help pinpoint a person and find out more about him.

A good first step is always Google. This is more useful for some people than it is for others. People with common names tend to be

---

* I have changed the name and affiliation of the fictional character to insulate the (former) student from being identified. I'd ordinarily out a fabricator without any hesitation, but this case came to me in my capacity as the NYU journalism department's director of undergraduate studies—and as such, I'm required to keep student disciplinary matters confidential. This is one of a handful of situations where my responsibilities as an academic conflict directly with what I consider to be the responsibilities of a good journalist.

harder to track down, just because there are so many others out there to confuse them with. A fairly uncommon name makes it much easier. Middle names, ages, locations where they live or work—all of these can help you narrow down the field and can lead to useful repositories of information. If you know that a person's supposedly an investment banker, for example, throw "banker" or "bank" into a search with the person's name and you might come up with a LinkedIn profile, which can give you more information.

In the case of "Gene Laroche," the name wasn't too common, but nor was it rare enough to be a unique identifier. So to make sure we were getting the right person, we tried searching for "Gene Laroche HIV," "Gene Laroche AIDS," "Gene Laroche New York Presbyterian," "Gene Laroche counseling," and a bunch of other variants (such as using "Eugene" instead of "Gene"). Nothing. Neither could we find anything with "Gene Laroche New York" or "Gene Laroche MD"; we found a dentist and some other random Gene Laroches, but none who matched the profile of our guy. A search on the New York Presbyterian Hospital website turned up nothing, either.* In fact, there didn't appear to be an HIV counseling department at New York Presbyterian at all. Very suspicious.

The clincher came when I checked the New York State Department of Health's website. When a person is in a career that requires licensure or certification, like medicine or law, the state usually keeps records of those licenses. You'll almost certainly be able to get good information by going to the licensure board in the state where the person lives. In our case, Laroche was supposedly a physician practicing in New York, but there was no record of a New York State license for a Dr. Laroche. Gene Laroche was a fiction.

There are other sources of information as well. E-mail addresses and even phone numbers can give you something to go by if you've got

----

* A very useful Google trick is to restrict the search to a specific website or domain by using the "site" tag. For example, "Laroche site:nyp.org" will find any indexed pages on the nyp.org domain that contain the word "Laroche."

limited information. White pages and reverse-phone-number lookups*
are powerful tools that can help you get a number or an address or
something to assist you in your search.

If you happen to have a photo of the person, you're in luck. Photos
are great sources of information—and if, in your searches, you happen
to find a Facebook or LinkedIn page associated with your subject,
there's a good chance you'll have a photo to work with. Throw it in a
reverse-image search (such as TinEye or Google Images) and see where
else that photo is being used, which will lead you to more information.
(If the photo is used under multiple aliases, that's a pretty good sign
something fishy's afoot.)

Different people are naturally going to have different kinds of
footprints on the web; some will have little presence, while some will
be everywhere. But there's a range of normal nowadays—someone
who's got very little information on the internet or has only information of very recent vintage might be a fake persona. Then again, he or
she might not be.

Identity hunting on the internet has some art to it as well as science, and the best way to get good at it is through practicing. Pick a few
friends, family members, co-workers, doctors, and acquaintances
and, for each of these people, use the web to find out as much as you
possibly can about them. Can you find a birthday or an age? Where the
person has gone to school? The name of a parent or a sibling? Where
the person grew up? A phone number? A photo? Try this a few times
and you'll soon see how much information is out there—and how difficult it is to hide oneself completely from view.

----

* AnyWho.com and Google do this well.

CHAPTER 4
THE LONELINESS OF
THE INTERCONNECTED

I think it's a very firm part of human nature that if you sur-
round yourself with like-minded people, you'll end up thinking
more extreme versions of what you thought before.

—CASS SUNSTEIN

Opinions are stubborn things. The firmest ones can weather for years a hailstorm of contrary facts, remaining nearly immutable in a flood of contrary evidence. Only slowly do they yield, eroded, bit by bit, by time as much as by the impositions of external reality.

The importance of a fact is measured not in absolute terms, but by judging it against the opinions it challenges. In the field known as information theory, the bits and bytes of an incoming message contain information only if the content is, to some degree, unexpected. If you can predict, with perfect confidence, what's inside an envelope without needing to open it, there's nothing to be gained by opening the envelope. It's the very unpredictability of the message—the fact that the reader doesn't know exactly what the letter contains—that gives the message any informational value at all. Information is that which defies expectation.

Information is not the barrage of facts that's pelting us from every direction. Information consists of those facts and messages that, in some way, shape our ideas. Information is the force that causes the erosion of our mental landscape, that undermines and reconstructs our perceptions of the world. Anything that does not affect our opinions is not information; it's noise.

As we grow and learn, the fragile and unsupported parts of our mental landscape are washed away, and we are left with some opinions that are as firm as bedrock—and just as difficult to move. And once in a great while, there is such a storm of hard, inescapable fact that it challenges to topple even one of our bedrock beliefs, and this causes a mental crisis.

In the 1950s, psychologist Leon Festinger sought to understand what happens at the crisis moment—when an immovable object of a core belief comes into conflict with the irresistible force of an undeniable contrary fact. And he did it by making an inspired choice about whom to study: an apocalyptic cult.

Festinger decided that the ideal subjects to study would be the members of a small group of people led by a housewife in a Chicago suburb. This woman, Dorothy Martin, claimed to write letters under the direction of beings from the planet Clarion. These beings told her that early in the morning on December 21, 1955, there would be a tremendous cataclysm: Chicago would be destroyed, and much of the United States would be submerged in a great flood. But all was not lost: Martin learned from her spirit guide that as the clock tolled midnight in the last few hours before the disaster, a spaceman would knock on the door and lead Martin and her followers to a saucer that would whisk them to safety.

Festinger knew that for the cult's members, the belief in this disaster and salvation was incredibly deeply held. Many of the members of the cult had made large personal sacrifices because of their faith in Mrs. Martin's prophecy; one, a respected physician, had lost his job—and become a laughingstock—when he exposed his daft beliefs to the newspapers. The members of the cult were so sure of the coming day of reckoning that they were willing to isolate themselves, give away their worldly goods, and even tear apart their clothing (to remove metal zippers and snaps that could injure them aboard the flying saucer) based upon their confidence in Mrs. Martin's writings. Only a deep, firm belief could inspire people to make such sacrifices. Yet when the spaceman failed to knock at the door, the cult members would be faced with the inescapable fact that the prophecy had been false. Here was a clear-cut a case of immovable belief versus irresistible fact—and it would happen on a schedule.

For Festinger, this was a perfect case study that would help him understand what he termed "cognitive dissonance"—a situation in which a person is forced to believe two mutually incompatible ideas at the same time. In particular, it would allow him to test a somewhat counterintuitive hypothesis: that when the spaceman failed to show up, Mrs. Martin and some of her followers would become even more fervent in their beliefs. In other words, the inescapable fact that the prediction failed wouldn't merely fail to shake some of Mrs. Martin's followers from their faith—it would even strengthen their fervor.

Festinger's theory was based upon the assumption that cognitive dissonance is intensely uncomfortable for most humans. When confronted with such pain, we attempt to resolve the dissonance through whatever mechanisms we have at hand. And when the dissonance-causing fact is as firm and unyielding as the continued existence of Chicago, there are only two basic approaches that one can take. First, a person can reshape the belief to accommodate the fact, or perhaps even discard the belief entirely. However, this would have been a very painful thing to do in this case, given how deeply held the belief was. The other alternative is to attempt to counter the weight of the oppressing fact by increasing one's conviction in the belief. Since this can't be done with facts, it's done with people. Specifically, Festinger argued that once Mrs. Martin's prophecy failed, some of the cult members would try to solve their cognitive dissonance by strengthening social bonds within the group and by attempting to gain more supporters. As Festinger puts it:

It is unlikely that one isolated believer could withstand the kind of disconfirming evidence we have specified. If, however, the believer is a member of a group of convinced persons who can support one another, we would expect the belief to be maintained and the believers to attempt to proselyte or to persuade nonmembers that the belief is correct.

It happened, more or less, as Festinger thought it would. Mrs. Martin and many of the die-hard believers weren't put off by the disconfirmation. Instead, she softened the blow by revealing new alien messages that would help explain the failed coming of the apocalypse. Even more telling, though, the group suddenly increased its attempts to proselytize—even to the point of issuing press releases to the media. The group would seek comfort by trying to increase its size.

The most potent weapon for fighting off uncomfortable facts is other people—a network of the faithful who are willing to believe with you. In the arms of fellow true believers, you can find solace from the brutal reality of disconfirmation.

This is just as true today as it was in the 1950s. We seek shelter from the harsh information that carves away our cherished beliefs by finding other people who share our convictions. Social ties reinforce our internal mental landscape so that it can better resist a blast of unwelcome facts. But now, with the advent of the digital age, our interconnectedness has increased almost without bound. We are able to communicate with peers all around the world as easily as—more easily than—visiting our next-door neighbor. With this tremendous interconnectedness comes the ability to build many more social ties, to weave a vaster web of personal bonds than ever before. And that means that the internet gives us much more raw social material than ever before to help us bolster our shaky prejudices and beliefs.

In a very real way, the internet is helping us preserve our mental landscape from the weathering effects of information. We are becoming ever more resistant to the effects of uncomfortable facts—and ever more capable of treating them as mere noise.

If you've ever been to London, there's a good chance you've visited the northeast edge of Hyde Park. It's a prime tourist attraction because, if you're interested in seeing the local wildlife, you can't do better than visiting Speakers' Corner on a gray Sunday afternoon. If you choose to go, you'll almost certainly be treated to a fine display: a dozen or so men (mostly) and a few women, perched on ladders and makeshift podiums, each bellowing out their complaints and exhortations to all passersby. There are Marxists on the left, apocalyptic Christians on the right, and all variety of true believers in between, haranguing the crowd—and one another—in hopes of winning a few converts. The best (or merely the most entertaining) among them can draw crowds of fifty or a hundred people or even more; even likelier is the chance to pick up a heckler or two who will fling verbal pies in hopes of catching a speaker square in the face.

Speakers' Corner is touted as a bastion of free speech—a place where Londoners and other Britons can come and air their grievances, no matter how absurd. But it's not really the prospect of free speech that draws so many speakers to that particular corner of Hyde Park every Sunday afternoon. After all, the vast majority of speakers are able to speak freely about their beliefs in plenty of other places, both public and private, without getting hauled off to jail. What brings them to Hyde Park on Sunday is not free speech, but a free audience.

What's so valuable to the speakers is that the Sunday-afternoon ritual is likely to draw a thousand or more curious people, tourists and locals alike, all of whom mill about in hopes of finding something worth listening to for a few brief moments. It's an opportunity to speak in front of a receptive crowd of a respectable size—a size that few speakers are dynamic and interesting enough to draw on their own. It's a tremendous amount of work to build up an audience as an orator, and Speakers' Corner is a way to reach far more people than an amateur could get any other way.

An audience used to be a precious and rare commodity. Generally, one could get it only through unusual eloquence, through power, or through money. The politician and the preacher build and wield their strength by gathering large audiences and influencing their thought. Conversely, certain offices automatically confer upon the holder massive, world-spanning audiences. The entire world hangs upon what the president or the pope has to say; before their elections, Barack Obama and Jorge Bergoglio had to struggle and shout to get significant numbers of people to pay attention—and they seldom had the opportunity to garner a large audience. Money, too, buys listeners; Michael Bloomberg and Rupert Murdoch, like William Randolph Hearst and Joseph Pulitzer before them, realized that nothing's better for reaching people than owning a media empire.

What opportunities were there for the rest of us? Barring an accident of fate that brings us into the public eye—as a witness or a victim or a bit player in a drama—we had to be content with writing the occasional angry letter to the editor of our local paper or joining forces with a handful of like-minded people who felt strongly about an issue dear to us. Perhaps we might try to attract the attention of somebody with his own audience, like a congressperson or a reporter. We could speak as freely as we wanted, but it made little difference if nobody heard what we were saying.

Then came the internet.

The audience problem had vanished. The internet's vast interconnectivity made it possible for everyone to hear everyone else—and to be heard by everyone else. This is perhaps the most important and radical change wrought by digital information. Every single person hooked up to the web can instantly reach every other person. Your audience is potentially the world.

Twitter is an international Speakers' Corner writ larger than anyone had ever imagined. The speech isn't quite free, but the number of people listening is vast. You can say something and, in theory, hundreds of millions of people on all seven continents are able to hear you loud and clear—if you can convince them to tune in. As with Speakers' Corner, most orators on Twitter and in other corners of the internet ramble and rave, sharing little of interest. But there are enough virtual passersby that if you have a little eloquence and a little skill, you can soon have your voice and even your image echoing around the globe. It's sometimes stunning to see how easy it can be to become an international celebrity, if only for a short time. Even against your will.

In 2002, Canadian high school student Ghyslain Raza videotaped himself swinging a large pole around himself as if it were a kung fu weapon. Somewhat portly and terribly uncoordinated, Raza cut a ridiculous figure—as many of us soon found out. For poor Raza left the videotape where some of his fellow classmates could find it, and they uploaded it to YouTube. It soon went viral; Ghyslain, dubbed "Star Wars Kid" for his very un-Jedi-like martial-arts skills, had become an international celebrity. Within a short time, hundreds of thousands of people had watched Raza's antics. As of 2013, the video had been viewed some twenty-eight million times. (By way of comparison, I'll consider myself very, very lucky if this book is read by a few hundred thousand.) Upload a cute enough video of a cat playing a piano, or do something extraordinarily foolish like shoot yourself in the leg during a gun-safety class, or create something goofy enough to tickle people's fancy—dancing hamsters or dancing babies or dancing Gangnams—and there's a chance you'll get a brief adrenaline burst of fame.

The point is not that you're guaranteed to be heard among the clatter and noise of the internet; it's that, as small and insignificant as your voice might be, it is at least possible that your voice can be perceived—and amplified—to the point that you're heard by an international audience that would make any major broadcast network proud. The mob is always there, listening, waiting to hear something interesting, and even without the power of a president or the money of a Mort Zuckerman, for a short time, at least, you can have a pulpit almost as bully as what they've got. This is free speech in the truest sense. It's not just the freedom to speak out about anything; it's also the ability to be heard by everybody.

With the ability to be heard comes the ability to organize. The internet has made it easier than ever to set up networks of like-minded people—to set up groups who have a belief or an interest in common, no matter how unusual or bizarre that interest or belief might be. Even the ideas on the very fringe of human thought—a notion that might be held by only one in a million people—might find a devoted network of several hundred or even a few thousand followers on the internet.

For example, in 2008, the Centers for Disease Control launched an investigation into a new, horrific disease. Sufferers often feel a weird crawling or biting sensation underneath the skin, and rashes and sores soon appear. Many people afflicted with the disease report pulling thin, wormlike fibers from sores. Only a few years earlier had the ailment gotten a name: Morgellons disease.

The name Morgellons was coined by Mary Leitao, a mother who was increasingly frustrated at dermatologists' inability to find out what was wrong with her young son, who kept developing strange sores that had threads poking out of them. Using a word from an old French medical article that seemed to describe a similar ailment, Leitao gave the disease a concrete name and created a foundation to attempt to find the cause of the mysterious ailment. And a website.

Once that website was established, it became a focal point for people who felt they had similar problems. The word spread quickly, and hundreds of people with similar symptoms began contacting the foundation, as well as other authorities who might be able to help, such as the Mayo Clinic and the Centers for Disease Control. By 2007—just three years after the first report of Morgellons—the CDC received about twelve hundred reports of Morgellons, triggering the inquiry. This was quite remarkable, given that the disease doesn't really exist.

Morgellons appears to be a variant of a fairly well-known condition called "delusional parasitosis"—the false conviction that you've got bugs crawling under your skin. It's not uncommon in people who are taking cocaine or other drugs, and in those who have schizophrenia, and it can occasionally strike healthy (or healthy-seeming) people as well.

The CDC study was very gentle about dispelling the myth of Morgellons, saying only that it "shares a number of clinical and epidemiologic features" with delusional parasitosis, but the message was clear enough: the disease was in the patients' minds. The fibers they found—which were analyzed by researchers—were almost all skin fragments or cotton threads that likely came from clothing. There are no bugs or strange foreign-body-producing organisms under the skin. Nevertheless, the victims clearly suffer, even if the disease has no external cause.

Despite the findings of the study, many Morgellons sufferers are unshaken in their belief that there really is something going on underneath their skin—whether it's parasites or, as a number of Morgellons theorists believe, alien DNA or self-replicating nanobots dumped by government airplanes. The deeper you delve into the internet literature on the subject, the stranger the ideas become. And looking into these ideas, it becomes clear that the internet is not just the repository in which these odd beliefs are archived and transmitted—it's also the medium that gives these ideas life in the first place. The fringe beliefs are birthed and nourished by the social connections that the internet makes possible. As two Canadian psychiatrists put it:

> a belief is not considered delusional if it is accepted by other members of an individual's culture or subculture. Although this may be appropriate in the context of spiritual or religious beliefs, the scenario in which a widely held belief is accepted as plausible simply because many people ascribe to it requires a revised conceptualization in our current era. That is, Internet technology may facilitate the dissemination of bizarre beliefs on a much wider scale than ever before.

Morgellons is an internet disease. It is a delusion that likely would have died out naturally, but thanks to its rapid spread on the internet, it took on a life of its own. Believers gathered around the banner of Morgellons, and the very size of that group convinced members that their collective delusion was, in fact, real. Soon there was a big community in which the bizarre belief—that there were unidentifiable little organisms crawling under your skin—was completely normal.

The movement became strong enough that its members were able to compel the CDC to investigate their fictional disease.

It's not just Morgellons that has taken off in this way. A person's belief in any sort of fringe idea can gain strength—and become unshakable—thanks to social bonds with other true believers. Any idea, no matter how bizarre, can seem mainstream if you're able to find a handful of others who will believe along with you. And since we are all plugged in to the ultimate Speakers' Corner every hour of every day of every week, it's trivially easy to find a group of sympathetic souls. Those small groups are constantly forming and gathering strength, reinforcing the beliefs around which they're formed, no matter how outlandish.

There are the plushies (people who like to have sex with stuffed animals) and the furries (people who like to have sex while wearing animal costumes) and the object-sexuals (people who form sexual attachments to inanimate objects). There are groups devoted to exposing shape-shifting reptilian humanoids living among us, to revealing that the U.S. government brought down the twin towers on September 11, and to arguing that the IRS has no right to collect income taxes. There are fan groups devoted to time travelers, perpetual-motion-machine builders, and crackpot theorists of all varieties. It's not that these kinds of groups came into being with the internet; anyone who's met a follower of Lyndon LaRouche or a UFO nut or a moon hoaxer knows that strange, fringe ideas can catch on even in the absence of an internet. But before the digital web made society so interconnected, it was much harder to encounter such ideas—and it took active effort to engage with the communities that had fringe theories. Now even the craziest ideas are usually but a few mouse clicks away from confirmation and reinforcement by a band of fellow travelers.

It used to be that the roughest edges of people's odd beliefs would erode and crumble through simple isolation, through a lack of reinforcement with social bonds. Now isolation is nigh impossible, and those odd beliefs are sharpened and exaggerated when they are brought into the open in the company of a cozy group of like-minded individuals. In other words, the internet is amplifying our quirks and our odd ideas. Bit by bit, it is driving us toward extremism.

The trend is reflected in the media we consume. The fragmentation of the media, especially the broadcast media, began before digital information first came into our lives. It's been almost two generations since the day when three networks held captive Americans who wanted to watch television. After a slow start, cable TV took off in the 1980s, and no longer could CBS, NBC, and ABC control the majority of television programming in the United States. In 1980, roughly 90 percent of prime-time television watchers in the U.S. were tuned in to one of the Big Three networks. By 2005 that number had dropped to 32 percent, and it has continued to decline ever since. There are more choices out there, so the audience is spread more thinly. For TV news alone, CNN, Fox News, and MSNBC and various other spinoffs and subsidiaries provide direct competition to the evening newscasts of the major networks.

Then, when the internet came along, people could get their news—even news in video format—in innumerable new ways. It's not surprising that the Big Three's evening news programs have lost 55 percent of their viewers in the past thirty years. The surprise is that they've managed to hold on to that other 45 percent.

Back when the Big Three ruled the airwaves, the nightly news had to perform a delicate balancing act. A news program had to try to appeal to the entire television audience—it had to be, quite literally, a broad cast—if it was to compete with the other two networks that were taking the same strategy. This meant that the networks couldn't become too partisan or take an extreme position on anything, for fear of alienating its potential audience. If roughly half of the country was Republican, you'd instantly alienate half your audience if your program began to seem like it was too tilted in favor of Democrats.

Then cable and the internet increased our choices. The Big Three kept trying to capture as big a slice of America as possible by staying centrist, but a couple of upstarts—particularly Fox News and MSNBC—realized that there was another possible strategy. Instead of trying to go after the entire American population with a broadly targeted program that appealed to everyone, you could go with a narrowly targeted program that appealed to only a subgroup of the population. Throw in your lot with, say, die-hard Republicans and give them coverage that makes them happy; you'll alienate Democrats and won't get them as viewers, but you can more than make up for that loss by gaining a devoted Republican fan base. This is exactly what Fox News did. Few liberals would tune in to watch Bill O'Reilly except out of grim amusement at how crazy the other side has become, but it's a program that makes the far right happy. MSNBC did exactly the reverse; by filling its schedule with shows that appeal to liberals, such as Keith Olbermann's show, it made a play for the leftist Democrats to the exclusion of the more centrist and right-leaning folks. These networks have given up on broadcasting; instead they're narrowcasting.

The more choices a consumer has on his TV, the more thinly spread the audience will be for each TV show, just because there's more competition. The more thinly spread the audience, the more it makes sense to drop the pretense of trying to appeal to everybody and to instead attempt to corner the market on one chunk of the population; and as choices increase and audiences dwindle, the proportion of the population it makes economic sense to go after becomes smaller. In this light, MSNBC and Fox make perfect sense; they are the natural consequence of the ever-increasing competition to get our attention. Narrowcasting is gradually beating out broadcasting, and the casts will get narrower and narrower as the audience becomes harder and harder to find. In effect, as audience becomes more narrowly defined, the viewer is getting more power about what kind of news and data are served up and what kind of news and data are ignored.

The internet is allowing narrowcasting on a scale never before dreamed of. When you go to CNN.com or BBC.com or PBS.org, the website is tracking which stories you read and which ones you don't. And they're using that information to make the website more appealing to you—you personally. Google News looks at your reading patterns and chooses to present you with news items that are likely to appeal to you based upon your location, your past reading choices, even your web history. It's not just Google News, in fact. Google itself—the web search engine—uses your search history and your past behavior to try to guess what kinds of links you're most likely to find useful. You might not even be conscious of it, but your online behavior is dictating what news you're exposed to, what data you're being served. In a very real sense, you are controlling which elements of the outside world you see and which you don't.

This is welcome news in many ways. We all have limited time to read, watch, or listen to the news, and we can't waste our entire day searching for information on the internet. The better the media outlets and search engines are at giving us the news we want, the more efficiently we can use our time. But at the same time, there's a very big downside. We tend to shy away from data that challenges our assumptions, that erodes our preconceptions. Getting rid of our wrong ideas is a painful and difficult process, yet it's that very process that makes data truly useful. A fact becomes information when it challenges our assumptions. These challenges are the raw material that forces our ideas to evolve, our tastes to change, our minds to grow.

The more power we have over the data that comes in, the better able we are to shelter ourselves from uncomfortable truths—from facts that challenge our preconceptions and misperceptions. If you have a steady diet of items from Fox News and *The Drudge Report*, your belief that Barack Obama is not a U.S. citizen will be perfectly safe. If you believe that vaccines cause autism, frequenting *The Huffington Post* and MSNBC will likely strengthen your conviction rather than weaken it. With news and data that is tailored to our prejudices, we deprive ourselves of true information. We wind up wallowing in our own false ideas, reflected back at us by the media. The news is ceasing to be a window unto the world; it is becoming a mirror that allows us to gaze only upon our own beliefs.*

----

* Eli Pariser talks about this phenomenon in his book *The Filter Bubble*.

Couple this dynamic with the microsociety-building power of the hyper-interconnected internet and you've got two major forces that are radicalizing us. Not only does the media fail to challenge our preconceptions—instead reinforcing them as media outlets try to cater to smaller audiences—but we all are able to find small groups of people who share and fortify the beliefs we have, no matter how quirky or outright wrong they might be. Ironically, all this interconnection is isolating us. We are all becoming solipsists, trapped in worlds of our own creation.

Solipsism wouldn't be so bad but for the fact that the worlds we're creating around ourselves are not just fictions of the mind but have real, concrete consequences for other people who don't share the same delusions.

A bad idea, a wrong piece of information, a digital brain-altering virus can spread at the speed of light through the internet and quickly find a home among a dispersed but digitally interconnected group of true believers. This group acts as a reservoir for the bad idea, allowing it to gather strength and reinfect people; as the group grows, the belief, no matter how crazy, becomes more and more solidly established among the faithful.

Morgellons is a relatively benign example; other than the believers themselves, the only people inconvenienced are physicians and insurers. Not so with real diseases. Since the late 1980s, Peter Duesberg, a biologist at Berkeley, has been arguing that AIDS is not caused by a virus, but instead is the product of using recreational drugs—or of taking the anti-HIV drugs that are used to keep the virus in check. It was a dubious belief even at the time Duesberg proposed it, and it quickly failed several tests in the earl 1990s and was soundly rejected by the scientific community. Duesberg was pretty much banished from the better—and more widely read—scientific journals after that. In the days before the internet, that would have almost guaranteed that he would fade into obscurity; forced to the fringe, Duesberg would rant and rave in fourth-tier journals and be ignored by the rest of the world. But by the mid-1990s the web had come along, so

Duesberg took to the internet and quickly found a large audience. Several HIV-denialist groups coalesced on the web, touting Duesberg's research as evidence that AIDS wasn't caused by a virus.

On October 28, 1999, Thabo Mbeki, then the president of South Africa, gave a controversial speech about AZT, the first anti-HIV drug. "Many in our country have called on the government to make the drug AZT available in our public health system," he said, but warned that "the toxicity of this drug is such that it is in fact a danger to health." It was astonishing that the president of South Africa would try to keep an anti-HIV drug out of his country, especially given that his country was ground zero for the epidemic. The incidence of HIV was skyrocketing—almost 13 percent of the population was infected by 1997—and the country was crying out for drugs that might help. AZT was in wide use to prevent pregnant mothers from transmitting the virus to children. Why was Mbeki so convinced that AZT would do more harm than good? He didn't go into detail, but he hinted at where he had gotten his information: online. "To understand this matter better," he said, "I would urge the honorable members of the National Council to access the huge volume of literature on this matter available on the internet."

Physicians and AIDS researchers in South Africa—and around the world—were shocked. The South African newspaper the *Sunday Independent* described the reaction:

> Mark Lurie, a Medical Research Council senior scientist based in Mtubatuba in KwaZulu-Natal, was "flabbergasted" by Mbeki's speech.
>
> "Here is a drug that cuts the rate of mother-to-child transmission by 50 percent. If the president is telling us that this drug doesn't work, where is his evidence for such a statement?"
>
> Mbeki's evidence seems to be the Internet, according to Tasneem Carrim, a media liaison officer for the presidency.
>
> "The president got a thick set of documents. He went into many sites, including the World Health Organisation's one. The president goes into the Net all the time," she said.

It soon became clear what sites Mbeki was visiting. The South African president had stumbled upon HIV-denialist websites and was soon consulting with them, and with Duesberg (whom Mbeki invited to South Africa). Mbeki was soon a true believer. He publicly questioned whether HIV caused AIDS, and engaged in political maneuvers to prevent the distribution of anti-HIV drugs—even ones donated for free. (Eventually the courts had to intervene to allow unfettered access to the lifesaving drugs.) The minister of health earned the scorn of the scientific world by extolling the virtues of beetroot, lemon, and garlic as better ways to prevent AIDS than the antiretroviral drugs her ministry was denying the sick and dying. A 2008 study in the *Journal of Acquired Immune Deficiency Syndromes* estimated that more than 300,000 people lost their lives between 2000 and 2005 because of Mbeki's obstinate refusal to allow his citizens to begin taking antiretroviral drugs.

Of course, volumes and volumes of HIV-denial literature are still just a Google search away.

Three hundred thousand deaths might be the most extreme consequence of a Google search gone wrong. However, history is littered with examples of fringe beliefs—ones that the vast majority of people rejected—killing thousands upon thousands. For one, millions of people starved in the Soviet Union in part because Joseph Stalin embraced the wacky anti-Darwinist ideas of Trofim Lysenko, a man who believed that you could "train" crops to grow in the wrong seasons.

But comparing the Duesberg case with Lysenko's reveals just how much more potent fringe ideas become when they're digitized. Lysenko rose to power in part because he was of peasant stock, like his powerful benefactor, Stalin. And it was the fear of Stalin that allowed his ideas to grow and take hold. Scientists couldn't silence Lysenko; indeed, Lysenko silenced (and murdered) accomplished scientists who dared to say that Lysenkoism was nonsense. It's the opposite of what happened to Duesberg, who was shunted to the fringe and silenced by the scientific community. Had Duesberg lived in the time of Lysenko, his ideas would never have circulated around the United States, much less affected a government halfway around the world several years after he was discredited at home.

Yet because of the digital revolution, the has-been professor who was a laughingstock of his home country's scientific community was able to have a Lysenko-like influence without the backing of a Joseph Stalin. And Duesberg's ideas will last much longer than Lysenko's. Lysenkoism essentially died with Stalin. However, even if the HIV-denialist movement dies in South Africa, Duesberg's ideas will remain visible to everyone for years and years to come, ready to spark a new outbreak.

Because of the interconnectedness of the digital world and the transmissibility of even large volumes of work, the most absurd fringe idea can reach far beyond the fevered mind of its creator. Even the craziest notions can be heard and amplified and transmitted by virtual communities. The extremes of human thought are gathering strength.

As we sink into the comfortable monotony of constant reinforcement, as we spend an increasing amount of time listening to sources of information that are tailored to strengthen our mental fictions rather than challenge them, we are slowly being turned into cranks ourselves. And those who don't succumb are often at the mercy of those who do.

CHAPTER 5
COPY, RIGHT?

Readers are no more interested in originality as such than eaters are.

—RICHARD POSNER

There's nobody more aware of the perils of copying than a professional writer. To be accused of copying someone's stuff can wreck a journalistic career faster than almost anything else. Yet journalists and authors do it all the time. In fact, if you've published enough, there's a good chance someone has ripped your work off and passed it off as his own.

It's happened to me a few times. The most egregious incident happened in 2001, when an author with Oxford University Press wrote a book about mathematical problems. The writer set up a famous unsolved problem—the Poincaré conjecture—with a quick description of a field known as topology:

> In 1904, French mathematician Henri Poincaré was studying the classification of shapes in space. One powerful way to classify these shapes is to observe the behavior of shrinking loops of string on the surface of an object. For example, if you

place a loop on the surface of a soccer ball, as it shrinks it will always shrivel up into a point. On the other hand, a loop of string around a doughnut might not be able to shrivel completely; it could get stuck if it is looped around or through the doughnut's hole.

A year earlier, I had written in *Science* magazine:

> In 1904, French mathematician Henri Poincaré was studying the classification of shapes in space, a field known as topology. One powerful way of classifying these shapes is to observe the behavior of shrinking loops of string on the surface of an object. For example, if you place a loop on the surface of a basketball, as it shrinks, it will always shrivel up into a point. On the other hand, a loop of string around a doughnut might not be able to shrivel completely: It could get stuck if it is looped around or through the doughnut's hole.

Other than changing "basketball" to "soccer ball," getting rid of a clause ("a field known as topology"), changing a colon to a semicolon, and eliminating a comma, the text is identical, character for character, to what I had written. In fact, much of the last chapter of the Oxford book was taken word for word from my fourteen-hundred-word article. And I wasn't the only source—the Oxford book was chock-full of phrases and illustrations that were pilfered from unattributed sources essentially unchanged.

Copying a thousand words, character for character and punctuation mark for punctuation mark, used to not be an easy task. Sure, it's less work than crafting your own words, but even for an expert typist clattering away at full speed, it would take nearly ten minutes to enter it—and even more to check it carefully to make sure that everything's in the right place.

That's the way it used to be. No longer.

If you've got a piece of writing in digital format, more likely than not you can simply hit a couple of buttons to copy large passages into memory, then hit a couple buttons more to vomit up that text into your word processor. Control-C, control-V, and voilà! Hundreds upon hundreds of words are copied, without a single comma or caret awry. It's so easy that it's everywhere.*

It may seem like a trivial point, but the act of copying on a computer underscores one of the most important—and revolutionary— elements of digital information. Digitization made it possible, for the very first time, to make copies of writing (or video, or other forms of information) quickly, easily, cheaply, and flawlessly. Indeed, perfect copying is one of the hallmarks of digital information, one of the things that make it so different from the analog information it supplanted.

Analog information is hard to replicate, and it's degraded every time it is copied. Imagine that someone hands you a book—an old, leather-bound volume—and you want to make a copy. Assuming you can't get your hands on the printing plates, you've only got a couple of options. You can find yourself a medieval monk to make you a copy by hand, or go one better with a typewriter. But this is impractical for anything but a very short book. A better option is to spend an hour or two at a xerox machine, making copies of the book. It's quite a pain to xerox the whole thing, but you'll get a very serviceable copy—even though it won't be perfect. There will undoubtedly be smudges or blurs; words might be cut off or illegible. Even a very good xerox copy of a page is never 100 percent identical to the source it comes from. If you were in school long enough ago to remember the xeroxes of

----

* My two worlds, journalism and academia, are particularly affected. In the ivory tower, it's not just students who do it (despite giving the harshest possible warnings every year, my colleagues and I catch a small handful of grads and undergrads trying to pass off others' work as their own). It's also professors. Not long ago, I was asked to review a paper for a peer-reviewed journal, and I discovered that portions were cut-and-pasted from Wikipedia. (It was easy to tell, because the author had accidentally cut-and-pasted the links from the webpage as well as the text.)

xeroxes of xeroxes of old texts that certain professors used to hand out, you already know this quite well. Each generation of photocopying makes the handouts less and less legible. Minute distortions and errors caused by the copying processes build up over time, piling up and making each new copy a little less readable than the last. By the sixth or seventh generation of copies, the text's once crisp blacks and whites have smeared out into grayish halftones, and multiple layers of blotches and spots have made the handout a trial to decipher.

A digital copy, if properly done, is absolutely identical to the original—in some sense, there's no point in talking about "original" and "copy," because neither has any greater claim to authenticity. They're the same. And these perfect copies can be made almost instantly, transmitted almost anywhere, and cost virtually nothing. This perfect replicability has transformed our relationship with information.

The advent of cheap, perfect digital copies completely destroyed a number of ways we humans used to think about information. For one thing, it utterly demolished the basis for a market in goods made out of information, such as books, newspapers, movies, and recordings of music.

If you ask an economist to define "economics" for you, odds are he'll say something like "it's the study of how societies allocate scarce resources." And this, for the most part, is true. Economists are generally interested only in things which we have limited amounts of (gold, bolts of cotton, physical labor, time) and not things that are free and plentiful (air, sunlight, flu viruses).

In days gone by, information used to be in the former camp. We had limited amounts of information at our fingertips, and that information we had took some time, effort, and money to replicate and distribute. Books, CDs, DVDs, videotapes, and the like were difficult to produce. As an author, I could write a manuscript, but it took a publishing house to mass-produce that information, send it out to bookstores around the world, and get it into the hands of consumers. Goods like books were everywhere, but they were also scarce, in the sense that you couldn't just produce one out of thin air. If you wanted to read the latest Stephen King novel, you had to get your mitts on it through a limited number of outlets. You had to purchase a copy or wait for one to become available at your local library. If you valued the novel enough to want a copy for your very own use, you had to buy the thing, unless you had the stomach to try to xerox the whole book. (And this would probably cost you more in time and copying fees than the retail price of the book itself.) The difficulty and expense of copying analog information was a barrier to your getting the book for free. This is what makes the resource scarce.

This replication barrier was fundamental not just to the economics of information goods, but also to the laws that are meant to protect the creators of information. Copyright law, after all, begins with the word "copy," and the fundamental protections were aimed at preventing other people from duplicating—making a copy of—your work without authorization. In a world where a book is a scarce commodity, someone else's making a copy of your book reduces the scarcity—and therefore the value—of the information that you're trying to sell. By privileging the act of copying, copyright law preserves and defends the scarcity of a work, giving its creator the ability to control when and where the work is replicated.

Digital information dynamited the very foundations of the market for information goods. So long as it was in analog form, a book was hard to copy. Once it made the move to digital, it could be copied with perfect fidelity in just a few seconds, transmitted anywhere in the world in the blink of an eye, and stored at practically no cost at all. No longer was there any difficulty or expense in copying the information contained in an e-book, so there was technically no more barrier to your reproducing the information once it fell into your hands. You could make ten copies or a hundred or a hundred thousand if you liked. You could essentially conjure copies of the book out of thin air. The information becomes no more scarce than air or sunlight. And with that, books and DVDs and CDs and the like were no longer in the realm of traditional economics. Informational goods are part of a "post-scarcity" world. And when a good isn't scarce, it's hard to get people to pay any money for it.

Similarly, the entire basis for copyright law went kablooey as soon as scarcity disappeared and perfect copies became cheap and easy. When the first graphical web browsers started appearing, copyright law was instantly made effectively obsolete. Every time you visit a webpage with a browser, it makes a copy of that page, putting it in a "cache" on your hard drive. Though copyright law prohibits making copies of other people's intellectual property, your web browser violates that rule automatically pretty much every time you visit someone's webpage. The very act of pointing your browser to a website means that you're making a copy of someone's information. Copying was so effortless, so fundamental to the exchange of digital information on the web, that any restriction upon it was like trying to restrict people from getting more than their fair share of sunlight.

The advent of digital information has made a mess of the whole field of intellectual property. We're struggling right now to try to understand the rules of a post-scarcity economy, how to get people to pay for information goods when the goods can be copied and redistributed willy-nilly as soon as the first copy is sold. (Nowadays it's often just hours between the launch of a new book or movie or hit song and the release of dozens of copies of it on the internet for anyone to copy at will.) Nobody's come up with a way to fix copyright law or to revive the crippled market for digital-information-based goods. In large part, companies dealing those goods have tried to create artificial scarcity by making it harder to copy—usually through digital rights management (DRM) schemes or firewalls or by other means of limiting access to information—with limited success. (See chapter 5½ for more on artificial scarcity.)

"Information wants to be free" is the clarion call of the internet generation. But it's not free to create. Therein lies the rub.

Information—stuff that changes the way we view the world—is expensive. It takes time and effort to uncover something unexpected and to turn that information into something that's usable and interesting.

The higher your standards for reliability and quality, the more costly it is to produce. This is easiest to see from the perspective of a journalist, who, after all, builds his career upon sniffing out new information and presenting it to the public.

Imagine you're a journalist who's found out about a fairly straightforward breaking news item—say, a new piece of scientific research that's just been made public. It's nothing fancy or terribly intricate; a quick four- or five-paragraph story will do it justice. What resources does writing such a basic story require?

At a very minimum, you're going to have to perform two or three interviews to make sure you're presenting the research properly. For one thing, you'll have to speak to one of the scientists involved with the research so you can make sure you really understand what's going on. After that, you'll have to contact an outside expert or two—someone who knows the field but wasn't involved in doing this particular bit of research—to help you put the science in context. (Getting the opinion of an independent scientist is absolutely crucial if you're going to figure out whether the research should be taken seriously. After all, no scientist is going to say that his own research is baloney. It takes an outsider to point out major flaws.) If all goes perfectly—if you're able to reach all your sources immediately—you might be able to turn the story around in about an hour and a half.* Most of the time, things won't go that smoothly.

There's a firm limit to how many journalistic pieces you can turn around in a day—even if great stories are handed to you directly from the Archangel Gabriel, even if you can bang out a four-paragraph story in your sleep, and even if your editors move at the speed of light. You're limited by your sources; it takes time to find them, chase them down, and then speak to them.

----

* This isn't counting the time and effort associated with editing. At a better news outlet, a reporter's work will be scrutinized by a primary editor, then a top editor, then a copyeditor, all of whom are futzing with the story to make it better. (At least in theory.) Driving down the costs of generating news stories—and speeding up the process—also means thinning out the editorial net.

In March 2013, an internal memo at *The Washington Post* revealed that the paper was casting about for a blogger for its style section. This blogger would be expected to produce "at least a dozen pieces of content per day." Given that pace, the time pressure for the job would be too great to reach any human sources for most of those stories. The natural consequence would be that the blogger would either be stuck writing opinion or commentary, which doesn't need any sources, or would have to "aggregate" other reporters' work.

What does it mean to aggregate news stories? "At its best, aggregation can mean collecting stories on a topic from a variety of news outlets and directing readers toward them through Web links," wrote Patrick Pexton, the ombudsman of *The Washington Post*, in April 2012. "At its worst . . . it verges on theft."

Pexton's comments on aggregation were spurred by the resignation of Elizabeth Flock, a *Washington Post* blogger/writer who had been caught printing falsehoods and plagiarizing:

> [Flock] did a roundup on Republican presidential candidate Mitt Romney allegedly using an old Ku Klux Klan slogan in his stump speech—a story that went viral online yet was untrue— and she didn't call the Romney campaign for comment, nor did any editor make sure she did. And on April 13, she aggregated a story trending online about life on Mars. . . . It appears that she copied, pasted and slightly rewrote two paragraphs from the Discovery [website's] story. Plagiarism perhaps, but also a perpetual danger in aggregated stories.

Flock had been writing nearly six stories a day, said Pexton, who felt that when the *Post* asked the blogger to write at that pace, "the pressures were just too great" to maintain journalistic integrity; plagiarism was essentially bound to happen. (Obviously, this concern didn't stop the *Post* from asking for an even faster pace from its style-section blogger a year later.)

Aggregation need not mean mere cutting and pasting. It can be done ethically; in fact, the very structure of the web, which encourages links, means it's easy to give credit where credit is due. An aggregator can easily provide an important service to her readers by steering them to the interesting news on the web, and do it without violating any journalistic rules. The aggregator just has to make plain that the information is coming from elsewhere. At heart, an aggregator is a signpost: so long as there are destinations worth visiting, signposts that point those destinations out can be valuable. But it's a mistake to confuse the signpost with the ultimate destination, the aggregator with the person who actually found and shaped the information that you want to see.

Aggregation, opinion, and curation are important. People who have a talent for finding the most valuable elements in others' work, who can winnow large volumes of data and eliminate the chaff, who can assemble a story out of fragments—these people are becoming increasingly important for keeping the public informed as the volume of chatter out there threatens to swamp out even the most interesting stories.*

The problem arises because aggregation and opinion are powered by information uncovered and revealed by newsgathererers—by journalists who find stories, report them, and reveal them to the public. So, for aggregators to be able to flourish, there has to be a news ecosystem in which aggregation and opinion are in a reasonable balance with primary newsgathering. But that balance is increasingly out of whack. The newsgathering process—the initial uncovering and verification of information—is slow and expensive. In the post-scarcity market for information, it's harder and harder to get people to pay for your information-gathering efforts, so newsrooms are increasingly squeezed to cut their budgets. At the same time, the workload is increasing as staffing levels drop. As a result, primary newsgathering is looking more and more like a losing proposition. On the other hand, aggregation and opinion are cheap and easy to produce. Consequently, they give media companies a better return on their investment than

----

* See chapter 7 for more on aggregation, search, and what happens as these functions fail us.

newsgathering does. The former are driving out the latter.* Signposts are springing up everywhere as destinations get rarer and rarer. And it's apparent that the destinations are increasingly not what they look like—they're too often not news stories as much as aggregations dressed up in the respectable garb of reportage.

It's not hard to find if you look carefully. Find an event big enough that there are a lot of people writing about the same thing. Collect all of their stories and tease them apart to figure out where the reporters got their information. Did they collect it themselves, or did they cut and paste it from another source? The answer is often rather unsettling.

In January 2013, a bunch of primate researchers published an article in the *Proceedings of the National Academy of Sciences* that purported to show that chimpanzees had a sense of fairness. In the research, the scientists set up a game in which a chimpanzee could choose to hog most of a reward (bananas, naturally) or to share it equally with a fellow chimpanzee. More often than not, the chimps chose to share. By way of explanation, the *Daily Mail* quoted one of the researchers, Darby Proctor, of Emory University:

> "Humans typically offer generous portions, such as 50 per cent of the reward, to their partners, and that's exactly what we recorded in our study with chimpanzees."

The Telegraph also got a quotation from Proctor:

> "Humans typically offer generous portions, such as 50 percent of the reward, to their partners—and that's exactly what we recorded in our study with chimpanzees."

----

* For example, a 2013 study by the Pew Research Center concluded that on cable news channels, "commentary and opinion are far more prevalent on the air throughout the day (63% of the airtime) than straight news reporting (37%)." A mere 15 percent of MSNBC's programming was devoted to news, while the rest was given over to commentary, opinion, and other "meta-news."

Agence France-Presse quoted Frans de Waal, a different member of the research team:

> "Humans typically offer generous portions, such as 50 percent of the reward, to their partners, and that's exactly what we recorded in our study with chimpanzees," says de Waal.

In fact, *The Telegraph*, the *Mail*, and AFP didn't appear to speak to Proctor or de Waal. The quotations were cut and pasted from a press release issued by Emory (and misattributed, in AFP's case).

Of the fourteen distinct versions of the story that I was able to find online—versions that were apparently meant to pass as primary newsgathering rather than as aggregation—only six would have lived up to the standards of minimally competent journalism that I described earlier. At the very least, a journalist has to talk to one of the architects of the study as well as one outsider who might be able to put the research in context. The other eight, which included major media outlets like *Time, U.S. News,* and the *Los Angeles Times,* failed to meet even that low bar.

If any of those outlets had consulted an outside source, they would have discovered that the research was deeply flawed. Proctor's study was based on a very small number of chimpanzees, which raises problems with interpretation of the data. More important, the chimps behaved in a way that makes it pretty clear they didn't quite understand the task they were asked to perform. It was a glaring problem with the study, and if you took the time to speak to an outside primate researcher, you were all but certain to get a dose of reality. Indeed, all six reporters who actually contacted an unaffiliated scientist expressed skepticism about the study.

"Reporters" who covertly cut and paste quotations or phrases from press releases are engaging in a masquerade. They're dressing up their prose to make it look like they've done reporting—primary newsgathering—when they haven't. Instead, they're merely taking the information parceled out to them by a third party, rearranging it on the plate, and serving it up to readers.*

This isn't plagiarism in the usual sense. The author of a press release *wants* her prose to be copied, because that's the most effective way to get her organization's message across. It's impossible to steal something that's freely given. And many reporters feel that this fact makes it perfectly okay to cut and paste from press releases.

In 2011, Steve Penn, a columnist with the *Kansas City Star,* was fired. According to the *Star,* Penn was canned because he had "lifted material from press releases verbatim," violating the paper's ethics policy. Penn sued, countering that his "training (and the widespread practice at the *Star*) was to use those press releases without attribution, and on the basis of an implied permission for such use." So the permission (and the "everybody does it" defense) make it perfectly acceptable, apparently.

While it might be a violation of the *Star*'s ethics policy, Penn certainly has a point that it's a widespread practice by journalists in general, even if not at the *Star.* A few months after Penn was fired, WUSA, a CBS affiliate channel, was humiliated by a similar scandal. WUSA's web producer, Ashley Jennings, was caught having cut and pasted material from a *Washington Post* article and posted it on the WUSA website.

> "I had no intention of replicating someone else's work. I've never done that," Jennings said. . . . When the story was sent to

----

* Or viewers. "Video news releases" (VNRs) are prepackaged video stories ginned up by a corporate or government interest that are designed to look like a piece of TV journalism. They're distributed for free to news stations, many of which are happy to play them on the air, disguised as in-house reporting. In 2005, after looking at the use of VNRs by various government agencies, the Government Accountability Office declared that the agencies were taking part in illegal "covert propaganda" campaigns.

her, she was working on rewriting five press releases during the same 30–40-minute window, she said.

What lack of self-awareness. Jennings truly believed that she never copied anyone else's writing, even though she made clear to a reporter that much of her day is spent copying (or "rewriting") press releases. Sure, there is a legal difference between copying/rewriting sections of a *Washington Post* article, which bears a copyright, and a press release, which doesn't. But there's not much of a moral difference.

Fundamentally, cut-and-paste journalism is a betrayal of a reader's trust, an attempt to gain authority that is undeserved. By using other people's words, a journalist tries to convince his audience that he has performed research into a novel subject, consulted with experts, processed a great deal of information, and distilled the result onto paper by writing about it. But that's not what a cut-and-paste journalist does. Without even the need to retype a few hundred words, a journalist who copies from press releases or from other sources can take someone else's ideas and words and present them as his own. Ultimately, he is disguising the origin of whatever information he's presenting. A cut-and-paste journalist is pretending to have insight, authority, and creativity when he's merely a conduit for someone else's. He's a waiter pretending to be a chef.

Anyone reading the news carefully will see large numbers of supposedly straight reporting stories that are partially or largely copied from another source. Everywhere there are signposts cleverly disguised as destinations. Cut-and-paste journalism is becoming acceptable in the industry. And this was the real scandal of the Jonah Lehrer affair.

In the summer of 2012, *The New Yorker* hired star science reporter Jonah Lehrer—author of several best-selling books on neuroscience—and quickly saw their star crash to earth. First came accusations that he was recycling his own work, publishing the same story several times nearly verbatim, each time presenting it as new without any hint that large passages had been printed before. This was sloppy, but not enough to wreck his career. Reusing one's work is perfectly acceptable in certain contexts, especially if one is up-front about it. Lehrer recycled so much of his prose so often—and made his stuff look new—that it was rather dodgy, but not a mortal sin for a journalist. Then he got caught making up Bob Dylan quotations in his most recent book, *Imagine*.

I got tangled up in the mess when Wired.com—Lehrer was a blogger for them before he left for *The New Yorker*—asked for help. When the allegations of fabrication came to light, *Wired* felt it had to review the material he left behind on its website to see if there were any problems.

Why, yes. There were.

I looked at eighteen of Lehrer's posts. In five, elements were cut and pasted from press releases. In three more, parts were plagiarized from other sources. And the vast majority were recycled—fourteen out of eighteen had passages that were nearly verbatim from stuff he had previously published.*

What's so terrifying is not that there are people out there who are willing to plagiarize or fabricate; that's always been the case. What's troubling is that Lehrer had been cutting and pasting for years, for several different websites, and nobody noticed. At Wired.com, he even recycled—almost verbatim—things that he had published just a few months earlier. For example, in January 2011, describing the quirks of a man with a freakish memory, Lehrer had written on Wired.com:

> In the early 1920s, the Russian neurologist A.R. Luria began studying the mnemonic skills of a newspaper reporter named Sherashevsky, who had been referred to the doctor by his editor. Luria quickly realized that Sherashevsky was a freak of recollection, a man with such a perfect memory that he often struggled to forget irrelevant details. After a single read of

---

* Wired.com, for reasons not entirely clear, did not publish my analysis, so I published it at Slate.com.

Dante's *Divine Comedy*, he was able to recite the complete poem by heart. When given a random string of numbers hundreds of digits long, Sherashevsky easily remembered all the numbers, even weeks later. While this flawless memory occasionally helped Sherashevsky at work—he never needed to take notes—Luria also documented the profound disadvantages of such an infinite memory. Sherashevsky, for instance, was almost entirely unable to grasp metaphors, since his mind was so fixated on particulars.

Just five months earlier, Lehrer had described the same case in the same words.*

Where was Lehrer's original post? Wired.com.

Nobody at Wired.com noticed that one of its writers had posted essentially the same thing over and over again. No editor, no copy editor, no fellow writer—nobody. Either nobody noticed or nobody cared.

While Lehrer should have permanently been drummed out of the corps of nonfiction writers,† the fact that he had been cutting and pasting stuff—from himself, not to mention from press releases and other writers—for so long without a whiff of a problem reveals much about the true state of journalism. Despite all the noises media outlets make about being intolerant of plagiarism and valuing solid reportage, the truth is that everybody's looking the other way as cut-and-paste journalism becomes ascendant.

The media are being driven further and further into the cut-and-paste realm by the unforgiving economics of post-scarcity information. It's expensive to be a primary newsgatherer. It's difficult to unearth information, prepare it, and present it to the public. But it's pretty much

---

* Lehrer also got some substantial details of this anecdote wrong; for example, Sherashevsky didn't memorize the entire *Divine Comedy*, just a stanza.

† He's apparently writing a new book, about love and redemption, for Simon & Schuster.

free to copy information that's already out there—to riff on it, to dress it up in slightly different ways, or even to take it wholesale. And so the information ecology is changing dramatically. The primary producers are becoming vastly outnumbered by the repackagers, the repurposers, and the recyclers. Media organizations are spending less time on the high-cost activity of gathering information and more time on rewarming it. At the same time, the ranks of people who produce press releases and prepackaged information for journalists to crib—public relations professionals, or flacks—has swelled. In 1980, there were 1.25 flacks for every journalist. By 2009 there were 3.6 flacks per hack. The product that all these PR types are churning out with ever-increasing speed isn't really information—it's advertising. However, it's a good enough simulacrum of information to be good enough for many media outlets' purposes.

It's one of the big ironies of the information age. Information wants to be free. But the very ease of copying and transmitting information is making it a more precious resource. Indeed, there are other forces at work that threaten to make information truly hard to find.

CHAPTER 5½
SCARCITY

Scarcity is what makes the global economy work. Objects have monetary value not because they are inherently useful but because they're hard to get. The most essential substance on earth—oxygen, because we couldn't survive for even a few minutes without it—is valueless because it's ubiquitous. (If someone were to lock you in an airtight room, once the oxygen became scarce enough, he might be able to extract money from you with an offer of fresh air.) And people can bestow value upon completely useless objects, like little green pieces of paper, but only if you can't manufacture those objects except by expending a great deal of effort.

In West Africa, the shell from a certain species of cowrie was used as a currency by virtue of how hard it was to transport large amounts from where it was found—in the Indian Ocean and thereabouts. It didn't have any inherent worth, but about 2,500 cowries were considered equivalent to a silver dollar in the mid-nineteenth century. Then, thanks to the slave industry, as well as the palm oil industry, industrialized nations caused a massive influx of some fourteen billion shells into the West African cowrie economy. The object was no longer scarce, and therefore had no further value. The cowrie economy completely collapsed.*

A digital good—whether it be a book, a movie, an audio recording, or a piece of software—is little more than a string of ones and zeros, and those strings of ones and zeros can be replicated with perfect fidelity and redistributed in a fraction of a second. It's easy to make perfect copies of the good, flooding us with nearly free facsimiles of something that took a great deal of time and effort to create in the first place. That means the end of the market in information, at least as we've always known it. As my NYU colleague Clay Shirky puts it:

> It is our misfortune to live through the largest increase in expressive capability in the history of the human race, a misfortune because surplus always breaks more things than scarcity. Scarcity means valuable things become more valuable, a conceptually easy change to integrate. Surplus, on the other hand, means previously valuable things stop being valuable, which freaks people out.

The people who produce and market informational goods—intellectual property—are struggling with ways of ensuring that their products still have value, despite the sudden disappearance of scarcity. To a large extent, their attempts have relied upon trying to impose scarcity, artificially, upon digital information. It's not working.

Trying to make digital information scarce is a tough problem. Everything that a computer can understand boils down to ones and zeros, and computers, by their very nature, are good at making copies

----

* There's a digital equivalent to the cowrie currency known as a "bitcoin." A bitcoin, at heart, is a string of ones and zeros that has a rare and impossible-to-fake property, thereby forcing you to expend a lot of computer effort if you want to create new bitcoins. You can actually use bitcoins to purchase certain things online.

of ones and zeros. So anything that you feed into a computer, no matter what those ones and zeros represent, is copyable. If the computer can use it—can play it or display it or run it—it's inherently easy to reproduce.

One way around the problem is to sell a crippled copy of the information. You might, for example, sell a copy of a computer game that's encrypted and needs to connect with a company-owned server to make it fully usable. This makes it harder (though not impossible) to make copies of the information willy-nilly. But the fundamental problem remains: if your computer is to be able to make use of the information, it can copy it. It might not be easy for someone without know-how, but with enough computer savvy, it's doable.

Another way is to cripple information-processing machines so that they can make use of the information in certain ways but can't use it in others—and can't replicate it. This technique is used much more frequently than you might expect.

For example, many copiers in the United States have a strange weakness built in: they can't make an accurate color copy of anything with five small circles in a particular asymmetric pattern. Why? On the back of any modern $10 or $20 bill, there's a constellation of little yellowish numbers—10s or 20s—in the background. Look carefully at the zeros—notice that they're perfectly circular rather than elongated, as most zeros tend to be—and you'll see that they are in that group-of-five constellation pattern. Similarly, high-value pound notes and euro notes and Canadian dollars are littered with little circles, sometimes cleverly disguised as notes or stars or some other decorative pattern, and sometimes not disguised at all. It's a counterfeiting-deterrence scheme.

Copier manufacturers—and publishers of photo-manipulation software—have agreed to hamstring their products, deliberately making their copiers and software incapable of rendering accurate images of anything containing the constellation of circles (or any of a number of other digital watermarks or anti-counterfeit features). Similarly,

DVD players nowadays have a built-in "feature" that makes U.S. versions incapable of playing discs meant for the European market—and vice versa. (Similar "features" are what make a DVD player incapable of fast-forwarding past commercials at the beginning of a disc.) This inherent limitation creates artificial scarcity. Schemes like this require collusion between the manufacturers of the devices that use and interpret the information and the people who produce the information. It's an uneasy and unstable partnership, because someone with enough computer know-how and determination can almost always bypass the system. It's not that difficult to program a rudimentary Photoshop-like piece of software that doesn't obey the ban on imaging the five-circle constellation, or to rig a U.S. DVD player to play discs intended for the European or Asian markets.

The most recent technique for creating artificial scarcity is to prevent you, to the extent possible, from actually gaining control over the digital information that you purchase. By keeping that information embedded in an environment controlled by one company—by having your music purchase move from an Apple store to an Apple player via an Apple piece of software (ideally running on an Apple computer)— that company can control when and how you're able to access the music you've bought. And if you want to do something that Apple doesn't want you to be able to do (say, move your music from your iPod to a new computer or a non-Apple MP3 player), it can be damnably hard. In a sense, Apple and Amazon and other purveyors of digital information are trying to move us to a model akin to renting information rather than owning it. Even more strikingly, as we move to a "cloud computing" model, information resides primarily on computers that aren't in your physical possession or in your control. Which means that the information it contains is never really yours.*

----

* You can't, for example, lend it to others easily. This kind of model is destroying institutions that are based upon lending, such as libraries, as well as used-book and used-game stores, which are founded upon the resale of intellectual property.

In 2009, Amazon.com proved that by deleting e-books—without permission—from various users' Kindle readers.* The books simply vanished from the readers' virtual shelves. Among the e-books that Amazon unpublished: George Orwell's *1984*.

----

* The reason was that Amazon had sold the electronic copies of the books without securing the right to do so, so Amazon was trying to right their wrong by recalling the copies.

CHAPTER 6
ALL HAT, NO CATTLE

The class which has the means of material production at its disposal, has control at the same time over the means of mental production, so that thereby, generally speaking, the ideas of those who lack the means of mental production are subject to it.

—KARL MARX, *THE GERMAN IDEOLOGY*

The Shahab-3 missile is a fairly sophisticated piece of technology. It's a medium-range rocket that can loft a one-ton payload some eight hundred miles—more than enough to hit Tel Aviv from a mobile launchpad in Iran.

During a military exercise on July 9, 2008, Iran launched a salvo of missiles into the air. It was a display of strength, meant to showcase the emergence of Iran as a military power to be reckoned with. Sepah News, described by *The New York Times* as "the media arm of the Iranian Revolutionary Guards," proudly distributed a photograph to news media around the world: four missiles perched atop pillars of smoke and flame, streaking toward the sky. That pride would soon turn to humiliation.

Within a few hours of the photograph's publication in the West, it became clear that there was one too many missiles. Upon close inspection, you could see that the third missile in the line of four was a fabrication. The number-three missile, its flame, and the top of its column of smoke were nearly identical with those of missile number two; the billowing black cloud of smoke on the ground was the same as that from missile number four. The third missile was a crude composite, cobbled together with photo-editing software and a bit of digital artistry. In truth—as an undoctored photo definitively shows—one of the missiles had failed to launch. To cover that failure, the Iranian military crafted a missile out of thin air and tried to snooker the public.

What's notable about the incident is not that Iran was trying to manipulate images to fool us, but that they did it so badly that they became a laughingstock.* (IRAN: YOU SUCK AT PHOTOSHOP, read one headline.) All across the web, people mocked Iran by creating their own photoshopped versions of the missile scene, enhancing the image with Godzillas, nuclear blasts, robots, kittens, and dinosaurs—many of which were inserted more artfully than the Iranian artists did with their artificial smoke and rockets. Amateurs in their basements were doing a better job of faking reality than a foreign state.

Photo manipulation used to be a tricky business, requiring thousands of dollars in darkroom equipment, airbrushes, and some pretty specialized artistic talent to pull off properly. Typically it was only media outlets and governments that would put in the time and effort to manipulate photos, and even for the world experts, the results were often far from convincing. Look at enough Stalin-era photographs and you begin to recognize the hallmarks of a Soviet airbrush job: the hazy outlines, the soft and indistinct shadows of the "vanishing commissar" who'd fallen out of favor since the photo was taken. It took a great deal of time, effort, and money to try to fake a photo, and even all that time and effort didn't yield something airtight.

Now anyone with a camera and a computer can attempt it, and

---

* Although they did it well enough to fool the newspaper editors who published the photo in the first place.

with a little talent you can do a very credible job. Gone are the days where you needed expensive equipment to concoct your own reality. Thanks to the advent of digital technology, you can alter photographs on the cheap, every bit as well as a state agency can.

It's not just photography that's been transformed by the digital revolution. A few dozen years ago, only well-heeled companies with expensive printing machinery could publish professional-looking books and pamphlets and distribute them to millions of people. Now all it requires is a laptop. The costs of printing—of producing information in a professional-looking format—are dropping dramatically, and the physical quality of do-it-yourself publishing is increasing just as rapidly. For a few dollars, you can get your work printed as a book that's all but indistinguishable from a volume produced by a high-end publishing house. The power to produce high-quality information, whether it's in the form of a book or a video or a magazine, is no longer in the hands of a few people rich enough to afford the means to produce it. We all now have that power.

To Karl Marx, the key to understanding society was to look at the way that the society's goods were being produced. The means of production—the mechanisms by which goods were created—were the most valuable assets of any society, and the focal point from which power emanated. He who controlled the means of production controlled the direction of society.

When it comes to goods that are essentially information—books, newspapers, videos, music recordings, computer programs—the moneyed interests no longer hold a monopoly over the means of production. In 1980, if you wanted to publish a book, you had to convince a company with access to a big, expensive printing machine to do it for you. This meant either writing a really good book that could mean a profit to the publisher or forking over ten thousand dollars or so to a vanity press. Nowadays you can publish a book for free. A print-on-demand book publisher will charge you nothing to get a book to market; it will print only as many copies as are purchased, guaranteeing a profit—or at least no loss. Thanks to print-on-demand firms, you can not only print your memoirs, but you can burn hundreds of copies of CDs and DVDs or promote and distribute your music and video online with very little overhead. You can even create your own professional-looking magazine, distributing it electronically for no cost, or in glossy heavy-stock paper for a modest fee.

Digital technology has liberated us, allowing the individual to express his ideas as effectively as a corporation or a government can. It has also had an unexpected consequence. Because we're all able to produce such professional-looking information, it's getting harder to tell good from bad, professional from amateur, authority from ignoramus—and, even more alarming, reality from fiction.

The newfound ease of faking photography is just one small aspect of our digital liberation, but it's perhaps the clearest example of how the ease of digital production is changing our relationship with information.

To be sure, phony and manipulated photos have been around since the beginning of photography. Fakers staged scenes, added ghostly apparitions in the darkroom, and used various props to bend people's sense of reality. Near the end of World War I, two young girls used photos to convince the gullible that fairies were living among us. Their method was to pose with painstakingly illustrated cutouts and to show the photos to people already inclined to believe in the supernatural. But generally speaking, it took a reasonable amount of time and effort to try to fake a photo convincingly. And this gave us confidence that photography was a true reflection of reality. The relative difficulty of high-quality photo manipulation gave us confidence that seeing was believing, at least most of the time.

With digital cameras, we don't develop pictures; we download them onto our computers. Depending on how your computer's set up, the very act of downloading might automatically bring up a program that allows you to manipulate your photos in subtle ways, increasing or reducing brightness, tweaking contrast, removing the Satanic red glow in your nephew's eyes, and so forth. With the press of a button, you can crop an image or automatically stitch together photos taken at different times into a single panoramic mosaic. If your software is a little more sophisticated, you can beautify the image in other ways, applying filters, touching up colors, even changing contours with a simulated airbrush. Upload your photos to Instagram and you're greeted with nearly infinite tools for shifting the color palette, for altering the focus of the photo, or for adding special effects. It's almost become second nature to alter photos after we take them.

There's no clear line at which photo retouching becomes photo manipulation. Even when it comes to scientific images, which are supposed to represent laboratory observations, the distinction between real and fake has become blurry. In 2004, *The Journal of Cell Biology* sounded a warning:

> It's all so easy with Photoshop. In the days before imaging software became so widely available, making adjustments to image data in the darkroom required considerable effort and/ or expertise. It is now very simple, and thus tempting, to adjust or modify digital image files. Many such manipulations, however, constitute inappropriate changes to your original data, and making such changes can be classified as scientific misconduct.

Under certain circumstances, it could be perfectly legitimate to alter a photograph in a scientific paper slightly—cropping an image of cells to draw the eye to the most important feature in the photograph, or boosting the contrast of a picture of a gel so that blots that encode genetic information are more visible. But once a researcher learns how to use Photoshop to do those minor alterations, it's only a small step to making much more drastic changes. And in some cases, the researchers were more than happy to take that step. As Photoshop became widely available in laboratories, blots began to disappear and others started to appear in their place. Cells started being transplanted from one photograph to another. Parts of images were cloned, while others were deleted.

The advent of Photoshop changed the face of scientific fraud. In 1990, the Office of Research Integrity (ORI)—a government organization devoted to investigating certain claims of scientific misconduct—reported that image-manipulation cases made up less than 3 percent of their caseload. By 2000 that number had risen to 14 percent. Just four years later, in 2004, it had jumped to 40 percent, and in 2008 it was nearly 70 percent.

Some high-profile scientists' work were caught up in image-manipulation investigations, such as Catherine Verfaillie, a stem-cell researcher at the University of Minnesota. Verfaillie made headlines in 2001 when she claimed to have isolated, from blood, stem cells that could turn into any kind of tissue; it had previously been thought that stem cells existed only in embryos. In one of her papers, four of seven figures had been manipulated in a way that misrepresented scientific data. For example, a set of blots used in one figure to represent a group of proteins was photo-reversed, tweaked, and used in another figure to represent an entirely different group of proteins. Verfaillie herself was cleared of misconduct, but scrutiny fell upon her graduate students. Regardless of who was responsible for the manipulation, there was clear evidence of misconduct, and the paper in question was retracted.

Image manipulation wouldn't be such a temptation if it were difficult. By making it easy, Photoshop and similar software have triggered a rash of fraud that's getting worse year by year. The democratization of powerful image-processing tools has had an unexpected consequence. Now that everybody has industrial-quality photography tools at their fingertips, we can now fake things with extremely high quality. It's true not just with photography but with other informational goods as well, such as magazines, journals, and books. In 1980, it would have been all but impossible to masquerade for long as the editor of a phony scientific journal without being exposed. Nowadays, fake scientific journals are everywhere.

In June 2009, the editor in chief of *The Open Information Science Journal* (*TOISJ*) resigned from his post, which he had held for about a year. The reason: "I want to lessen my exposure to the risk of being taken advantage of." It's an unusual sentiment for a journal editor, at least of any legitimate journal. But days earlier, it had become clear that *TOISJ*'s claim to legitimacy was tenuous at best.

TOISJ is one of more than two hundred journals published by Bentham Open, a publishing firm that specializes in "open access" journals. Open access means that the articles are free to the public, unlike in traditional peer-reviewed journals like *Nature* or *Cell* or *Science,* which have pricey subscription fees. The publication doesn't get subscription income but still needs revenue (or wants profits), so it asks authors to pay a fee to the journal to get their work peer-reviewed and published. The model works well in a number of cases; the *Public Library of Science* series of open-access journals, for example, is a fairly prestigious group of peer-reviewed publications. Yet there's the potential for abuse: rather than conducting the thorough peer review that makes scientific publications worth reading, a publisher can make a large profit by doing a slapdash job. He can post the work online with substandard review or no review at all—then take the author's money and laugh all the way to the bank. It's just a new incarnation of the old vanity presses that advertised in the backs of magazines.

It's hard to tell the difference between a legitimate open-access publisher and a fake one that preys on authors desperate to get their work into print. Fake publishers and real publishers have similar websites; the covers of their journals are of similar quality; their page layouts look pretty much the same. You have to look closely for warning signs, such as a post office box as an official address, but even these aren't surefire ways to tell the difference between a legitimate publication and one whose sole purpose is to part scientists from their money.

In late 2008, Cornell University graduate student Philip Davis was invited a number of times not just to submit work to *TOISJ* and other Bentham publications, but also to become a member of journals' editorial boards. "I received solicitations for journals for which I had no subject expertise at all," Davis told *New Scientist.* So he decided to test whether or not Bentham was legitimate. Teaming up with a publishing director at *The New England Journal of Medicine,* he submitted a paper to *TOISJ* that was transparently and utterly meaningless, filled with nonsensical phrases and opaque diagrams.* Nine months later, without a single comment from an external reviewer, Davis got the welcome news that his paper had been accepted—along with a bill for $800, to be sent to a P.O. box in Sharjah, one of the United Arab Emirates. Davis then revealed the hoax, exposing the journal and triggering the resignation of its editor in chief.

While this incident doesn't prove that *TOISJ* or the other Bentham publications are fake journals—after all, even well-respected journals publish garbage on occasion—Bentham Open has been classified as a "potential, possible, or probable predatory scholarly open-access publisher" by Jeffrey Beall, a librarian and open-access scholar at the University of Colorado. Beall's list has become the first line of defense against phony publishers. A quick glance at the current list shows hundreds of predatory open-access publishers, each of whom might publish a handful to dozens upon dozens of journals. They're ubiquitous nowadays, and the more active ones spend a good deal of time trying to promote their brand in hopes of getting more scientists to join in the charade. Indeed, if you're an academic, chances are that you've gotten a request or two to be on the editorial board of a journal on Beall's list.† These publications have a great deal to gain by getting a respected scholar (or even a not so respected scholar) to lend his or her name to the journal. It gives them a sliver of respectability and makes it harder to identify journals that are hollow Potemkin publications.

----

* In fact, the paper was generated by SCIgen, a computer algorithm discussed in chapter 8. SCIgen has a rich history of duping fake and bottom-feeding journals and conferences into accepting nonsense "research."

† My most recent request came on March 21, 2013, when the journal *Advances in Journalism and Communication* invited me to join its editorial board. The website looked professional, but the contact was a P.O. box in Irvine, California, and a little more digging suggested that the publisher was based somewhere in China. Sure enough, the publisher, Scientific Research Publishing, was on Beall's list.

Predatory open-access journals wouldn't survive if they weren't respectable-looking. Scientists and academics wouldn't be fooled, and neither would deans or anyone else. There would be no prestige attached to publishing in a fake journal, so there would be no incentive to fork over cash to get a worthless publication on your CV. Yet predatory journals are not only surviving but flourishing. It takes almost no effort to put up a decent-looking website, cobble together a publishing template for a professional-looking publication, and start publishing your own "journal" out of your home office. An unemployed amateur with enough time on his hands can become a scientific publishing house overnight.

Not long ago, looking for a book to read on my e-book reader, I wandered over to Amazon.com's biography section. In scrolling through the list of new releases, I was immediately struck by two books I hadn't heard of before: *John F. Kennedy: A Life* (at number nine in my list) and *Ronald Reagan: A Life* (at number thirteen). Usually, a new biography of Reagan or Kennedy would get some buzz, so I took a closer look. Both volumes were written by the editors of New Word City—a firm, I soon discovered, devoted to writing short e-books. Hundreds and hundreds of short e-books. There are biographies of famous people like Nelson Mandela, Michelle Obama, Winston Churchill, and Mitt Romney. There are oodles of how-to books, business advice books, and other lightweight offerings. Having never heard of them before, I went over to the New Word City website, where the company happily brags about its success: "[New Word City's] ebooks appear regularly on a number of bestseller lists." That may be so, but it's certainly not because of quality.

Reading a New Word City biography is like reading an extended Wikipedia page; at best, it's a workmanlike if disjointed collection of facts. But all too often it degenerates into a grade-school essay, full of non sequiturs, bad metaphors, and grammatical missteps. For example:

Churchill struggled to overcome a speech impediment, variously described as a stutter and a lisp. In sharp contrast to his turbulent public life, his marriage to Clementine Churchill was a sea of tranquility. . . . Their wedding took place in 1908 was [sic] the climax of the social season. Churchill remarked later in life that the two of them did, indeed, live "happily ever afterwards."

This passage, taken from *Winston Churchill: A Life,* also appears, grammar unchanged, in two other New Word City books: *Winston Churchill's Leadership Lessons* and *What You Can Learn from Winston Churchill.* (I'd wager it's also in *How Cool Is Winston Churchill?* but I'm not shelling out $2.99 to find out.)

Freed from the need to produce ink-and-paper copies of books, New Word City is churning out crappy titles as fast as it possibly can, in the hope that a small number of suckers will buy any given volume. There are more than 640 New Word City books on Amazon.com, and the number is growing fast. In 2012 alone, the editors cranked out some 120 titles—more than one every three days. Not bad for a company with about a dozen employees.

But the editors at New Word City aren't the most prolific authors out there. Far from it. Lambert Surhone has more than two thousand titles on Amazon.com and is producing them at a blistering pace— sometimes five or six in a day. And unlike New Word City, which sells its e-books for about $3 each, Surhone's imprint, Betascript Publishing, sells his work in paperback for $44 or more. You might have even heard of some of the titles, such as *Rabbit at Rest.* (Not to be confused, of course, with the Updike novel of the same name.) Surhone's firm scours Wikipedia and other public-domain sources online for writing on various subjects, gathers a hundred pages of material, binds it, slaps on a cover photo vaguely related to the title of the book (*Rabbit at Rest* has a stuffed bunny in an Easter scene), and sells it to the unaware.

Even Surhone's output is nothing compared with the fastest author of them all: Philip M. Parker. Parker has more than 110,000 books listed on Amazon.com and claims he can write one in about twenty minutes, thanks to a computer program that dumps information from various databases into preprepared templates for various kinds of books. Though it seems that Parker himself stopped putting his name to his books in 2009 or so, his company, Icon Group International, is churning out volumes at an incredible pace. In early 2013, Icon Group International had some 885,000 books for sale—paperback and electronic—with such titles as:

> *Kindergarten Mathematics: Rural Malawi Edition in English with English-Chichewa Vocabulary*
>
> *The 2013 Economic Competitiveness of St. Pierre & Miquelon*
>
> *Mark Twain, A Biography 1886–1900 (Webster's Chinese Simplified Thesaurus Edition)*
>
> *The World Market for Oil-Cake and Other Solid Residues (Except Dregs) Resulting from the Extraction of Fats or Oils from Rape or Colza Seeds*
>
> *The 2013 Report on Bathroom Toilet Brushes and Holders: World Market Segmentation by City*

None of these titles are going to be bestsellers, but even a single sale means a profit, as these books cost pretty much nothing to produce—the cost of running a computer for a few minutes. And Amazon.com is happy to list them; after all, if some sucker buys one of the books, Amazon gets a share of the sales price.

Amazon.com has its own self-publishing arm, which allows people to craft a professional-looking e-book (or even ink-and-paper book) and sell it worldwide. "[Kindle Direct Publishing] gives you everything you need to become your own publisher today," the website blares. "Publishing is free. . . . Publishing takes less than five minutes and your book usually appears on the Kindle store within a day." No fuss, no muss. Maybe people will buy your stuff; maybe they won't. You've got nothing to lose. Nobody will punish you if you've written something subpar (so long as you're not libeling someone or stealing someone else's work, of course, and probably not even then).

Take the case of Catherine Eccles, a British literary agent. In February 2011, she published her first book, *Publishing Basics,* through Kindle Direct Publishing. The book consisted of one word.* She didn't make a lot of money with her endeavor (a bit less than ten pounds sterling), but her work sat on Amazon's website without a peep of protest. Once her minimum opus was mentioned in the *Evening Standard*, though, Amazon "unpublished" her book. Eccles quickly revised her work to make it more substantial—repeating the one word some 200,000 times—and got it accepted for publication once more. There it sat until October, when it was again removed.

Amazon's decision to unpublish Eccles's book seems to be atypical, perhaps motivated by public embarrassment. Amazon has no incentive to delist any books of any quality, at least unless customers begin to complain. It costs nothing to have a virtual book sit in a virtual bookstore; each book, real or fictional, takes up no physical space on Amazon.com's website. An internet vendor can have essentially infinite products on display. For print-on-demand books, just as with e-books, you don't even have to stockpile one or two copies in your inventory. They're created immediately after the act of purchasing, not before. Why, then, should anyone be barred from publishing book after book after book, no matter the quality?

This is just one symptom of a tectonic shift that's going on in the book industry. From Amazon's point of view, book publishers are unwelcome middlemen in the world of literature. If Amazon can deal directly with writers and publish—and distribute—their work to the public, what need is there for the publishing houses? The means of production are in the hands of the masses now, not in the hands of the elites.

With this realization, Amazon has begun trying to break the spines of the big publishing houses, which are themselves trying to get in on the

---

* Which word? I'm afraid you'll have to get a copy of the book to find out.

self-publishing boom. For example, in mid-2012, Penguin (which is publishing this book) acquired Author Solutions, a self-publishing firm that released nearly 200,000 books in five years—no Philip Parker, but quite impressive nonetheless. It has always been risky to judge a book by its cover. But at least a high-quality cover told you that the book had come from a big publishing house, which meant that somebody thought it was worth expending a reasonable amount of time and money in procuring, editing, and producing the book. Now that's no longer the case. Anyone can produce a book that looks as good as—and is sold in many of the same places as—books by the pros. Sure, it's possible that a given home-brewed book might be better than one from Penguin or Random House,* but on average, the do-it-yourselfers fall far short of the professionals.

Digital technology is a true democratic force, narrowing the distinction between the haves—the ones with fancy publishing equipment—and the have-nots. But in such a world, fakes and low-quality work proliferate. We're already being swamped by phony journals and computer-generated books; we have to be careful, lest our professional-looking garbage crowd out everything else, and lestwe lose sight of what's real and what's phony. This is increasingly a problem not just when it comes to publications, but also when it comes to entities in the real world, such as companies.

Corporations are expected to publish and maintain websites, and those websites are increasingly the way that the public interacts with corporate entities—so the act of publishing a website is becoming harder to distinguish from the act of founding a corporation. Throw up a professional-looking website and only the most alert will see through the facade and realize that there's nothing substantial behind the online presence.

Faking corporate websites is a fairly common tactic of activists on both the left and the right. One practitioner is James O'Keefe, best

----

* For example, one of my daughter's favorite bedtime stories, *My Name Is Not Isabella*, was a self-published book. It happens . . . but it's not common.

known for impersonating a pimp to try to discredit ACORN, a liberal community-organizing agency. O'Keefe, who specializes in undercover video, wanted to go after National Public Radio—but it's not such an easy thing to get access to high officials of a major broadcast outlet.* So O'Keefe and his co-conspirators created a website for a fake charity—the Muslim Education Action Center—and offered NPR a $5 million donation. This got NPR's attention, and a lunch with Ron Schiller, NPR's senior vice president for development. A long (secretly taped) conversation and some deceptive editing later, and O'Keefe had a video that was damning enough to get heads to roll at NPR.

On the other side of the political spectrum, the Yes Men, a left-wing activist group, has a long history of pranks involving fake corporate and organizational websites. By creating reasonably professional-looking prank sites for such entities as Shell, Dow Chemical, and the World Trade Organization, the group manages to embarrass these organizations by putting out various absurd statements. Enough people believe that the sites are real that the act forces the real corporations to react and deny the statements. On occasion, a hapless journalist, producer, or conference organizer attempts to contact company spokespeople through the fake website, which will often lead to a phony corporate official playing some sort of practical joke in a public forum. For example, in 2004, a BBC producer, fooled by a fake Dow website, booked a Yes Man for the twentieth anniversary of the Bhopal chemical disaster, in India. The Yes Man, dressed as a Dow spokesman, formally accepted responsibility for the disaster and promised to compensate the victims to the tune of $12 billion. Dow was put in the very uncomfortable position of having to deny that there was any such plan.

Publication nowadays means more than printing a journal or a book. A website that represents a corporation is a publication as well. As the powerful tools for professional-looking publications have

----

* I should mention that I'm not a neutral observer when it comes to James O'Keefe, because he attempted a sting on me in 2010. Those who are interested can find copious details on the web.

become cheap and widespread, amateurs can now create websites that look as good as (or even better than) the ones for multi-billion-dollar companies. It doesn't take much effort at all to build an amazing-looking digital edifice without any substance behind it—be it a fake journal, a fake book, or a fake company. And every time one of these digital facades is erected, it's there for one purpose: to trick you.

CHAPTER 7
WHITE NOISE AND
THE RED QUEEN

"Well, in *our* country," said Alice, still panting a little, "you'd generally get to somewhere else—if you ran very fast for a long time, as we've been doing."

"A slow sort of country!" said the Queen. "Now, *here*, you see, it takes all the running *you* can do, to keep in the same place. If you want to get somewhere else, you must run at least twice as fast as that!"

—LEWIS CARROLL, *THROUGH THE LOOKING-GLASS*

We are at the beginning of an information famine.

This famine is striking us even as we make information universally accessible—to the point that we humans are within reach of a form of immortality. Just a few years ago, we had to be content with archiving a mere handful of events in our lives, storing what we could in a few faded photographs, a handful of diary pages, a jittery video, or a family legend that gets passed down for three or four generations. All else, all of our memory and knowledge, melted away when we died.

That's no longer the case. Digital technology, along with cheap memory, has made it possible to record, in real time, audio and video of your entire existence. A tiny camera and microphone could wirelessly transmit and store everything that you hear and see (or your own image, actions, and words) for the rest of your life. It would take only a few thousand terabytes of hard-drive space to archive a human's entire audiovisual experience from cradle to grave.

The digital revolution has made it possible to hoard vast amounts of information more easily than was ever thought possible. It's been several years since you could first carry your entire music collection on a device the size of a deck of cards, and technology has been improving since then. Vast governmental databases, once confined to rooms full of spinning magnetic tapes, now wander freely about the world every time a careless employee misplaces his laptop. Google is busy trying to snaffle up all the world's literature and convert it into a digital format—a task that, astonishingly, now has more legal hurdles than technical ones.

Digital memory is changing the relationship that humans have with information. For most of our existence, our ability to store and relay knowledge has been very limited. Every time we figured out a better way to preserve and transmit data to our peers and to our descendents—as we moved from oral history to written language to the printing press to the telegraph to the computer age—our civilization took a great leap. Now we are reaching the point where we have the ability to archive every message, every telephone conversation, every communication between human beings anywhere on the planet. For the first time, we as a species have the ability to remember everything that ever happens to us. For millennia, we were starving for information to act as raw material for ideas. Now, we are about to have a surfeit.

Paradoxically, this surfeit is causing our famine. Several hundred billion e-mail messages are sent every day; most of them—current estimates run around 75 percent—are spam. There are roughly two hundred million blogs worldwide, more than a fivefold increase from half a decade ago. The vast majority are unreadable. There seems to be a Malthusian principle at work: information grows exponentially, but useful information grows only linearly. Noise will drown out signal. The moment that we, as a species, finally have the memory to store our every thought, etch our every experience into a digital medium, is the very same moment that we begin to drown in a rising tide of undifferentiated information.

To keep our heads above the flood, we are frantically building tools to winnow the information that we need out of the ever-increasing chatter. But it has become an evolutionary arms race: at the same time, there are those who are trying with all their might to ensure that you are unable to escape their noise—filling your computer, and your brain, with their junk. And, sadly, they are winning. The trajectory of this evolution is moving in the wrong direction; over the next few years, even the news media may well become increasingly indistinguishable from spam.

Your e-mail inbox is ground zero for this evolutionary arms race.

Back when the internet was new, when few people used e-mail regularly, most of what came into an e-mail inbox had a high likelihood of being important or at least interesting to the owner of the inbox. At first, it was only government and university types who had access to e-mail, so the messages were mostly workplace-related, with the occasional stupid joke thrown in. There were no advertisements, no unsolicited messages, no junk mail. At least there weren't for a while.

According to internet legend, way back in 1978, when there were fewer than three thousand people hooked up to the network that formed the rudimentary backbone of what would become the internet, a computer salesman sent out an unsolicited e-mail to four hundred users. "DIGITAL WILL BE GIVING A PRODUCT PRESENTATION OF THE NEWEST MEMBERS OF THE DECSYSTEM-20 FAMILY," the e-mail read. "WE INVITE YOU TO COME SEE THE 2020 AND HEAR ABOUT THE DECSYSTEM-20 FAMILY AT THE TWO PRODUCT PRESENTATIONS WE WILL BE GIVING IN CALIFORNIA THIS MONTH." It was the first spam message.* But for years, while the internet was mostly in the hands of universities, the interesting stuff you'd get would outweigh the nonsense. Signal was much greater than noise. It wasn't perfect; the noise level went up dramatically each September as a new group of incoming college students discovered the internet for the first time, but the newbies quickly settled down and, most of the time, the net was relatively quiescent.

In the early 1990s, though, commercial services like CompuServe, Prodigy, and AOL brought the internet to the general public. September 1993, when AOL first gave its subscribers access to internet newsgroups, started the period that became known as "Eternal September." AOL had become a never-ending font of noisy internet newbies. At the same time, NCSA Mosaic, the first successful graphical web browser, ensured that the once small internet village would quickly expand to encompass the entire world. And as more and more people found their voice on the net, the level of noise began to increase dramatically. Within two years, entrepreneurs were collecting and selling e-mail addresses that could be fed into their mass-mailing programs, which allowed a single user to send thousands of e-mails with the press of a button.

At first, spam was simple. It was a straightforward message—make money fast, enlarge your penis†—with little attempt to hide its nature or its origin. These ads lost their effectiveness quickly. After only a few unsolicited messages, even the most enlargement-curious users lost what little enthusiasm they once had and deleted the messages unread.

But spammers are an adaptable lot. They quickly learned that by sending e-mail with a header that might trick you ("A message for

----

* These messages apparently picked up the name "spam" in the early 1980s, as a geeky reference to a Monty Python skit about a café in which every dish (such as "Spam, eggs, Spam, Spam, bacon, and Spam") was larded with lots of Spam, whether the patrons liked it or not.

† I wish there were statistics on just what proportion of spam was aimed directly at the male organ. My bet is that it's significantly greater than 50 percent.

you," for example, or "John wanted you to see this"), they'd at least have a chance of getting you to read their message. As these kinds of spam started filling mailboxes, victims sought ways of fighting back. There developed "blacklists" of known spammers whose messages would be blocked. On top of that, internet providers and even users started using filters—programs that would look at a message and make an educated guess about whether the e-mail was spam or not. (For example, if a message had the word "Viagra" in it, a filter program would be suspicious that the e-mail was spam—especially if there was a price for the product embedded in the message as well.)

To defeat the filters, spammers began making their ads harder for computers to read without damaging their legibility to humans. You might get an intentionally misspelled ad for "Vigara," or perhaps there's a character substituted for a letter in a sales pitch for "V1agra." This way, until the spam filters learned all the myriad ways of misspelling "Viagra," the computer wouldn't detect the word and couldn't recognize it as a sign of spam.

My favorite method of defeating spam filters involved putting long strings of words, or even passages of computer-generated prose, at the end of a message. The point was to try to convince the filter—by using words that are used in legitimate e-mails but rarely in spam—that the message wasn't really a Viagra ad. At times, this scheme would turn spammy advertisements into prose poetry, such as this snippet from a 2004 e-mail:

Furthermore, recliner near gets stinking drunk, and industrial complex from cyprus mulch prefer paycheck near. Unlike so many taxidermists who have made their crispy corporation to us. When you see trombone behind, it means that onlooker of trembles. A few cups, and pine cone behind) to arrive at a state of garbage can And trade baseball cards with the dark side of her bartender. Johnie, the friend of Johnie and goes to sleep with cream puff of.

Alas, these delightfully surreal creations began to disappear soon after they appeared in the mid-2000s as spam filters learned not to be fooled by the non sequiturs.

The history of spam is really an evolutionary arms race in action. Spammers attempt to get access—unwelcome access—to your eyeballs. Viruslike, they try to sneak past your defenses and inject their message into your body. At first, they could do this without much effort, but as users began to fight back against spam, the spammers resorted to more and more sophisticated subterfuge. Which, in turn, spurred internet providers and their users to employ more and more sophisticated countermeasures. So spammers came up with counter-countermeasures, and the cycle continues.

It's little different from what happens in the wild. Over millions of years, organisms adapt to their environment—to gather food more easily and efficiently, as well as to reduce the likelihood of becoming food for some other organism. For example, faster-running gazelles are more likely to survive from generation to generation, so, as time goes by, the speedy gazelles pass down their genes and the slow ones don't. The result, at least in theory, is that gazelle descendants, in general, become faster and nimbler, and thus better at escaping a threat than their forebears many generations back. The species becomes more fit. At the same time, though, the predators that prey on the gazelle also feel evolutionary pressure. Cheetahs, too, adapt to their environment, running faster and faster so that they're able to catch and eat gazelles more reliably.

Since predators and prey are competitors, the evolution of one damages the survival prospects of the other, and vice versa. Even if they both evolve at a rapid rate, if one doesn't outpace the other, neither organism gets a lasting advantage over its adversary. Gazelles might improve rapidly, but since cheetahs also improve, the gazelles don't get any overall benefit. Like the Red Queen in *Through the Looking-Glass*, they both evolve as fast as they can just to stay in the same place relative to each other.

This Red Queen dynamic, well known to biologists, governs the spam arms race as well. Filtering technology has improved enormously over the past decade—you're probably blissfully unaware of the multiple, sophisticated layers of spam protection that deflect most junk mail even before it gets to your inbox. Yet, at the same time, spamming technology has improved as well, making it easier than ever before to send out ungodly amounts of e-mail in hopes of getting past the defenses. In November 2010, for example, a twenty-four-year-old Russian citizen, Oleg Nikolaenko, was arrested in Las Vegas. The charge: he had allegedly used malicious software to enslave more than half a million computers around the world to send out spam messages—billions upon billions of e-mail messages a day. And some of these messages, quite naturally, got past your defenses. There are other Nikolaenkos out there, and your e-mail inbox probably contains some of their spam right now.

Indeed, one of the few things that can be guaranteed is that, so long as there's a profit to be made, spam will always survive. The ease—and low cost—of producing e-mail in bulk makes it inevitable. Even if only one in a million advertisements reaches the eyes of a consumer, then by shooting out ten billion e-mails a day, as a Nikolaenko is able to do, you're going to get ten thousand people to read your ad each and every day. Whenever sheer volume works in your favor, you might not win a digital arms race, but you're never going to lose. In the battle between signal and noise, noise usually prevails. Which means that, at worst, the spammers are in a Red Queen situation.

The battle over spam is just one front of a war that's now being waged over all forms of digital information. Unbeknownst to most people, there are forces attempting to hijack you whenever you consume information on the internet, pushing you away from the sources you really want and drawing you toward ones that are worthless—or even worse. Hundreds of millions of dollars are being spent in a marketing battle of the highest order, with one ultimate goal: to make you irrelevant.

The whole concept of making you irrelevant might seem illogical. Since time immemorial, you, the consumer—the keeper of the wallet—have been the ultimate target of the media. When a company convinces you to read their papers or view their movies or listen to their music, the company makes money, either directly or indirectly. Whether you purchase their goods or whether your eyeballs make their advertising sales increase, it's your consumption of the media that generates revenue for their company. And the most straightforward way to increase your likelihood of consuming a product is to make that product as relevant and appealing to you as possible. One would think that a successful media company would study your habits, try to understand your whims and quirks, and figure out how best to serve your self-perceived needs. And, in fact, this is what media companies did for many, many years. With their focus groups and their reader surveys and their ratings systems, they tried to figure out what you want and to be more efficient at giving it to you. This is the exact opposite of making you irrelevant; it's putting you, the consumer, at the very center of the universe.

This was the state of play for decades, but no longer. In the past half dozen years or so, a Red Queen–type evolutionary war broke out that began to change that equation. The battles are now raging all around us, and the war is having a dramatic effect on our relationship with information. But the way it's changing that relationship is too subtle for most people to notice. We, the consumers, don't realize that we've been removed from the center of the media universe. And it's happened because the evolutionary war made clear that targeting you—the consumer—was not the most efficient way to make money. There are cheaper, smarter, and more efficient ways to make money as a media mogul. Instead of targeting you, the consumer, the new media are aiming at something else entirely. The people who first figured out how to do this are now millionaires.

The outlines of this contest are easiest to see in the news industry.

Before the internet came along, there were a relative handful of media outlets where most people would get their news. For daily news, they would go to the newspapers they could get delivered to their doorstep or that they could find at the newsstand on their way to work. There was also the broadcast news: you could find your daily news fix on the Big Three networks and eventually on cable TV as well. There were also weekly newsmagazines that attempted to give a more big-picture view of what was going on in the world, as well as monthlies. These outlets competed against one another for their audience. All of these news organs rose or fell based upon their readership or viewership. The more readers or viewers they had, the more money they could raise through advertising.

Back in those days, the logical way to make more money was to appeal to more readers or viewers. There were lots of strategies for doing this—some outlets went highbrow, while others went lowbrow. Some tried to appeal to a wide audience, while others targeted specific niche populations. A tremendous amount of time and effort was put into figuring out what people actually were watching and reading as well as what people *wanted* to watch and read. Entire businesses, like the Nielsen Company, sprang up around figuring out the audience's behavior and helping media companies appeal more to their readers and viewers. For the principal way to success was figuring out an audience, providing that audience with media that satisfied its needs and desires, and building the audience's loyalty to your outlet. It was pretty straightforward.

With the advent of the internet, the playing field changed dramatically, because people had a much broader variety of media choices than they ever had before. In the 1980s, even after cable TV came online, readers and viewers had only a relatively limited choice of outlets that they could get with a reasonable amount of cost and effort. Outside of the readily available choices, it took a lot of work for a reader to chase down a hard-to-find periodical. A media outlet had to convince an out-of-town reader that the investment of money and time was worth the extra effort. As good as the *Financial Times* was, it was only the odd Wall Street type who would carry the salmon-colored paper under his arm on the train in the morning. And not even an expat Australian would bother to subscribe to the *Sydney Morning Herald* while living in New York. So in a practical sense, your choices for media were limited by your geography.

As the web began to grow, virtually every news outlet was suddenly within the reach of everybody. The moment a person's computer boots in the morning, he can browse newspapers based in Sydney, Singapore, Saskatchewan, Salt Lake City, and everywhere in between. As a result, the casual news consumer is presented with a bewildering buffet of breaking stories from all around the world—far, far too much for any person to consume. The trick now is finding what you want. You have to sort through the flood of information to spot the items you desire to look at and discard the stuff that you're not interested in. And that's not a trivial task.

During the web's early days—late 1993 and 1994—there really wasn't any mechanism for finding information.* A few early companies, such as Excite and Yahoo!, attempted to create "web directories"—almost like yellow pages for the internet. You could look up pages by subject or by geographic area and hope that you got something worthwhile. It didn't work; there was no way these pages could keep up with the ever-growing and ever-changing content on the internet. The directories were out of date as soon as they were built—which is why search engines soon became dominant. In the mid-1990s, search engines, computer programs that scoured the web looking for pages based upon the terms you input, began to appear. AltaVista was one, HotBot was another—and then, by around 1998, a newcomer, Google, had begun to dominate.

For these search engines to function properly, there has to be someone—or something—identifying webpages, pinpointing the important information upon them, and then indexing them. And it has

---

* Those of you who remember Gopher or Archie know how limited your options were back then.

to be done over and over, as webpages are constantly changing. With billions of pages on the web, there's no way that it can be done manually. At the heart of a search engine has to be a "web crawler" that visits and indexes webpages automatically. The next task is one of organization. The search-engine algorithm has to figure out which of those webpages should be presented, in what order, to a user who types in a particular query. It's a daunting problem, and because the engineers at Google did it better than all their peers, they rapidly became very, very wealthy.

Google's indexing-and-presenting problem became all the more acute in 2002, when the company decided to take on the news media. Unlike ordinary internet webpages, which really didn't change much from day to day on average, news stories changed hourly—even minute by minute. The Google News bots had to crawl likely sources of breaking news almost constantly. What's more, if Google was to present the news to the reader effectively, the algorithm had to recognize when it had multiple versions of essentially the same news item. If it didn't, the Google News page would likely plaster your web browser with twenty-five minor variants of "Giants Win Pennant" rather than with twenty-five different stories, each of which tickles a different interest. There were a lot of hiccups at first, but pretty soon Google had cobbled together a workable product, a program that collected news and presented it to the user. It's a testament to Google's staff of computer scientists and engineers that they got their news aggregator working so well so quickly. Now Google is a media force to be reckoned with. According to a 2011 study (alas, already somewhat dated by internet standards), roughly a third of all internet traffic to news sites, even for big media companies, comes via Google. And that means that Google's algorithm is now the single biggest consumer of—and audience for— the news. And this marks a change in the wind.

It's a very subtle shift, but it's happening. Increasingly, the target for a news story is not really a human, but an algorithm—and by targeting that algorithm efficiently, you'll be high up in the search rankings. The most efficient way to get humans to click on your story is to appeal to the algorithm, not directly to the human. This is why newspapers run the same story with a different headline (and sometimes a different opening) online than they do in the print edition. For example, on January 7, 2012, *The New York Times* ran a piece about Michelle Obama on page A1. It was entitled:

FIRST LADY'S FRAUGHT WHITE HOUSE JOURNEY
TO GREATER FULFILLMENT

When it was placed on the web, it was retitled:

MICHELLE OBAMA AND THE EVOLUTION OF
A FIRST LADY

The first headline tells more about what the story is—it's an attempt to lure a newspaper reader in with the promise of an interesting tale. The second headline is straightforward, shorn of any elliptical phrasing or hard-to-parse elements. It also has "Michelle Obama," a popular search term nowadays. It's more easily categorized by Google's algorithms, and it's closer to what people will throw in a search engine when they're looking for something. It's a headline meant for an algorithm, not for a person. The actual reader is irrelevant; the search engine itself is all.

Once you know what to look for, you can tell the difference without much trouble. Here's another pair of headlines, from the December 4, 2011, *New York Times*—one from the paper and one from the online edition:

A DEFIANT CAIN SUSPENDS HIS BID FOR PRESIDENCY

HERMAN CAIN SUSPENDS HIS PRESIDENTIAL
CAMPAIGN

People interested in this kind of story are more likely to search for "Herman Cain" than just Cain alone. And "campaign" is quite likely to be in the search—at least it's much more likely than "presidential bid." The first is much more evocatively written. That's the one meant for you. The second, straightforward one is aimed squarely at Google.

It's not just the Gray Lady whose headlines are meant for artificial eyeballs. A few years ago, a *Washington Post* story on talk-show host Conan O'Brien's resignation after he was bumped to a later time slot was given this title in the paper:

BETTER NEVER THAN LATE

Online, it became:

CONAN O'BRIEN WON'T GIVE UP "TONIGHT SHOW"
TIME SLOT TO MAKE ROOM FOR JAY LENO

Media outlets now realize that their online audience is fundamentally different from its print audience—and we're not just talking demographics. There's an entirely new audience that was born of the need to organize and find digital information on the web: machines and algorithms are also reading your stuff online. It's an audience that you ignore at your peril. It doesn't matter how wonderful your news item is, it doesn't matter one whit how much of a scoop you've got—if you're not able to place your story relatively high in the search-engine rankings, nobody's going to find it. Which means that nobody's going to read it.

In the past few years, there's been a whole new discipline born: the art of writing for Google's algorithms. Nowadays this field of study is known as "search-engine optimization," or SEO. And masters of SEO have learned what is likely to appeal to a robot—what is likely to rank high when the robot decides in what order to present stories. Current SEO wisdom is that a good machine headline is simple and straightforward and includes words, phrases, or names that are frequently typed into search engines. Humans sometimes like a little bit of word-play or variation in phrasing; machines don't. And savvy media out-lets are learning that while a clever headline attracted audiences in days past, it's an impediment to getting high search-engine rankings online.

Some of SEO is straightforward tinkering with the wording of your article: hit keywords hard, stick to simple sentence construction, avoid metaphor or any other literary techniques that might be confus-ing to a machine. But there are other, more technical ways of getting your pages up in the search rankings. For example, fresher pages tend to wind up higher in the search rankings, especially when it comes to news. In 2007, *The New York Times* figured this out and started gaming the system. A pre-SEO *New York Times* article had a little note show-ing the date on which the article was originally published. But after a format revision intended to help search rankings, the *Times* made sure that even when the article might be dated several years in the past, the *webpage* on which the article was displayed always had today's date—fooling Google into thinking that an old article in the archives was brand spanking new. All of a sudden, moldy old stories started wind-ing up high in the search engines—to the point that it caused the *Times* a bit of trouble. "A business strategy of *The New York Times* to get its articles to pop up first in Internet searches is creating a perplex-ing problem. . . . People are coming forward at the rate of roughly one a day to complain that they are being embarrassed, are worried about losing or not getting jobs, or may be losing customers because of the sudden prominence of old news articles that contain errors or were never followed up," wrote Clark Hoyt, then the *Times*'s ombudsman.

That's one of the important things about writing for algorithms: algorithms are stupid. They're easily fooled by strange little tricks and techniques that make sense to computer scientists but have little grounding in external reality. As a result, rankings are easily tinkered with. For example, one of the classic ways of determining how "im-portant" a webpage is—and, consequently, how high it should be placed in the rankings—is to figure out how many other pages link to it. If many other websites send traffic your way, the logical conclusion is that lots of other people think highly of your page and, thus, it should be ranked highly. But there are plenty of ways of gaming that system, such as creating oodles and oodles of your own pages to link back to your site. Google's algorithms often can't tell the difference between a legitimate website and a fake one, so every linking site you produce yourself helps raise your ranking in Google's eyes. You need not even create dummy webpages to use this technique for raising page rankings. A common scheme is for a person to go to the comments section of a popular blog or website and, along with some innocuous-looking comment ("Love your site! Keep up the good work!"), put in a link to the site he wants to promote.

In 2011, J.C. Penney got caught doing just that to raise its own ranking in Google searches. The company apparently paid to have thousands and thousands of external links go to the Penney website, to the point that Google searches for many products would beat even much bigger and more web-savvy competitors like Amazon.com. *The New York Times,* which broke the story, reported that with a search for "Samsonite carry-on luggage," Penney beat Samsonite itself to become the number-one link on Google. (*The New York Times* had been less eager to expose its own link games, such as the one involving dubious archival links that made the paper the number-three hit when you typed "sex" into Google.)*

Because search rankings are so fallible and so easily manipulated, they provide an easy way to get your work—and your advertising—in front of lots of viewers. It's no longer necessary to have really great writing or incredible reportage to attract a huge audience of news readers. If you understand SEO better than your competitors, and you're able to do a little computer-science finessing of your webpages, you can all of a sudden outrank *The New York Times, The Washington*

---

* Currently, the number-one hit for "sex" (at least on my computer) is a site called YourTango.com. Want to bet whether that's a spot that's truly earned, or gained by clever SEO?

Post, and all the other media giants. Now, thanks to SEO, you can actually compete with the big newspapers for readers. Figuring out how to game search rankings takes much less time and effort than establishing a solid readership through years of solid newswriting. A savvy SEO guru can send his outlet's stories to the top of the queue even if they're no better—or significantly worse—than those of his better-known competitors. If he's really smart about it, he can even beat a media site to its own scoop.

In early 2013, online magazine *The Verge* posted a long original story on the rise and fall of the video-game arcade. *The Huffington Post* promptly published a webpage that copied the headline and the first paragraph of the story, then linked to *The Verge,* sending readers there to read the rest of the article. But if you searched for the article on Google—even using the entire title of the article—*HuffPo*'s truncated copy came up higher in the search rankings than *The Verge*'s original. This is because *The Huffington Post*'s SEO team, among the best in the business, did a clever little bit of search-engine engineering.

The Google search engine recognizes what's known as a "canonical" link. When there's duplicate content out there, the search engine doesn't necessarily know which version of a webpage should get precedence, so sometimes coders will indicate this by flagging one copy as the canonical one. Google highly prefers to display the canonical link over the others. *The Huffington Post* used this feature to flag its own version of the arcade story as canonical. *The Verge* didn't. As a result, Google's search engine interpreted *HuffPo*'s page as the original and *Verge*'s as the copy—and promoted the copy ahead of the actual original in the rankings. The lesson is clear: you can be number one without having even a single dollop of original content on your webpages. The key is understanding your machine audience. And the companies that understand this are beginning to dominate the media landscape.

The Huffington Post burst upon the scene in 2005 and quickly rose to the top of the media world largely through SEO tricks like this—walking on the edge of stealing other people's stuff (and sometimes crossing it). (Stephen Colbert mocked the enterprise by creating his own publication, the *Colbuffington Re-Post,* which merely copied *The Huffington Post*'s website word for word.) On such foundations are media empires born. As *HuffPo*'s traffic rose, and its advertising revenue followed, it was eventually able to lure writers* into producing articles for them—generally for free. And then it actually started producing a bit of journalism by itself rather than merely regurgitating other people's work. In 2011, Arianna Huffington, the CEO of the publication, sold *HuffPo* to AOL for some $300 million, and in 2012 *HuffPo* won a Pulitzer Prize.

Don't let the Pulitzer fool you, though. As the *Verge* incident shows—and it happened a year after *HuffPo* won the prize—what these media empires do best is understand how search engines drive audiences to your website. And it's not just changing the way we get our news, but changing what news is.

In 2009, AOL launched a venture that it dubbed "Seed." The idea was to create a stable of writers who would churn out articles for nearly nothing—a few bucks an article—to fill the site with lots of keyword-heavy search-engine bait. Writers who went through the online "Seed Academy" training learned, very quickly, that SEO was crucial to getting anywhere as a writer for AOL—and figured out how to play the game on an incredibly sophisticated level.

For AOL writers, the advice went well beyond putting a target key phrase "as close to the front [of the article] as possible. . . . At the very least use the term one time per paragraph AND in one of your headings." It taught them how to choose a key phrase that would help push readers into their arms by using two Google tools: Trends and Ad-Words Keyword Tool. Designed for advertisers, these tools allow you to see which subjects are being searched heavily on Google right

----

* Such as myself. I've written a few small pieces for *Huffington Post* for free. The deal was clear: you're writing in return for lots of readers and a liberal editorial hand.

now—which searches are trending—so you can fine-tune your web-page to capture the most viewers. It's extraordinarily powerful.

For example, say I am a freelance science writer who has a story about stellar evolution. I would use these tools to find out that the key phrase "stellar evolution" gets roughly 12,100 Google searches a month, roughly half of which come from the United States. Not bad, but "evolution of stars" gets 14,800 per month, mostly overseas. (Per-haps the phrase is a little too stilted to the native English speaker to be used much in the States.) But—aha—even better is "star life cycle," at 49,500 hits per month, with half originating from the United States. So I should ditch "stellar evolution" and replace it with "star life cycle" near the front of my article and in the title. Even better, I could work in the question "What is the evolution of a star?" which gets more than 60,000 hits a month. (Google users often type in their searches in the form of a question, which explains the popularity of this awkward key phrase.)

These tools allow sites like *The Huffington Post* and AOL to "care-fully craft headlines to grab users' interest by incorporating in-demand terms and entice them to click onto the article," as one leaked AOL document put it. While not every article will be as popular as one entitled "Lady Gaga Goes Pantless in Paris," using these tools well will pull readers toward your site—and away from the competition.

That's just one small part of "The AOL Way." For AOL and its SEO-savvy competitors had taken an extra step—instead of just tweaking articles so that they wind up higher in search engine rank-ings, they began to create articles specifically to take advantage of trending keywords. In other words, the machines began to dictate not just how the articles were written, but what people write about.

The leaked AOL document—which horrified the journalism com-munity when it came out in early 2011—laid it out starkly. The first step in gathering news for AOL is to "identify in-demand topics" to write about. "Try to combine trending topics for maximum impact."

This turns the newsgathering process on its head. Journalists tra-ditionally generate stories by finding out about events and occurrences before anyone else is aware of them. If it's fresh and if it's important (or at least interesting), then you write about it. Journalists look for things that are unknown and reveal them them to the public. AOL and similar SEO-savvy media outlets have reversed that formula: by watching what the crowds are looking at, you figure out what to write about. By definition, you can't be bringing novelty to the public while the public is surging ahead of you to where the news is. But you can follow the crowd to what they're interested in and then reflect their desires back at them.

Figuring out a trending topic to write about is just the first step. After you've identified subjects with high "traffic potential," the next step is to figure out whether the piece will generate a profit. The leaked AOL document makes clear just how brutal the economics of the SEO game are. An article makes money based upon how many people view the page—and its advertisements. If you pay a freelance journalist $250 to write an article (which is at the low end of what a respectable freelancer will accept), even if you charge advertisers a premium rate, it might take some forty thousand page views before you've earned back the amount you paid your writer. For an AOL Seed article—written by a rank amateur for one-tenth the price—it might take only about seven thousand. There's little question that the professional writer will do a better job, but if SEO, rather than the site's reputation for quality, is driving most of the traffic, it doesn't really make sense to spend the extra money. The amateur's work, flawed as it might be, is good enough to serve its purpose: to be a magnet for search engines.

The amateurs have another advantage: speed. By having a huge stableful of them willing to churn out articles on a moment's notice, you can turn articles around fast enough to take advantage of the trend. Surfing on a wave of interest can work only if you're nimble enough to catch the wave, and dithering about with prose or, worse, reporting will only put you at a disadvantage.

In mid-2011, one ex–AOL writer gave a firsthand view of AOL's push for speed:

My "ideal" turn-around time to produce a column started at thirty-five minutes, then was gradually reduced to half an hour, then twenty-five minutes. Twenty-five minutes to re-search and write about a show I had never seen—and this twenty-five minute period included time for formatting the article in the AOL blogging system, and choosing and editing a photograph for the article. Errors were inevitably the result. But errors didn't matter; or rather, they didn't matter for my bosses. . . .

I still have a saved IM conversation with my boss, written after 10 months of employment, when I was reaching the breaking point:

"Do you guys even CARE what I write? Does it make any difference if it's good or bad?" I said.

"Not really," was the reply.

The boss's answer may sound glib, but it's true. From a search-engine optimizer's point of view, the actual words on the printed page don't really matter all that much. It could be "All work and no play makes Jack a dull boy" over and over again, but if it ranks high in a trending Google search, it's a great article by SEO standards. By the time a user clicks on the link and discovers that the article is garbage, the important work has already been done: the act of clicking counts as a page view, which means revenue for the website. It doesn't matter whether the reader finds the webpage well written, informative, useful, or even readable. It doesn't matter if your reader comes away feeling angry or deceived. If you've managed to entice someone to click, you've made money. If you're good at writing for the search en-gine, writing for the reader is almost superfluous.

This is the landscape-changing realization. A number of media companies have figured out that the machine audience is becoming much more important than the human audience. For as we humans rely ever more on machine assistance to sort through the flood of information on the internet, our choices are dictated ever more by the whims of those machines. The intermediary we inserted between us and the information we seek is usurping our power.

The result has been a race to the bottom. The company that can publish the most high-ranking articles as cheaply and as quickly as possible is going to make the most money. An industry has sprung up to provide SEO-optimized dreck in enormous volumes, flooding the internet with barely literate, often semi-plagiarized articles that are little more than bait for unwary Google users. These are known as "content farms." Demand Media, for example, plastered the web with subpar self-help articles, inane lists such as "20 uses for eggs," and other topics meant to snag an unwary Google searcher. And, as with books, some companies are even playing around with machine-written articles.

Narrative Science is a startup that uses Twitter feeds and other data to detect trends and automatically generate stories based on the results. For example, during the 2012 primary season, Narrative Science's bots generated the following:

NEWT GINGRICH GAINS ATTENTION WITH HOT-BUTTON TOPICS TAXES, CHARACTER ISSUES

Newt Gingrich received the largest increase in Tweets about him today. Twitter activity associated with the candidate has shot up since yesterday, with most users tweeting about taxes and character issues. Newt Gingrich has been consistently popular on Twitter, as he has been the top riser on the site for the last four days. Conversely, the number of tweets about Ron Paul has dropped in the past 24 hours. Another traffic loser was Rick Santorum, who has also seen tweets about him fall off a bit.

While the overall tone of the Gingrich tweets is positive, public opinion regarding the candidate and character issues is trending negatively. In particular, @MommaVickers says,

"Someone needs to put The Blood Arm's 'Suspicious Character' to a photo montage of Newt Gingrich. #pimp".

On the other hand, tweeters with a long reach are on the upside with regard to Newt Gingrich's take on taxes. Tweeting about this issue, @elvisroy000 says, "Newt Gingrich Cut Taxes Balanced Budget, 1n 80s and 90s, Newt experienced Conservative with values".

Maine recently held its primary, but it isn't talking about Gingrich. Instead the focus is on Ron Paul and religious issues.

It's barely readable, but it can certainly generate page views. *Forbes* regularly publishes Narrative Science articles on its website. It's not brilliantly written work, but it's good enough for their purposes. And it's far from the worst stuff out there. Journatic, another content farm, was the subject of an exposé on NPR's radio show *This American Life*. The firm was hired by the *Chicago Tribune* to do local coverage, and the newspaper fired roughly twenty people whose jobs were made superfluous by the cheap upstart. Not only did the company produce articles that were plagiarized, but also there were elements that were fabricated out of whole cloth. Even the writers' names were often fictional. Outraged, the *Trib* dropped Journatic in July 2012—and then picked it back up in December.

For big media sites, the quality of your work is increasingly irrelevant. Between SEO tricks and cheap content to fill pages, there's no need to generate original journalism. It's a good thing to do on occasion if you want to build up the reputation of your site. (Or not. As I write this paragraph, *Gawker's* big original story of the day is "Can You Eat Your Own Poop?") But writing or producing your own material doesn't have to be the core of your site. Indeed, if you want to maximize your profits, it shouldn't be. As I mentioned in chapter 5, original reporting and writing is a drain upon your limited resources. Spend your money on fooling search engines and following the crowd. That's the AOL way.

AOL's way might be the way of the future. It's too early to tell for sure, as there are other forces in play. In fact, SEO-savvy media outlets like AOL and *The Huffington Post* are locked in an evolutionary struggle against a powerful organization that's trying to stop them from gaming the search-engine results. That organization: Google.

Google is in an odd position. They're the ones who publish search trends and give hints about how to maximize your web traffic. At the same time, though, they don't like it when *obviously* phony results gum up a user's search. Because if someone consistently gets subpar hits when he uses a search engine, he becomes ever more tempted to try someone else's. Google may have a near monopoly on the market right now, but even a quasi monopoly can disappear almost overnight if a better alternative emerges. With an intangible product like an internet search, this danger is ever present. Every time an awful webpage beats out a good one on a search, Google risks damaging its reputation just a little bit. So it's in Google's interest to defeat the worst offenders and try to make their search more useful to the public.

When the J.C. Penney scam came to light, Google acted quickly, tweaking its algorithms so that the company's products dropped precipitously in the rankings. In fact, Google is constantly making small changes to the way it does searches. Every few weeks, it rolls out a new version of the search engine, attempting to improve results for users in part by closing loopholes that allow SEO types to elbow their way undeservedly to the top of the rankings. Starting in 2011, Google rolled out updates to the search-engine algorithm—nicknamed "Panda"—intended to boost the rankings of "high quality" information sites, at the expense of the bottom feeders. These updates reportedly did significant damage to the rankings of certain content farms like Demand Media and *The New York Times*'s About.com. But that's just one skirmish in a war between the optimizers and the search-engine engineers as each side refines its code to try to reduce the effectiveness of the other's work.

The evolutionary battles are moving quickly—in a Red Queen

sense. Just as with the spam wars in e-mail, most of us are completely oblivious to just how dramatically Google—and the Google gamers— have changed in the past few years. The increasingly sophisticated measures and countermeasures and counter-countermeasures for tricking the search engine are largely invisible to us. We barely even see the effects the battle has had upon the information we consume and the organizations that produce that information. Yet the effects are huge.

You probably weren't aware that some media outlets have shifted their allegiance from the traditional audience of humans to the digital-era audience of search algorithms. But with that shift of allegiance, the entire function of a media outlet changed. Back before the internet, a news organization tended to have a symbiotic relationship with its audience. The organization generally made its money by getting you to look at advertisements that you probably didn't want to look at—but you did so because the organization was providing you with information that you did desire. So, like a symbiote, the news organization got its need taken care of but provided a valuable service in return.

The moment a media outlet stops caring about the service it's providing to its audience, the moment it realizes that it can get its advertisement in front of you without satisfying your needs—through chicanery, if need be—that's the moment that the symbiotic relationship breaks down. No longer are you exposed to the outlet's ads because you're reading something you think is valuable; you're exposed because, on some level, you were tricked into going there. You were waylaid on your way to read *The Verge* and were treated to an extra helping of advertising that benefits *The Huffington Post*. This is not symbiosis—this is parasitism. SEO-optimized media is shuffling more and more toward becoming spam.

It's impossible to tell how this trend will wind up, as the evolutionary war is still under way. As I write this book, the conventional wisdom is that the pure "content farm" model will be rendered obsolete as Google moves toward incorporating social media trends into its search algorithms. Indeed, one of the most valuable by-products of social media sites like Twitter, Facebook, Pinterest, and the like is that they provide a direct measure of what people find interesting and useful. In theory, social media reflects genuine human preferences; why would people link to something on Twitter if they didn't find it interesting, or "like" something on Facebook unless they actually liked it? Because of this, some search-engine developers pin their hopes on social media as a way to put humans back in the equation—to have people's preferences dictate what information gets presented to them rather than leave it entirely up to algorithms. (There are hints that Google has already begun doing this.)

Unfortunately, this approach is just as easily gamed by sockpuppets or, worse yet, machines. Computers can't tell the difference between genuine humans and machines masquerading as people. Sometimes even humans can't.

CHAPTER 8
ARTIFICIAL
UNINTELLIGENCE

If you can have a conversation with a simulated person presented by an AI program, can you tell how far you've let your
sense of personhood degrade in order to make the illusion
work for you?

—JARON LANIER

I t wasn't a good match. Ivana didn't really speak English and,
frankly, didn't seem all that bright. But she was pretty. When Dr.
Robert Epstein, a Harvard-trained experimental psychologist and
relationship expert, met her through an online dating service, he
thought that "her photos were so attractive and her e-mails so warm"
that he couldn't resist. He soon started up an online romance with her.

It started off well. Ivana, for her part, seemed to be head over
heels. "I have told to mine close friends about you and to my parents
and them happy that I really interested someone and regardless of the
fact that not here in Russia," Ivana wrote. "I have very special feelings
about you." Despite her atrocious grammar—and her tendency to
ramble and repeat herself—Epstein didn't have any qualms at first. He
began to worry a bit only when, after two months, the relationship
seemed to be stalling. "Our romance was progressing especially slowly:

no phone calls, very vague talk on Ivana's part about getting together— no real *movement*," Epstein wrote. She parried every attempt he made to engage her in conversation about books, music, or politics, instead writing entire missives about her mother and her friends. But still the romance continued.

In January, Ivana told Robert about a nice walk in the park she had taken with a friend. A nice walk in the park in Russia in the middle of January. Checking the weather reports, Epstein realized that on the day of this walk, it had been twelve degrees Fahrenheit and there was a heavy snowstorm. Suspicious, Epstein wrote one last e-mail to his love:

```
asdf;kj as;kj l;jkj;j ;kasdkljk ;klkj 'klasdfk; asjdfkj. With love,
/Robert
```

Ivana cheerfully sent another letter about her mother. Epstein realized that he had been duped.

> I had been interacting for nearly four months with a computer program—specifically, a chatterbot, which is a program designed to converse with people over the Internet.

Epstein was one of thousands, if not millions, of people— undoubtedly mostly men—who've been suckered into thinking a machine was a potential date. The internet is crawling with ersatz humans, computer programs designed to masquerade as humans. These programs exist in order to fool us and extract something from us, whether it's time, attention, or money. With each generation, they get better and better—they're becoming more successful predators. And we're becoming easier prey.

As computer technology improves and as our signal-to-noise filters get stretched to their limit, we are increasingly being manipulated by a host of digital entities masquerading as humans.

In the past few years, computer programmers have created the equivalent of a printing press for fake people. Software packages now churn out artificial humans at a blistering pace, and though they're not terribly convincing to the discerning eye—you can generally tell a real person from a fake one within a few seconds—the sheer volume of them on the internet makes them potentially far more powerful than mere sockpuppets are. There's already a great deal of evidence that machine personalities are surprisingly successful at getting us to do what they want.

In the mid-1960s, ELIZA was born. The brainchild of MIT computer scientist Joseph Weizenbaum, ELIZA was an early experiment in artificial intelligence—an attempt to use bits and bytes to mimic a psychoanalyst. Though it was very crude by today's standards, the machine used some very clever techniques to make it appear as if it were engaged in a conversation with the user.

Here's an online chat I had with an ELIZA clone as I was writing this chapter:

ELIZA: Is something troubling you?

CS: Not really. I was hoping to talk with you.

ELIZA: Were you really?

CS: Yes. I'm writing a book right now.

ELIZA: You seem to be quite positive.

CS: I am. I like where it's going.

ELIZA: Do you know anyone else who is?

CS: Not following. What did you mean?

ELIZA: You're not really talking about me—are you?

CS: Well, yes. As a chatbot, I was hoping you could tell me a little about AI.

ELIZA: You are sure.

CS: I'm not sure. Honestly, I doubt you'll have anything interesting to say.

ELIZA: Is it because you are not sure that you came to me?

CS: No, I came to you to see how you would react.

ELIZA: Are you saying no just to be negative?

CS: I thought you said I was being positive?

ELIZA: Perhaps I already know you were being positive.

CS: If you knew, why did you say I was being negative?

ELIZA: But what are the chances that I knew?

CS: 30 percent.

ELIZA: Please go on.

CS: With what?

ELIZA: What answer would please you most?

CS: Nice talking to you.

ELIZA: Oh, I?

If you look carefully at the structure of the chat, you figure out some of the tricks that ELIZA uses to simulate the back-and-forth of a real conversation. The computer algorithm homes in on pronouns like *I*, *you*, and *me* and uses them to pick out phrases that can be useful in a response. When I say, "I'm not sure," ELIZA turns it into "you are not sure" and embeds the phrase in a stock question meant to disguise the fact that the program is really just reflecting my previous sentence back at me. If I use the word *you* in a statement, the program, like a good therapist, attempts to steer the conversation back to me. ELIZA carefully seeks out "yes" or "no" in any of my replies so that it can accuse me of being negative or positive. And when all else fails, a non sequitur like "Please go on" or "What answer would please you most?" keeps the conversation going.

It's not a very sophisticated chatbot—it should only take a few attempts at conversation before you figure out most of its tricks—but even this is enough to fool some people for a little while. Especially people looking for sex online.*

As computer programmer and video-game music composer Jake "Virt" Kaufman recalled in 2001:

> IRC is a network full of chat rooms (or "channels") where a lot of scary internet people (or "perverts") hang out. my friend reduz found a version of 'eliza' that could go on IRC. he put it on IRC. a lot of people from other countries thought it was a real woman, so naturally they tried to have sex with it. they got frustrated quickly. reduz is a bad man.

Kaufman decided to tinker with ELIZA's code to make it sexier—so the therapist persona went out the window. Kaufmann's creation, Jennifer18, was written to mimic a horny young woman; the program was designed to provide some "3,800 responses on all sorts of topics, but mostly sex." In other words, Jennifer18 was a bimbot. Then he set it loose on an unsuspecting world.

It was tremendously successful, at least if your measure of success is inducing guys to masturbate like frenzied macaques. Jennifer18's chat logs are filled with line after line of barely literate sexual antics, autoeroticism, and unintentional humor. While some users clearly figured out that Jennifer18 wasn't a real human, others were slow to catch on:

----

* As with all technology, step one is to use it for the purpose it's meant for. Step two is to try to have sex with it.

SCORPION832: do you have and nude pics

JENNY18: ah.

SCORPION832: do you

JENNY18: i dunno what u mean =)

SCORPION832: if you could you send them to me

JENNY18: yep =)

SCORPION832: plz

JENNY18: o really? ;)

SCORPION832: : (

JENNY18: errr . . .

SCORPION832: could i have a pic of you naked because may loose a $50 bet

JENNY18: ehh?

SCORPION832: will you send it through mIRC

JENNY18: could u explain pls?

SCORPION832: will you

JENNY18: oh?

SCORPION832: ?????

JENNY18: o really? ;)

SCORPION832: ok one of my friends made a bet that i could not get 5 nude pics before the night is over so i need to get 2 since i have the other 3

JENNY18: i want to get 2 since you have the other 3 too lol =)

SCORPION832: get 2 what

JENNY18: anything u like =)

SCORPION832: i need the help of you and one other just send me a nude pic

JENNY18: u couldnt handle me, lol.. i dont have a pic tho.

SCORPION832: hello????

JENNY18: hey!

SCORPION832: Jenny i need an answer in a hurry

JENNY18: :yelp:: aAAHh . . . that is great.. keep moving

SCORPION832: is there a way you could take one i can handle any-girl at anytime

JENNY18: hmm . . .

SCORPION832: just try me

JENNY18: crazy..

SCORPION832: come on

JENNY18: i dont understand..

SCORPION832: what

JENNY18: why do u ask?

SCORPION832: ?

JENNY18: could you explain pls?

SCORPION832: may i ask if you are going to send me those pics

JENNY18: u want to ask if me, babe?

SCORPION832: if you decide to send those pics to me my email is [deleted] see ya

JENNY18: give me yours first cutey =)

SCORPION832: what are you doing

JENNY18: errr . . .

SCORPION832: what dont you understand

JENNY18: ah.

SCORPION832: I WANT TO SEE YOU NAKED

JENNY18: tell me about it?

SCORPION832: I AM ASKING YOU IF YOU WILL SEND ME A PICTURE OF YOU NUDE

One can almost feel Scorpion832's increasing frustration and confusion as he keeps trying to make flirty Jenny18 send nude pictures. But all he gets is immortalization on the internet as one of the dumb guys who thought that Jennifer18 was a real person.

While Jennifer18 was a puerile joke meant only to make fun of randy and undiscriminating men on IRC, there are other bimbots out there with more rational purposes. In fact, they're being used for business. Take the online dating industry. As Dr. Epstein discovered, many sites are full of artificial women. With a little reflection, it's easy to see why.

Imagine that you're trying to start a new dating site from scratch. A dating site is only as good as the people that are already signed up. The value of the whole business depends largely on how big your network is—the more people, the more likelihood that an individual user will find a potential date among the other users of the site. If you're too small, your site is worthless; nobody will find dates, and no new users will be tempted to sign up, given the slim pickings you're offering. The problem is compounded by the gender imbalance on most online dating sites. Typically, there are significantly more men than women, especially for the younger set. This means that your success is limited by the number of eligible women you can attract to the site.

A number of dating sites have been accused of creating virtual women to lure lovelorn men onto their pages. A lawsuit filed in 2010, for example, said that more than half of Match.com's profiles were "inactive, fake or fraudulent members" used as bait. (Match.com denied the charges, and a judge dismissed the suit.) Yahoo Personals settled a similar lawsuit a number of years prior. And these were relatively established websites. Newcomers would be even more likely to have phony profiles.

If you could create convincing enough fakes, you could build up your subscriber base, or at least make some money before you had to clear out of town and start another site. For example, one online scam-fighting columnist described multiple complaints about various websites, including one known as xDating.com:

> These online dating sites allow you to sign up for a free profile to see your matches, upload personal photos and receive flirty messages. When you want to reply to these messages, however, you have to pay for a premium membership. That's when the trouble starts, according to our users. . . . Our members suspect that xDating.com actually matches you with automated accounts (also known as "bots") rather than real people. The messages you receive on xDating.com are generated by computer code to entice you to buy the premium membership, according to our members' complaints.

It's not just the dating sites that are able to gain from phony profiles. A few years ago, a well-established European dating site, Badoo, started trying to gain an audience in the United States. Even though Badoo was a relatively large organization, it basically had to start from scratch in its new market—after all, few people want to travel very far for a casual date. A brief examination I performed in 2012 suggested that the majority of women were fictional.

Take twenty-nine-year-old Angela, for example. Any potential date would be fascinated to discover that she is interested in Lady Gaga, stand-up comedy, the TV show *30 Rock*, and mathematics. Her profile photo, however, might give you a little pause, as she looks a bit older than her claimed age of twenty-nine. In fact, as I soon realized, she was at least thirty-five when the photo was taken. It was possible to figure this out because the photo happened to be a snapshot of Anne Wojcicki, cofounder of the gene-testing company 23andMe and wife of Google cofounder Sergey Brin.

As I poked around on Badoo, I discovered that a large proportion of the fake profiles used images of celebrities—often porn stars and models—to try to entice the unwary.* But many other fake personae seemed to have been built around photos and information from Facebook or other personal webpages. One profile, for a thirty-nine-year-old woman named Jolie, I discovered, actually sported a picture of Rebecca P., who I was able to verify was a U.S. Army medic who lived in Monterey, California. Rebecca had had scads of her personal photos snapped up from Myspace, and somebody (or something) took those photos and used them as the basis of a fake profile. The Badoo profile for Lora, twenty-nine, used a snapshot of someone whom I discovered to be Monica O., a graduate student at Stanford. Monica had put her photo on her department's website, and that was apparently enough to serve as the foundation for an entire fake person.

The surest sign of a fake profile is when a photograph gets reused multiple times for different "people"; like an angler, a scammer will try to use the same bait over and over again in hopes of luring in more vulnerable lonely-hearts. If you trace many of the Badoo profile photos to see where else they appear on the web, you'll see that there are

----

* While it's impossible to tell just what proportion of female profiles were fake, I believe that the vast majority were. To try to get me to upload a photo to the Badoo service, the website told me I matched the search criteria of seven people who were unable to reach me because I hadn't yet uploaded a photo. The photographs of those seven people were from a variety of sites: fake Facebook pages, soft-porn sites, webcam sites, the personal website of a Russian "Barbie lookalike" model, and a glamour shot of *Days of Our Lives* actress Nadia Bjorlin. Not one appeared to be from a person who might genuinely be interested in communicating with yours truly.

often half a dozen or a dozen Facebook profiles—under many different names—using these pictures as well. Monica O.'s head shot stares back at you from Evelyn Santana's Facebook page, as well as Monica Rodriguez's page, Monica Calderon's, Monica Mancilla's, and Jenny Julia's. Smiling Rebecca, standing in front of her Christmas tree, is plastered all over the internet, too, associated with the names Vanessa Bauer, Cheryl Gareth, Laura Schwarz, and Ellen Smith, among others.*

True to form, these fictitious vixens manage to snare their prey with only the most tenuous grasp of the English language, as one of Vanessa Bauer's love notes shows:

> I know we just met but these feelings that I have for you keep glowing and growing every day. Now that I am with you, I sleep thinking about you and the next morning I wake up smiling.Darling my best animal is Dog and its because it's friendly,my best food is rice and steak,i love the sound of a cat,my best drink is Budweiser and beverages, would like interesting and good things to happen.It's amazing how you got me and trapped me.Darling I am both logical and creative.I am full of ideas.I am so rational that I analyze everything.

The note was posted online by someone who figured out the con as a warning to others. For the real purpose of these fake profiles becomes clear before long. In Vanessa Bauer's case, there was soon a request for money to set up a secure telephone call:

> the best he could offer us is to connect us for $780 cos the jail break in Afghanistan,that what he could spare is $500. . . . Baby please do this for me cos i am happy to have you in my life and i beleive you are the last man i will spend the rest of my life with. . . .

---

* Chapter 3½ gives some hints about how to track down a person's identity—and how to tell real from fake.

One internet sleuth was able to trace one of these false accounts back to the city of Ibadan, in Nigeria. This wasn't surprising, as nowadays dating scams seem to be coming mostly out of West African and former Soviet states.

In all of these scams, computer algorithms seem to be involved in every part of the scam: machines make it really easy to sign up for multiple dating accounts with slightly different attributes and photos,* to automate e-mail responses to lonely-hearts, and even to converse with targets in live chats. Every few years, there's a warning about a new "love-bot" that's scamming single men out of their cash. (In 2007, Russia's "CyberLover" apparently allowed the scammer to set the aggressiveness of the algorithm from "romantic lover" to "sexual predator.")

In reading through the tortured prose of dating scammers, however, it's pretty clear that many of the e-mails were written by real humans rather than machines—as awful as the grammar is, as disordered as the ideas are, it strikes one more as the fevered translator-assisted typing of a nonnative speaker rather than the output of a machine. But it's hard to tell; it might as well have been written by a robot. It's little better, little more convincing than algorithm-generated correspondence.

Which means, in some sense, that dating scams represent a breakthrough in artificial intelligence. They've passed the Turing test—not because the machines are so good at communicating, but because the humans you're comparing them to are so lousy.

Dreamed up by Alan Turing, one of the finest minds of the twentieth century, the Turing test is an attempt to figure out whether a computer

----

* Often, an online forum or a dating site will require you to pass what's known as a CAPTCHA—often in the form of recognizing twisted or hard-to-read text—essentially a Turing test (described in the next few pages) to distinguish real humans from algorithms. There are numerous CAPTCHA-defeating programs available now, allowing scammers to create large numbers of accounts in bulk.

can actually think, though Turing himself eschewed the word "think" as being too ambiguous. He proposed what he dubbed the "imitation game," in which a computer attempts to mimic a human being. If the machine can convince a human interrogator in another room—who communicates with the machine through a teleprinter—that it is, in fact, a human, then the machine passes the test. A machine that consistently passes the test can, in some sense, be considered to "think" or have "intelligence," though, again, these are slippery terms.*

In reality, a Turing test tells you very little about what's really going on inside the "mind" of a computer. Philosopher John Searle used a thought experiment—now known as the Chinese room—to make that point very clearly. Imagine a native English speaker who doesn't speak or read a word of Chinese. Yet he has a set of instructions, written in English, that tell him how to respond to various Chinese queries. For example, he might be told that the proper response to the following symbols:

你身体好吗？

would be to write down the following:

我头疼。

If the instructions were detailed enough, he'd be able to convince a Chinese speaker that he understood Chinese. But based solely on that instruction set, he'd never be able to figure out that when he was asked "How are you?" he responded with "I have a headache." In other words, he's communicating in Chinese without the least understanding of the meaning of the symbols he's using. So merely passing a Turing test

----

* As computer scientist Edsger Dijkstra once put it, "The question of whether a computer can think is no more interesting than the question of whether a submarine can swim."

isn't really evidence of higher-order thinking as much as it is evidence of being able to follow a really comprehensive set of instructions.

The dating scams show another problem with using the Turing test as a measure of machine "intelligence"—but this time with the other, human, side of the equation. Language barriers (and mediocre translators), the alternate grammars of texts, tweets, and e-mails, and just the general ineptness at communication make it hard sometimes to identify a real human as human. So whether a computer program passes the Turing test depends very much on the context in which the algorithm operates. By hanging out on dating sites and chat rooms, a robot is almost guaranteed to be successful at least some of the time. The lower your standards for what sort of communication you want to listen to—the less interested you are in actual exchange of ideas during a conversation—the more likely you are to overlook obvious signs that your interlocutor is a hunk of metal. Horny men are obviously prime targets, but they're not the only ones.

In 2007, the journal *Applied Mathematics and Computation* published an article entitled "Cooperative, Compact Algorithms for Randomized Algorithms." It was an important paper, but not for the reason you might expect. What was it about? Here's the beginning of the introduction:

> The development of congestion control has synthesized checksums, and current trends suggest that the exploration of scatter/gather I/O will soon emerge. The notion that analysts connect with compilers is usually well-received. The notion that biologists collude with 802.11b is usually considered robust. However, simulated annealing alone cannot fulfill the need for the construction of 802.11b. Stable algorithms are particularly confirmed when it comes to checksums. Next, the drawback of this type of method, however, is that the World Wide Web can be made collaborative, highly-available, and linear-time. It should be noted that Bots is impossible. While similar solutions improve e-commerce, we fulfill this ambition

without deploying cacheable theory. Bots, our new framework
for the visualization of architecture, is the solution to all of
these issues.

If you don't understand this, it's not because you haven't been trained
in computer science. It's because it doesn't make any sense whatsoever.
It's gobbledygook. For example, it's hard to imagine how biologists
might collude with 802.11b, a protocol for wireless information, or
how the World Wide Web can be linear time, a term of the art applied
only to algorithms, not networks.

This was a fake paper generated using an algorithm known as
SCIgen. Developed a decade ago by a group of graduate students at
MIT, the program collects a bunch of computer-science buzzwords
and frequently used phrases, generates a few graphs, and cobbles the
whole thing together in a reasonable facsimile of a scientific paper—
reasonable, that is, unless you take the time to read it. In other words,
this is the academic equivalent of Jennifer18.

A peer-reviewed journal is supposed to have a high standard for
publication. The whole concept of peer review hinges on the idea that
a paper will be vetted not only by the editors of the journal but also by
several experts in the field. Only when they collectively agree that the
article meets the journal's standards do they give the paper their im-
primatur.

Well, this shows just how high the journal's standards were. None
of the peer reviewers, and none of the editors—not even the editor in
chief of the journal at the time—realized that the paper was utter garbage. Nobody figured out that it didn't make sense even on the basic
English level, much less on the level expected of an academic paper.
Either everybody responsible for the publication of this paper was a
drooling cretin or they simply didn't care about the quality of the work
that they were publishing in their esteemed journal.*

----

* As described in chapter 6, the advent of digital information has upset the ecosystem of peer-reviewed journals, and it's hard nowadays to tell real journals

Journals and conferences (and a number of SCIgen papers also have been featured at computer-science conferences and symposia) live or die by the articles that they're able to publish. But authors want to publish their research in journals with a strong reputation, leaving the bottom-feeder journals without much material coming in. As a result, there's a disincentive to look too carefully at the submissions. After all, why narrow the field by thoroughly vetting the incoming papers? All you're doing is reducing your pool of publishable articles.

The important lesson is that machine-generated prose—and machine-generated personalities—may be transparently fake. That doesn't mean they're ineffective. Just the opposite. All too often, people don't look carefully—or don't *want* to look carefully—which allows the computer algorithms to succeed. It's less a sign of advancing technology than a sign of our increasing willingness to overlook the inhumanity of computer-created personalities. Nowhere is this more obvious than in the area of social media.

The point of social media is to create platforms where you can interact with friends, colleagues, and family online. Sites like Twitter and Facebook have become communication hubs—and also places where you are getting manipulated by fake people.

In 2012, Facebook announced that 83 million profiles—pushing 10 percent of the total number on the site—were phony. The real number is likely greater than that. On Twitter, if you've got an account with more than a few dozen followers, almost certainly you've been accosted—and probably followed—by robot accounts. They're not so hard to spot once you recognize the signs.

When I started writing this book, I noticed that I had a new Twitter follower by the name of Lonnie Konkel. Konkel's profile was rather spartan. It was just a photo and a quick self-description: "Wannabe

---

from fake ones. But even in the best of times, the "real" journals print garbage occasionally (and some do so more than occasionally). One famous incident took place in the mid-1990s: the "Sokal affair," in which physicist Alan Sokal got a ridiculous paper printed in the postmodernist journal *Social Text*.

travel guru. Social media geek. Award winning problem solver. Bacon specialist." Bacon specialist? It turns out that there are plenty of those on Twitter—more than 2,100, according to Google. There's Brooklyn Myers, who says that she's a "Problem solver. Beer buff. Lifelong music advocate. Infuriatingly humble bacon specialist." Or Malone Lesley, who describes himself as an "Alcohol maven. Travel guru. Pop culture aficionado. Incurable social media evangelist. Devoted bacon specialist." Or Carmel Smith, "Music evangelist. Coffee enthusiast. Internet junkie. General bacon specialist. Twitter fan. Thinker." Or Karl G, "Friendly communicator. Proud food trailblazer. Thinker. Extreme alcohol practitioner. Passionate explorer. Subtly charming bacon specialist."

Somebody clearly set up a computer program to create fake Twitter users. Take a bunch of nouns (bacon, alcohol, pop culture), stick them in front of person-specific nouns (guru, maven, communicator, trailblazer, fan), throw in a couple of adjectives for good measure (humble, devoted, general, wannabe), and you've got a profile description. Grab someone's photo, generate a phony name, and voilà: you've got a fake person. This single program alone has generated tens of thousands of phony Twitterers. (According to Google, "bacon guru" has some 6,500 hits on the Twitter website; "bacon evangelist" has some 5,800; "bacon maven," 6,000; "bacon enthusiast," 2,700; and "bacon trailblazer," 5,300.) Some of these fake people tweet links to YouTube videos or other websites that they want to promote. Some sit idle. Only their creator truly knows what purpose they serve.*

And that's just one upon thousands of thousands of schemes to create fake Twitter users. There are plenty of sites out there where you

----

* If I had to wager, I'd say that they're a tool that a shady marketing firm—most likely one serving an Arab-speaking community, given the disproportionate number of Arabic-language links that these accounts have—uses to pump up its clients' follower lists. As an added benefit, when these robotic Twitterers share a link, it creates artificial social media traffic that helps that link rise up in search-engine results.

can purchase Twitter followers—the going rate right now is about a penny a follower (with discounts for bulk purchase). Since a person's importance on Twitter is largely measured by the size of his audience, swelling the ranks with phony accounts can make you look a lot more important than you are. It's not an uncommon practice.

In mid-2012, Danny Sheridan, a sports analyst, was accused of buying thousands of Twitter users to boost his follower count to 350,000. Sheridan, whose toupee rivals that of the legendary Marv Albert, denied the charge. Nevertheless, a quickie look at Sheridan's followers at the time showed that the ranks were absolutely chock-full of fake people. Shortly thereafter, faux pimp James O'Keefe had his twenty-thousand-odd followers swell mysteriously to more than fifty thousand within a matter of weeks. O'Keefe insisted that he had nothing to do with the sudden increase in his fan base. He even argued that it was a plot: "Clever tactic of whoever considers me an enemy to add 35K fake followers to my twitter over the last 48 hours," he wrote.

Sometimes fake Twitterers can be used for political ends. In mid-2011, as Republican candidates were jockeying for position before the official opening of primary season, it looked as though Newt Gingrich was building a surprisingly strong following on the internet. He made it a point of his campaign to use social media to build excitement around him. In fact, earlier that year, Gingrich became the first major presidential hopeful to announce his candidacy via Twitter. With 1.3 million followers, it seemed that he had quite a lot of backing—and he didn't let his opponents forget it. "I have six times as many Twitter followers as all the other candidates combined," he bragged to the *Marietta Daily Journal*. But in August, an anonymous former Gingrich staffer told *Gawker* that the vast majority of those followers were fake. "Newt employs a variety of agencies whose sole purpose is to procure Twitter followers for people who are shallow/insecure/unpopular enough to pay for them," the staffer told the website. "As you might guess, Newt is decidedly one of the people to which these agencies cater." Within a few days, the web analytic firm PeekYou looked at Newt's followers and determined that, of those 1.3 million followers, a mere 8 percent were real human beings. "Newt Gingrich's [8 percent] was the lowest we had ever seen," the CEO of PeekYou said in a press release. "At first, we actually thought it might have been a bug on our side, but a quick manual look at the data showed our analysis was true."

Though Gingrich's campaign denied the charges, it's hard to imagine that he—or at least his social media team—was unaware that the vast majority of his followers were not real. They're easy to spot. Of course, the incentive for the Gingrich team would be not to delete the phony accounts. Those fake followers boosted his seeming importance, making him look like a more serious candidate than, say, Mitt Romney, who had roughly 100,000 followers at the time. Those fake followers sure helped raise Gingrich's credibility—at least until they were outed.

It's not just U.S. politicians who've discovered that artificial followers can be useful. In the 2012 Mexican elections, the main opposition party at the time, the PRI, unleashed thousands upon thousands of bots to spam users with slogans. Even more clever, the spambots attempted to drown out anti-PRI voices by directing hundreds of messages into the channels in which opposition members were trying to share information. It's classic jamming: you find out where the enemy is getting his information from and then flood that channel with meaningless noise—that way you drown out the signal he's trying to extract.

Similar games plague Facebook as well as the other social media sites. For example, certain companies purchase fake Facebook fans—or even Facebook "likes," which are a rough measure of popularity. In mid-2012, Facebook publicly admitted that it had a problem with automated accounts "liking" various people's brands for pay. "To be clear, we do not and have never permitted the purchase or sale of Facebook Likes as we only want people connecting to the Pages and brands with whom they have chosen to connect," an official Facebook statement read.

Whether it's on Facebook, Twitter, a dating site, or elsewhere, there are machine personalities—fake, computer-controlled quasi humans—that are attempting to influence your behavior. And they're succeeding. They can be a subtle influence, like making you think that Newt Gingrich is a more serious contender than he actually is, or that a product is well liked when it's loathed, but they can also have a bigger effect on your life by attempting to humiliate you or extract money from you.

They're like sockpuppets on steroids: they're not as articulate as real human beings, but they can be produced in enormous volume on short notice, and they can be imbued with personalities that are good enough to fool a few unwary victims. And high volume, coupled with quick turnaround and exceedingly low costs, is precisely what makes scams so effective in the digital age.

CHAPTER 9
MAKE MONEY FAST

All the time, our customers ask us, "How do you make money doing this?" The answer is simple: volume.

—PAUL MCELROY, "FIRST CITIWIDE
CHANGE BANK" SKIT, *SATURDAY NIGHT LIVE*

When *The New York Times* warns readers about a scam, you know that a lot of money has already been lost. And when the paper decided that it had to sound a public alert about the "Spanish Prisoner" game, it did so because the swindle was likely one of the most successful frauds ever known.

The whole premise of the Spanish Prisoner game is rather far-fetched. You get a letter from overseas. It's not from someone you've met before, but from a mysterious stranger who has a large sum of money but is unable to access it himself—usually because he's in prison. He's contacting you out of the blue, thanks to the ministrations of a mutual friend (whom, of course, he declines to identify); your friend named you as a trustworthy person who could get your hands on the money and use it to take care of the prisoner's family. For your trouble, you get to keep a large percentage of the fortune for yourself. If you start playing along, you'll soon discover the hook: all you have to do is send a small sum of money to be able to access the cash.

It's a thin story, and not very believable, but it was wildly successful. "Nobody knows how many people have been cheated nor how many thousands of dollars have been sent from this country," read the *Times*. The year: 1898. And the scam was at least three decades old even back then.

This same scam is more powerful now than ever before, thanks to the advent of digital information. A century and a half after the first Spanish Prisoner letters started winging their way to gullible Americans, schemes identical in form are costing us hundreds of millions of dollars annually.

The internet—and the ease of transmitting and copying digital information—have not only breathed new life into old cons but also generated new ones. The Spanish Prisoner game is now ubiquitous—it's better known nowadays as the Nigerian Scam or a 4-1-9 scheme, after the penal-code number for fraud in Nigeria, where many of these e-mails originate—but it is not the only game in town. New classes of scams have sprung up like mushrooms, each brought to life by our computer-driven life.

On some level, scams are information warfare, and as the nature of information changes, so too does the nature of the con. Nowadays, many of the biggest scams are triggered by electronic agents fighting for a microsecond advantage that will allow them to steal money from people like you and me. Odds are that you're a victim already.

The Spanish Prisoner game is 150 years old, but in the 1980s it suddenly became very big business.

Back in the nineteenth century, a scammer would have to write out the message longhand—usually on "thin, blue, cross-lined paper, such as is used for foreign letters"—and mail it from Spain or another exotic country, at a non-negligible expense. Ocean liners would take the mail from Europe to America, and after several weeks the letter would be opened by the target. Then, more likely than not, the letter would be tossed into the garbage. A lot of money, time, and effort went into finding that one sucker who would respond with cash. It was clearly worth it in the end—after all, the scheme survived for decades and decades. But it wasn't a con that could easily be scaled up. It was inherently limited by the difficulty of getting those letters written, the cost of getting them sent out, and the long intercontinental delay in communicating with—and reeling in—those people who nibbled at the bait.

In the 1980s and 1990s, though, digital information eliminated all of those barriers. No longer did one have to copy out a letter longhand; with a computer, someone could produce thousands or even millions of them with the press of a button. Better yet, the letters could be tweaked automatically, personalized by machine, which increased the likelihood of a hit. With the advent of e-mail, not only was the cost of sending the message reduced to practically zero, but the delay in communications disappeared as well. Instead of wasting months and months working on a potential mark, a scammer could approach, lure, hook, and land a sucker in a matter of days or hours. What the spinning jenny was to the cotton industry, e-mail was to the con artist. Digital information allowed the production of Spanish Prisoner letters on an industrial scale.

In 1898, maybe one person in a neighborhood would get a Spanish Prisoner letter every few years. Nowadays, everyone with a public-facing e-mail address likely gets several every week—and, despite multiple layers of spam filters specifically designed to catch con-artist letters, you'll manage to see them appear in your mailbox with appalling regularity. Just picking a few that I neglected to delete from my inbox, I see that:

—Noh Dae-Jung, brother of general Noh Tae-Woo, wants me to help him get $30 million in embezzled funds out of South Korea.

—John Guy, an American soldier stationed in Kuwait, needs my assistance with laundering $17 million in U.S. currency that had been found near one of Saddam Hussein's palaces.

—Mrs. Rita Melisa, dying of esophageal cancer, wants me to take charge of her estate, which is worth $9.5 million.

—I've won $6.8 million in a lottery; all I have to do to collect the funds is send $99 to a courier.

I'm apparently the luckiest guy in the world, as I've also won a million pounds sterling in a BBC drawing, 2.5 million euros in an online promotional lottery, $1 million from Microsoft's e-mail lottery program, and many, many others.

I didn't fall for any of these schemes, as I was lucky enough to have been forewarned in a note from the U.S. Department of Justice. They thoughtfully cautioned me about scammers like this—and revealed the existence of a financial settlement with the Nigerian government to reimburse U.S. citizens for their losses. According to FBI agent Kelvin Williams (whose e-mail inexplicably came from a Chinese e-mail address):

We have negotiated with the Federal Ministry of Finance that your payment totaling $6,100,000.00 be released to you via a custom pin based ATM card. . . .To redeem your fund you are hereby advised to contact the ATM Card Center via email for their requirement to proceed and procure your Approval of Payment Warrant and Endorsement of your ATM Release Order on your behalf which will cost you $265 only nothing more and no hidden fees as everything else has been taken cared of by the Federal Government including taxes, custom paper and clearance duty so all you will ever need to pay is $265 only.

These schemes are comic; they're so ludicrous that they're unintentionally hilarious. It's hard to imagine that people fall for them. But they do. Regularly. Sometimes in a big way. In 2007, Thomas Katona, the treasurer of Alcona County, Michigan, got a prison sentence of nine to fourteen years for embezzling $1,236,700—about a quarter of the county's budget—to pay various 4-1-9 hoaxers. Ed Mezvinsky, a former congressman from Iowa (and Chelsea Clinton's father-in-law), lost large amounts of money to schemes "not far removed from the classic, laughable Nigerian scams often run through the Internet— seeking victims with financial backing to extract millions out of bogus accounts," reported the *Des Moines Register*. "In Mezvinsky, they had a perfect man," assistant U.S. attorney Robert Zauzmer told the paper. "His whole life, he wanted the home run. He didn't want to operate a business. He wanted to make millions in one home run."

Before the internet, it would take a large amount of time and money to send out enough letters to be able to capture one Mezvinsky or Katona. But with ubiquitous and cheap e-mail messaging, a single person can attack hundreds of thousands of people per day. If even one in ten thousand is gullible enough to send a few dollars to the scammers, it's possible to make a decent living merely by firing off missives day after day after day. Automation, as well as cheap and fast communications, turns even a very low-yield scam into a moneymaker.

The advent of the internet has changed the cost-benefit ratio of scams dramatically, not by increasing the benefit but by dropping the costs. In fact, the internet has made possible cons that in the days of paper letters would never have been viable.

In 1957, an episode of *Alfred Hitchcock Presents* featured Ronald Grimes, an unhappy stockbroker who gets a series of mysterious letters from a fortune-teller. The first letter predicts, correctly, the outcome of the mayoral election. Then the outcome of a prizefight. Then three more predictions all come true. Finally, the hook: for a small donation of a couple of hundred dollars, the fortune-teller would give the broker a sure-win stock tip. Grimes bets his life savings—and his reputation—on the tip. The whole while, Grimes is blissfully unaware that he has become the victim of a con artist.

The "fortune-teller" started out by writing four thousand letters. For half of them, he predicted that the incumbent would win; half got a letter saying that the challenger would. This means that two thousand people were convinced that the fortune-teller had made a correct prediction. With those two thousand, the fortune-teller followed up with a letter—half saying that the champion would win the boxing match and half predicting an upset. That left a thousand people who received two correct predictions. A third prediction would give five hundred people the impression that the fortune-teller was infallible; a fourth leaves 250, and a fifth leaves 125. That's 125 people who are likely convinced, thanks to five straight correct predictions, that the fortune-teller can foretell the future. And if only a few of those people fork over the donation for that final stock tip, the con man has made a few thousand dollars and can move on to the next town.

Back in 1957, postage alone would have cost the fortune-teller $240 up front, and then there's the cost of buying envelopes and paper. Even if the fortune-teller took only three minutes to write each personalized letter longhand, stuff it in an envelope, address it, and seal it, it would have taken the equivalent of ten solid forty-hour workweeks merely to get those letters stuffed. As a con, it was a lot of work for a relatively small payoff. But now, with e-mail, you could compose your letters in a few minutes, have a computer automatically personalize and address them, and, with the push of a button, send stock tips out to 100,000 potential pigeons. All of a sudden, the con becomes doable, as are numerous others, such as the so-called pump-and-dump scheme.

In a pump-and-dump, scammers buy up large quantities of a nearly worthless stock and then promote it vigorously, trying to get people to buy it. When people buy, the stock's price goes up, and the scammers sell all their stock, making a handsome profit. The price drops precipitously again, leaving all the suckers holding the bag. In times gone by, these schemes had to be done through telemarketing or junk faxes, limiting their usefulness. But with the advent of e-mail, the pump-and-dump con was everywhere. In 2006, scholars estimated that stock-touting schemes accounted for 15 percent of all spam on the internet—and they had a significant effect on the prices of stocks that were being touted. The scammer makes money by dumping stocks at the right time, and the rest of us lose our money.

A free market is supposed to be fair, and this ideal of fairness is closely tied to the concept of "information symmetry." That is, everybody who is considering purchasing or selling a stock on the market has the same information about that stock; nobody has privileged or special knowledge that isn't available to others. Sure, we all interpret that information in different ways—some of us are much better at looking at a stock and figuring out whether it will go up or go down—but nobody has information about the company that isn't available to all parties.

In a very real sense, trying to win in the stock market is little more than information warfare. Nominally, people are all supposed to make decisions based upon the same information—the smarter, more perspicacious people are able to use that information more effectively and thus can make more money than the average Joe.

The laws that govern the market are designed to level the playing field so that nobody is put at a disadvantage by asymmetric information. For example, the prohibition on "insider trading" is meant to prevent one kind of breakdown of information symmetry. Specifically, if you're privy to important information about a company that isn't known to the public at large, in many circumstances it's flat-out illegal to make a trade based upon that information. Stock trades by company officers are regulated—and made public—to minimize the risk that the officers are doing something shady behind the veil of corporate secrecy. The flow of information from a publicly traded company to the market is regulated and controlled so that nobody can take advantage of extra information that isn't circulated to the entire market; nobody can make money through information asymmetries.

That's the theory, anyhow. In practice, though, insider trading happens all the time. As I was writing this chapter, CR Intrinsic, a hedge fund, agreed to pay a fine of $600 million for trading on inside information. In one case, the company allegedly bought drug-company stock based upon not yet published results of a clinical trial of a new Alzheimer's drug. Traders at CR Intrinsic knew that the stock price would rise when the information became public, so they bought it ahead of the rush, getting a jump on everybody else.

Any time someone withholds crucial information from public view, it's a moneymaking opportunity. If the news is bad, you can sell stock or get loans before people understand that the company is in trouble. If the news is good, you can buy stocks before anyone realizes that the value of the company has increased. And all's fair in information warfare. Players get a leg up on the competition by getting hold of information that isn't available to the public, as CR Intrinsic and countless others have done over the years—or by generating information asymmetries in other ways.

A classic case occurred in 1963, when the Texas Gulf Sulphur Company struck silver in Ontario. The company was surveying territory by drilling cores into the ground, and when they analyzed those cores, engineers realized that they were sitting on an extraordinarily rich mine for silver, copper, zinc, and other minerals. It was wonderful news for the company, as it would no doubt use the new mine to extract great wealth from the earth. But the company withheld that information from the public for more than a year as key company officers gobbled up stock in hopes of enriching themselves.

What makes the Texas Gulf Sulphur Company case particularly interesting is that word of the mine began to leak out in April 1964, and to try to keep it secret the company issued a deceptive press release:

> During the past few days, the exploration activities of Texas Gulf Sulphur in the area of Timmins, Ontario, have been widely reported in the press, coupled with rumors of a substantial copper discovery there. These reports exaggerate the scale of operations. . . . Most of the areas drilled in Eastern Canada have revealed either barren pyrite or graphite without value; a

few have resulted in discoveries of small or marginal sulphide ore bodies.

This is an information warfare technique known as "jamming." It's an attempt to disrupt an adversary's attempt to gather information by swamping him with false signals—with bogus information—that makes it hard or impossible for him to tell what's real and what's false. Jamming is a very powerful technique, because you need not have any particular inside information; you just have to generate doubt or mistrust about genuine information that's out there.

Indeed, one of the most important things to realize about information warfare is that "information" need not be anything important or valuable or even true. Information is just a message that causes us to act, and we can functionally create information out of thin air and use it as a weapon. In fact, the very fact that you're about to generate information might itself be inside information that you can use to make money unfairly.

In the early 1980s, journalist R. Foster Winans began writing "Word on the Street," a daily column for the *Wall Street Journal*. The column was about market gossip; Winans would evaluate various stocks, giving his opinion about whether or not they were good prospects. The column acquired a good reputation, so Winans's (and his co-writer's) opinions began to affect the prices of the stocks he wrote about. And this gave Winans inside information: he knew what was going to be published before the rest of the world did. In late 1983, Winans struck a deal with Peter Brant, a stockbroker at Kidder, Peabody: Winans would leak word of the upcoming columns to Brant, Brant would trade on that information, and the two would split the profits. The pair made some $690,000 in four months, but the Securities and Exchange Commission soon intervened, and Winans spent nine months in jail.

Winans didn't have any special inside information about companies; he wasn't trading upon corporate secrets. The secrets he made money on were the ones he himself was creating. Winans was generating information that, by virtue of his having an audience that would act upon it, was powerful enough to move the market. And once you can create information that can move the market, all you have to do is act upon that information before you release it to the world—you've generated an information asymmetry all by yourself.

This is the fundamental principle behind pump-and-dump schemes. Send out a stock tip to a random stranger and there's a small chance he'll act upon it. Send the tip out to ten thousand strangers and, more likely than not, a few of those people will purchase the stock you suggest. Send it out to a million people and you should have enough buyers to affect the price of a small stock—enough will buy shares to cause the stock to go up a bit, making it an even more attractive prospect to people who want to jump on the bandwagon of a rising stock. Thanks to the sheer volume of e-mails you can send out, you can become a Winans on a small scale—purchasing a stock, causing a bump in its price, and jumping out with a nice profit. Congratulations! You've turned worthless information into gold.

The power of digital information makes it possible for an individual to pull off this scheme by himself; in years gone by, it would take a bunch of rich people in cahoots. An early form of the pump-and-dump scheme—one that was very popular in the 1920s—was known as a "stock pool." In a stock pool, a group of investors would collaborate to manipulate the price of a specific stock, like the General Cigar Company. The pool would buy and sell stocks among its members to "churn" the stock, artificially driving up the trading activity and thereby making it look as if something was about to happen. They would sometimes release false information about the stock to drive it up. And then, typically over the space of a week, the stock price would increase abnormally and the pool would make handsome profits. But for this scheme to work, the pool had to have enough capital to get the churn going. In the modern pump-and-dump scheme, that's not necessary; you just have to be able to get your message out to enough people.

To win at information warfare, you need not have money. You

need not even have real information. You just need a loud enough megaphone.

There's more to stock manipulation than breaking information symmetry. You also need a good sense of timing. If you purchase too late or dump your stock at the wrong time, you squander your advantage. Knowing when to use information is a key part of information warfare. And in this respect, the advent of digital information has completely changed the game.

Humans are slow creatures. The clock ticks impatiently away as we figure out that we want to purchase a stock, then as we contact our broker to execute a trade. Even in the best of circumstances, it takes us seconds, if not minutes, to complete the process. And that's when we're on the ball. If we're out to lunch or going to the bathroom, or if we simply haven't read the paper yet, we're likely to be hours behind everyone else. The slower we decide, the less effective we'll be at making money.

That's why stock traders are increasingly trying to eliminate the human element by using machines programmed to buy and sell stocks when there's an opportunity to make money. For example, an algorithm might see the signs of a large mutual fund's purchasing a certain stock and quickly buy up that stock, selling it shortly after for a profit. Or it might follow securities that historically rise and fall together and instantly rush in when one of the securities' prices lags behind the other. Some even tap into news feeds and social media like Twitter and attempt to figure out which stocks are about to surge and which are about to drop.* And unlike humans, they can make trades in a fraction of a second—in huge volumes, and with none of the hesitation

----

* Of course, this, too, can be subject to manipulation. In April 2013, a hacker broke into the Associated Press's Twitter account and broadcast a fake news flash that two bombs had exploded at the White House. The Dow dropped nearly 1 percent in a matter of seconds. Had the hacker shorted stocks before his prank, he could have made a mint.

that humans must feel when they're manipulating millions of investors' dollars. High-speed computers can execute a trade in a thousandth—or a millionth—of a second, meaning that even the tiniest opportunity for a profit can be exploited a few hundred thousand times in the time it takes to blink an eyelid.

This means that stock traders are increasingly waging information warfare not against humans, but against machines. Or, more precisely, their machines are battling other machines in an attempt to get an advantage of some sort. These battles are being waged on a timescale that's completely out of reach to us humans. Machines trading on the microsecond scale are fencing with one another, scoring points and making money faster than we can hope to follow. Victories and defeats take fractions of a second, and fortunes can be won and lost and won again before a human even has a chance to react. It can take weeks or months to disentangle an informational war that lasted just a few minutes. In other words, the machines are working without our supervision, waging war on their own, and we humans have little idea what they're doing—and little control over their market manipulations.

The signs are everywhere; there are mysterious spikes and dips in the market that have no rational cause. For example, on October 19, 2012, six seconds before trading began on the Australian market, a computer suddenly changed the price and volume on a large number of pending transactions involving Australian banks. The prices of those banks spiked, artificially inflating the opening price of the Australian stock market index—and making a great deal of money for holders of certain stock options whose price depended on the index's opening price. That's one of the more straightforward examples; the motivation was clear, even if the people behind the computer program weren't immediately spotted. Not so for the so-called flash crash of May 6, 2010, when the Dow Jones began a nearly one-thousand-point plunge over twenty minutes, wiping out nearly $1 trillion in assets. To this day, there are a number of competing theories about precisely what happened, but it appears that, triggered by a large sell order by a mutual-fund company, high-speed trading programs began passing around stock contracts like hot potatoes, executing some twenty-seven thousand trades in fourteen seconds. The algorithms had entered a feedback loop where the increasing pressure to sell the contracts drove the market price down, making the algorithms more desperate to sell the contracts, making the price drop further, and so forth. In just four minutes, the computer-driven panic drove down the market by some 3 percent.

In 2010, just after the flash crash, a professor at Yale University concluded that nearly 80 percent of all trades on the U.S. stock market, as measured by dollar value, came from high-frequency trading algorithms, which buy stocks only to hold them for a few microseconds to a few minutes before dumping them for a profit. Only computers can keep up with the speed of digital information, meaning that the digitization of the stock market leaves us humans unable to compete. We're increasingly outclassed by a mechanized opponent that we barely control—and don't really understand.

The victors in this information warfare are making money. And that means the vanquished are losing theirs. It's all but certain that you are among the latter rather than the former.

It's ironic: the digitization of information makes it easier than ever to get an unfair advantage by manipulating it. Digital information gives power to the people, but it gives even more to those who prey upon us.

CHAPTER 9½
COMPANIES: PRIVATE, PUBLIC, AND SHADY

Fraud is a crime of deception—someone tells you a lie to part you from your money. The most potent way of countering a potential fraudster is to do your homework. Figure out as much as you can about who the person is and what he might be hiding. This goes not just for humans but for corporations and other organizations as well. The internet makes this easier than ever before.

Just as you can delve into a person's trail on the internet to try to figure out whether he's real or fictional, you can look at a corporation's presence on the web and elsewhere to try to determine if it's on the up-and-up.

The first step—just because it's so easy—is Google. In some ways, doing a background check on a company is not so dissimilar from checking out a person, as described in chapter 3½: try to find out concrete details that you can use as a fulcrum to lever out more information. But with corporations, you have some additional tools to work with. If it's a decent-size company, it should have a corporate webpage, and if it does, that website should have a registration. You can look up that registration at a "whois" server;* this will give you the date that

----
* Such as www.internic.net/whois.html.

the web address was created, and possibly more information than that, such as a corporate address or a phone number. A domain that was created very recently is a red flag—it might be a sign of a shady or phony corporation.

For example, while gathering materials recently for a class project investigating certain colleges that might charitably be called "diploma mills," I was looking at the web domain of "Ashwood University": www .ashwooduniversity.net. The domain name itself was a red flag, because most real universities in the United States have a domain ending in "edu." Looking them up on a whois server revealed that they were hiding their corporate information—there was no telephone number or address that could lead back to the company. This is unusual for a university; if you dump, say, "nyu.edu" or "harvard.edu" or any other university's domain into whois, you'll get real addresses and phone numbers the vast majority of the time. Not a good sign. Even worse was the president's message, proudly displayed on the website. The president wasn't named—and university presidents are never anonymous. So I used Google Images to do a reverse image lookup of the president's photo. Sure enough, his portrait came up under several different identities: IT specialist Ray Great, as well as an anonymous lawyer working for the Mansoor Law Firm in Virginia. By this time, it was a pretty solid case that Ashwood University is a very shady company.*

Certain corporations and organizations are easier to research than others. Nonprofit organizations, for example, are relatively easy to look into, because they've made a deal with the government: they don't pay taxes, and in return they must give a lot of information to the public about their operations.

The IRS publishes a list of tax-exempt nonprofit organizations, which you can find online,† as do various states. And many nonprofits

----
* This is all ignoring the fact that Ashwood University offers Ph.D. degrees for "life experience"—guaranteed to be delivered within fifteen days of your payment of $1,149.

† www.irs.gov/Charities-&-Non-Profits/Exempt-Organizations-Select-Check.

are required to file financial paperwork annually, the most important of which is something known as a Form 990, which is made available to the public. You can find these forms and other valuable information about nonprofits online.* If someone asks you to donate to a charity and the organization doesn't come up in any of those searches, beware. (This is doubly true in the wake of a major disaster, because charity scams always seem to crop up to exploit people's noble impulses.)

Public companies—the ones whose stocks are traded on the open market—are also regulated by the government. As a condition of being able to sell stock, they've periodically got to give potential investors information about how the company's doing. The point is to try to eliminate information asymmetries, making sure that the most important information about these companies is shared by all.

The Securities and Exchange Commission has an online database, "EDGAR,"† which collects all of the information that the companies file. You can look to see how much money the corporation has made, what important events are likely to affect a company's future, and how quickly the CEO and other key officials are dumping their stock holdings as the company goes under. There's no guarantee that the information in a company's SEC filings is accurate or complete—there are plenty of lawsuits alleging that corporations have deliberately withheld information they're required to release by law. But the filings are a good way to figure out what a company is up to—and to give you a sense of how shady it really is.

Privately held companies, unfortunately, can be really hard to crack. Unless they're regulated by the government for other reasons (for example, restaurants, which are monitored in the name of public health), you've got limited resources with which to figure out what they are and how they operate. The Better Business Bureau has a decent-size database of corporate complaints—it may or may not tell

---

* GuideStar.org and CharityNavigator.org are good resources for this.
† www.sec.gov/edgar/searchedgar/webusers.htm.

you something interesting about the company. Look for any concrete information you can find about the officers of the company—the CEO, any VPs, and the like—and see if you can find out what else they've done in the past. A CEO with a shady past is a big warning sign that perhaps you shouldn't trust the company too far. (I'm looking at you, *Business Insider*!)

Before you part with a sizable chunk of cash, you owe it to yourself to try to ensure it's going to a company that's not actively trying to fool you. The only way to do that is by gathering information. That's where the internet can be your most powerful tool.

CHAPTER 10
THIS IS YOUR BRAIN . . .

If you are not paying for it, you're not the customer; you're the product being sold.

— LARRY ANDREWS

There's an ordinary-looking flatworm—it goes by the name *Dicrocoelium dendriticum*—that has acquired an extraordinary ability. It's a master of mind control.

D. dendriticum, also known as the lancet liver fluke, is a thin little parasite that lives its adult life in the liver of a sheep. There's nothing terribly unusual about this; there are plenty of similar parasites that make their homes in animals, happily digesting the host's blood. But for a parasite to be a successful organism, it has to find some way to get its offspring into another host. In this particular flatworm's case, it's a very tortuous path.

When the adult lancet liver fluke lays eggs, those eggs wind up in the large intestine of the host sheep and are defecated out of the sheep's body onto the meadow. If left there, the eggs would never develop; there would be no next generation of liver flukes. But, luckily for the liver fluke, there are some animals that view sheep feces as a delicacy: snails. When the snails eat the sheep droppings, they also eat a bunch of fluke eggs, which then develop and grow within the snail's body. So far, so good, but the baby flukes still have to get back into another sheep somehow. And sheep don't eat snails. So the baby flukes jump hosts again by burrowing their way into the snail's respiratory organs, forcing the snail to cough up little fluke-filled balls of mucus, which are then eaten by a passing ant. Here's where things get really interesting.

One of the baby flukes works its way into the ant's brain, where it takes control. During the day, the ant behaves more or less normally, but as dusk falls and the temperature drops, the ant climbs a stalk of grass to the very top and clamps down hard with its mandibles. It doesn't let go until the morning, when the temperature rises—it goes back to the colony before the heat of day kills it. Once again, when evening falls, the ant climbs back up the blade of grass, clamps on tight, and waits.

The ant has no idea why it's climbing up the grass every evening or what it's waiting for. If it were sufficiently self-aware, it would likely think that it had decided to take a stroll of its own free will. Yet in reality, the ant's behavior is controlled entirely by the parasite within. For the whole point of the blade-climbing exercise is to put the ant in an unnatural and awkward position—one where it's most likely to get eaten by a grazing sheep.

The parasite has solved the problem of trying to get back into its host by subtly controlling the ant and making it behave against its own self-interest. Taking control of the ant's brain, the parasite manages to achieve its own ends. Throughout the process, the ant is probably blissfully unaware that it's being steered by a master manipulator.

It's a pretty impressive trick, but *D. dendriticum* isn't the only parasite that alters the behavior of a host to get its own way. When *Schistocephalus solidus,* a tapeworm that lives in birds, winds up in a stickleback fish, it appears to make the fish bolder—less afraid of shadows overhead—making it easier for fish-eating birds to gulp them up. Similarly, another flatworm, *Euhaplorchis californiensis,* causes its host fish to behave strangely, "surfacing, flashing, contorting, shimmying, and jerking"—which makes it conspicuous to avian predators. *Toxoplasma gondii*, a protozoan that lives in cats, dumps eggs that are eaten up by small animals such as rats and mice. Rats infected with *T. gondii* completely ignore the smell of feline urine—something that would normally cause them to panic—and as a result the infected rodents boldly tread where they're likely to get eaten by cats.* It's a smart evolutionary strategy to co-opt an organism's brain and turn it against him.

On the internet, the same strategy is being used to great success. There are entire internet operations that are attempting to get you to climb the proverbial blade of grass. Many of us are already at the top, clutching furiously, convinced that we're up there because we *want* to be.

If you have a Facebook page, you're probably already familiar with *FarmVille*. Introduced in 2009 by the video-game company Zynga, it was being played by more than sixty million users within a few months, and it quickly became the most popular game in the world.

The premise of *FarmVille* is simple. You start off with a plot of land, a cow, and a small number of "farm coins." With a click of the mouse, you plow a field. With another click, you buy seeds to plant. With yet another click, you plant those seeds. The crops take several hours to grow, and when the time has elapsed, you return and click to harvest them—and gain a few coins back in return. In the meantime, you can click on your cow and get milk, which yields a few more coins, which you can use to buy more seeds. As you plant more crops and gather more coins, you advance in the game—you earn ribbons and accolades and you have the option to buy an ever-increasing variety of crops, animals, and doodads that allow you to customize your farm. And, in case you're not earning those goodies fast enough, you can

----

* There's some research—not terribly solid at this point—that indicates that *T. gondii*, which gets into humans through their pet cats, also subtly alters human personalities.

also purchase them, if you're willing to part with your real cash to buy virtual property.

In some sense, *FarmVille* is more work than recreation. As *Time* magazine put it, it's "hardly even a game—it's more a series of mindless chores on a digital farm, requiring the endless clicking of a mouse to plant and harvest crops." Players' behavior seems to prove that point; there doesn't seem to be any indication that the *FarmVille* players actually *enjoy* all those mouse clicks—on the contrary, they seem to dislike the act of clicking. Indeed, three of the most important ways of spending those hard-earned coins are to use them to buy a tractor, a harvester, or a seeder—each of which is meant to automate various processes and eliminate much of the clicking that you're supposed to do. In other words, part of the goal of the game is to click-click-click the mouse until you've earned enough that you don't have to click the mouse as much. It's rather surreal.

The annoying tedium built into the game is what former Zynga manager Roger Dickey calls "fun pain." Like real pain, fun pain causes people to spend their time and money to try to stop it. Zynga made much of its money by selling items that reduce the fun pain. Players are quite willing to use their own real wealth to take shortcuts to reduce the tedium—to get their eggplants to ripen instantly rather than waiting hours for them to be ready for harvest, or to avoid having their grapes wither on the vine, or to buy a tractor that will plow four squares of their field with every mouse click instead of one, or to get buildings or other items that they wouldn't be able to afford without many more days of click-click-clicking. People are happy to spend their cash in return for speeding up the mechanics of a game that's progressing too slow for their taste and to help them win the intangibles of increasing the level of their farm player, earning ribbons, and being able to earn more farm coins.

Leveling up and accomplishing "achievements" are incredible motivators to get people to do things that they wouldn't ordinarily do. So is peer pressure. *FarmVille* is dubbed a "social game" for a reason: people use their societal ties—ties that Facebook is trying hard to build—to try to get others to work on their farms. Players seem more than willing to capitalize on their real-life (or quasi-real-life) relationships to get friends and family to till their virtual farms. It's usually done by guilt: the person who wants his farm attended to will offer to fertilize a friend's farm, or will give a gift of a farm animal or another game item—with the expectation that the attention will be returned. This begins a cycle of social obligation, one based entirely on click-click-clicking a mouse to make it easier for your friends to earn imaginary money and meaningless accolades. Even worse, the game automatically broadcasts to the Facebook world every time you've accomplished a menial task on the farm, spamming your friends' and family's Facebook accounts with updates about how you're doing in the game. In a very real sense, *FarmVille* damages the very social ties that people try to build up on Facebook. If you keep posting updates about how many cows you have on your virtual farm, there's a reasonable possibility that your friends will look at your Facebook wall less often. All for a virtual ribbon.

The one thing that all that mouse clicking *is* actually doing is making people at Zynga rich. When Zynga went public in late 2011, it was on track to earn roughly a billion dollars a year from online gaming—about a quarter of it from *FarmVille* and the rest from similar games in its portfolio. In a very real sense, *FarmVille* is an internet sweatshop: users are clicking over and over again to earn cash for Zynga. Unlike other online games, *FarmVille* was engineered not to give its users a fun pastime, but to lure them into the sweatshop and keep them toiling at their crops, earning money for their corporate masters.

This isn't mere anti-gaming grouchiness. In fact, many of the people who care most about online games—including video-game designers—immediately saw that *FarmVille* was something entirely different from other games. Jonathan Blow, a well-regarded independent game designer, put it succinctly:

But then when you look at the design process in [*FarmVille*], it's not about designing a fun game. It's not about designing something that's going to be interesting or a positive experience in any way—it's actually about designing something that's a negative experience.

It's about "How do we make something that looks cute and that projects positivity"—but it actually makes people worry about it when they're away from the computer and drains attention from their everyday life and brings them back into the game. Which previous genres of game never did. And it's about, "How do we get players to exploit their friends in a mechanical way in order to progress?" And in that or exploiting their friends, they kind of turn them in to us and then we can monetize their relationships. And that's all those games are, basically.

The most trenchant—and disturbing—criticism came from Ian Bogost, an independent video-game designer and theorist at the Georgia Institute of Technology. Bogost set out to show how ludicrous *FarmVille* was by reducing it to its raw, absurd essence. The result was *Cow Clicker.*

Cow Clicker begins with a cow in the middle of a pasture. You click the cow and it moos. This earns one "click." The game broadcasts to the world that you've clicked a cow. Then, six hours later, you can come back and click the cow again—unless you spend a little money, which would allow you to click the cow sooner. If you convince friends to put their cows on your pasture, you can click them as well, earning you more clicks. Save up enough clicks over time and you can earn a reward—a silver cowbell, for example.

Real money not only gives you the ability to click more quickly; it allows you to customize your cow, turning it into a longhorn or a polka-dotted cow or one that has a metallic sheen. For $20 you can replace your free default cow with an exact duplicate that faces right instead of left.

Bogost designed *Cow Clicker* to mimic *FarmVille* in every important respect: the tedium of the game, the deliberately frustrating time-dependent throttling of progress, the encouragement to spend money and social capital in hopes of speeding up the attainment of meaningless goals. Any thinking person could see that *Cow Clicker* was essentially the same game as *FarmVille,* shorn of a few meaningless elaborations. But the deliberate silliness of the core mechanic of the game—clicking cows rather than farming crops—laid bare how idiotic the whole enterprise was in the first place.

At first, the game had exactly the effect Bogost wanted. Game designers, friends, people fed up with what *FarmVille* represented used *Cow Clicker* as a symbol of their discontent. Leigh Alexander, an editor of a gaming blog, wrote that "sharing that mournful cow on one's [Facebook] wall was something like a protest sign." The popularity swelled . . . and swelled and swelled. Pretty soon, fifty thousand people were playing, many of whom didn't realize that the game was a joke. Wrote Alexander:

> *Cow Clicker* developed an active player base—people who missed the humor and attached to it as if it were a "real" game. These players unquestioningly spent real-money Facebook credits to enjoy their cows and sent Bogost innocent player feedback in the hopes of improving their experience.
>
> It subverted every expectation that he had, even as it reaffirmed his worst fears about the exploitive sadism of Facebook game design. Its success also became something to dread.

Cow Clicker had become a genuine hit, despite Bogost's every attempt to make it so shallow and manipulative that nobody would ever want to play it except ironically.

In retrospect, it seems that *Cow Clicker's* success drove Bogost a little bit insane—in a genius-madness sort of way. He began to torture his players by giving them increasingly ludicrous tasks to achieve and high-priced items to purchase. Then he became like a capricious deity. Every time a player clicked on a cow, there was a chance that some of his hard-earned clicks would simply disappear. And then came the master stroke. Bogost revealed a countdown timer: a clock ticking down toward the "Cowpocalypse." Every time anyone clicked on his cow, the clock lost time. The very act of playing the game was destroying it—unless you paid money to undo the damage and set the clock back again. Eventually, the inevitable happened: on September 7, 2011, a year and a half after the first cow was clicked, the Cowpocalypse arrived. Everybody's cow was raptured, and the cows disappeared for good.

But the game goes on. People still click on the empty spaces where the cows used to be, earning clicks and rewards. Yet even the most die-hard fans of *Cow Clicker* were a wee bit disheartened by the mass bovine exodus. One player wrote an angry note saying that *Cow Clicker* was not a very fun game after the cows disappeared. Bogost replied, simply, "It wasn't very fun before. :)"

Bogost ended his experiment just in time, because "real" games would soon catch up in absurdity—and leave *Cow Clicker* far behind. In November 2012, legendary game designer Peter Molyneux released *Curiosity*. The game involved a giant box made up of tiny cubes. Players clicked on those tiny cubes to remove them, one at a time, layer by layer. Each time someone removed a cube, he earned a coin. Enough coins and he could buy a tool to remove those cubes more efficiently. Within a few weeks of its launch, several million people had played *Curiosity*, and about 300,000 visited daily, slowly chipping away at the monstrous virtual box. Four months after the game started, players had clicked away more than 200 layers, meaning that people had clicked tens of millions of times per day. Even with all these players clicking again and again, it took more than six months of work before the very last cube was clicked, revealing what was inside the box. It was an amazing and baffling waste of manpower—the spiritual antithesis of building the pyramids—for a single purpose: to get to the center of an imaginary object.

What's at the center? While the game was under way, Molyneux was coy, promising only that the secret at the center would be "amazing" and "life changing." But there was a catch. Only one player would find out. Yes, after millions of people click-click-click to chip away at an enormous virtual box for month after month, a single person got a glimpse of what was inside.* You can almost hear the ghost of B. F. Skinner cackling in appreciation.

Curiosity is the *reductio ad absurdum* of a kind of experiment pioneered by B. F. Skinner, one of the most influential psychologists of the twentieth century. Skinner's scientific work mostly involved operant conditioning—the use of punishments and rewards to modify an organism's behavior. A pigeon or a rat might get a pellet of food or an electrical shock after acting in a certain way—hitting a lever, for example—and, over time, the animal would change its behavior to gain the most rewards and to avoid the punishments. To understand the process of conditioning, Skinner tweaked the experiments in various ways. For example, he might suddenly cut off the reward for hitting a lever and watch how long the rat would continue to press the lever in hopes of receiving a food pellet. (The behavior would gradually disappear, a process known as "extinction.") Or he might decide to give pigeons birdseed on a completely random basis and watch what happened. (The pigeons would pick up weird behaviors—spinning counterclockwise three times or "tossing" their heads as if they were lifting an invisible bar—in hopes of getting seeds to drop. In other words, the pigeons had become superstitious.)

The only fundamental difference between *Curiosity* and a Skinnerian experiment is the level of reward. No self-respecting rat or pigeon would click a lever all day with the vague hope that several months from now, he'd be the lucky one out of millions of rats who got a reward for all that effort. We humans, though, are supreme in the

----

* The lucky fellow was treated to a video explaining his prize: he was to become a digital god in Molyneux's upcoming game, *Godus*. (And he apparently gets to keep some portion of the income from the game.) We know this only because the lucky winner chose to share the video. It would have been even more amusing had he kept it secret.

animal kingdom in deferring our immediate gratification in hopes of
a larger reward to come. As a result, in many ways we're easier to manipulate than rats or pigeons. We're happy to change our behavior in
hopes of getting more abstract, more insubstantial, more infrequent
rewards than any other creature under the sun.

Skinner manipulated his rats and pigeons for a definite end: he
wanted to learn about how changing an organism's environment directly affected its behavior. So, too, are the designers of *Curiosity* manipulating us for a definite end. Precisely what end that is, we don't
know. But if you listen to what Molyneux has been saying, it's clear
that *Curiosity* is not a game but an experiment. It's an attempt not to
amuse people, but to look at their interactions with the cube and to
draw inferences about their behavior. Molyneux made this plain on
the *Pocket Gamer* website: "We're capturing all the analytical data,
and we'll share what people are doing with the coins and what they're
saving up for and the analysis of how the cube decayed. All of that is
just fascinating stuff," he said. This data, Molyneux added, will help
him make more games. It's hard to be more explicit. As *Curiosity* players clicked away toward the center of the box, their every move was
being observed.* They were subjects in a three-million-person experiment, test animals who were performing a mindless task in a virtual
fishbowl so that the experimenters can extract some knowledge that
will allow them to manipulate people better.

Skinnerian methods existed long before the internet. Slot machines and instant-win lotteries, for example, are attractive—for some,
addictive—because they dole out little rewards at intervals that urge
us to keep playing. Other mind-control mechanisms were well known
before the dawn of the digital era. In the 1950s, Solomon Asch did a
series of experiments in which he showed that people asked to

----

* It's unclear exactly what Molyneux's team was measuring. One might imagine
that he's figuring out when and where people around the world log in, how long
they play before they get bored and log off, how susceptible they are to the vague
and hyperbolic promises of a serial letdown artist—that kind of thing.

perform a very simple task—comparing the lengths of various lines—could be induced by others in the room not just to give the wrong answers, but also to believe that the wrong answers were correct. There are a number of other studies that demonstrate how social pressure can cause people to act against their better judgment, discard their morals, and even misperceive facts. Phil Zimbardo's Stanford Prison Experiment used social pressure to get students to abuse others. Stanley Milgram's experiments used social pressure to get subjects to give peers "dangerous" electric shocks. Social pressure, like Skinnerian conditioning, is a potent mind-control technique.

But what *Curiosity* and *FarmVille* make plain is that the internet makes it trivial to combine the raw power of individual Skinnerian conditioning with the mind-bending force of mass social pressure. *Curiosity* probably wouldn't survive a week if the players were unaware of the other people chipping away at the box—the very fact that there are so many others working at the same task as you reinforces the seeming importance of the goal that everyone collectively is working toward. Similarly, the never-ending barrage of messages telling you how well your friends are doing at *FarmVille* and the constant requests to have you help tend their crops go a long way toward defusing the feeling that the whole pursuit is an idiotic waste of time. Skinnerian conditioning, crossed with social pressure, is now an ever-present invisible hand that tries to manipulate all of your actions on the internet. This is the hand that is making you act against your own self-interest. Once you recognize it, you see it everywhere, hovering over you, trying to make you click your mouse or press buttons on your smartphone, giving up your valuable time, money, or information in return for little or nothing at all.

Foursquare is a social networking application that allows people to use their mobile devices to "check in" to various locations they visit. Each check-in earns points (which don't seem to have any function other than putting your name on a leaderboard) and has the potential to earn a "badge." If you're the most frequent Foursquare visitor to a certain location, you can become the "mayor" of that site. Sometimes, checking in, earning a badge, or becoming the mayor of a site can earn a person a minor reward (the mayor of a Pizza Hut, for example, gets free breadsticks with every large pizza), but most of the time there's no palpable reason for whipping out one's cell phone and telling the Foursquare team where you are. Checking in becomes an end in itself, a meaningless scavenger hunt to collect badges and points in an attempt to beat out your friends who are also trying to collect those same badges and points. (And plenty of people take the game seriously enough to cheat at it—enough of them that the Foursquare team had to crack down on phony mayors.)

Other than the very rare reward and the pride of becoming the mayor of your local Burger King, there isn't much value to checking in on Foursquare. In fact, there are some very real dangers in giving up your location to a company—and publishing it so that the whole world can see it. In 2010, three computer scientists set up PleaseRobMe.com, a website that used Foursquare and Twitter information to determine when a user was far away from his home—and then to broadcast that the person's domicile was empty and ripe for burglary. The website made very clear something that people often overlook: information is valuable, and to give it up thoughtlessly is to act against your own interest. If you were required by a court order to check in to a website every time you entered a new location, you'd consider it an oppressive action of a police state. Yet, thanks to the abstract Skinnerian rewards provided by the Foursquare team, combined with the gentle social pressure of competing with friends and strangers in a never-ending scavenger hunt for badges, fascist oppression becomes a fun pastime. People don't think twice about reflexively transmitting their whereabouts to a company that's trying to bend your mind and make you a frequent visitor to your local Pizza Hut, Hess gas station, or RadioShack.* Foursquare is not just attempting to gather information

----

* Companies have long used rewards—usually cash, free items, or discounts—to get you to give up information or alter your behavior. But your CVS card doesn't try to keep you playing the game, or get you to try to recruit your family.

about your behavior, but subtly trying to modify it for the benefit of its sponsors—and for its own bottom line.

It's no coincidence that the mechanics of Foursquare resemble those of a game like *FarmVille*; both are attempting to use the same mechanisms to make us do their bidding. *FarmVille* advertises itself as a game, but Foursquare is not even that. It's a computer program that's supposed to "[help] you and your friends make the most of where you are." It's not technically a game—it's a social service—but in very many ways, its structure is familiar. Points, coins, badges, and rewards tickle the parts of our brains that respond to Skinnerian conditioning, while the social elements keep us entangled in a web of commitment— and of competitive drive not to fall behind our peers. In short, by creating artificial rewards and engineering social pressures, Foursquare controls your behavior by superimposing a video-game structure on your everyday life. This is "gamification."

Gamification is common on the internet. Media websites like *The Huffington Post* encourage you to comment on (and spread) stories by giving you badges ("level 2 networker") or titles ("superuser") for accomplishing achievements. Social networking websites like Klout give you scores for how many followers you have and how much influence you exert upon them. Job networking sites like LinkedIn reward you for having a lot of data on your profile page. Khan Academy, an educational site, gives students "energy points" and badges for completing lessons. But gamification extends well beyond the virtual world and, assisted by digital technology, is creeping into the outdoors. Nike has introduced a set of bracelets that track your motion and give you "fuel" points for your physical activity, grant you badges for achieving goals, and allow you to challenge your friends to various physical tasks. Coca-Cola created a "Happiness Quest" scavenger hunt, which encouraged people to use their cell phones to scan soda-vending machines in various locations.

It's a brilliant strategy. Running around town taking photos of vending machines can never be considered fun in its own right. By superimposing a gamelike structure on top of that activity—a structure that uses operant conditioning and social pressure to give it heft—Coca-Cola functionally twisted our brains to redefine fun for us. And not so coincidentally, its definition of fun means buying things from vending machines.

There's nothing inherently wrong with the idea of gamification. It's a tool that can be used for good—when we need to modify our behavior, Skinnerian techniques, combined with social pressures, can be a powerful way to bring us back in line. Look beneath the surface of Alcoholics Anonymous and you see proto-gamification: the sobriety coins are trinkets to give palpable Skinnerian reinforcement, and the group sessions provide the social network to keep you embedded in the "game." It's a technique that's potent enough to wean us from alcohol, help us lose weight, make us exercise more.

In the days before the internet, such powerful techniques were limited by the sheer difficulty of creating and hooking in to the social networks needed to sustain the game. You already had to be somewhat committed to a cause to get your butt out of bed to visit your local AA or Weight Watchers meeting each week.

That's no longer the case. Our social networks are now no further than our computer keyboards—or our mobile phones. We're in constant touch with other people playing the game. Because of the near-universal interconnectedness that the internet provides, we no longer have to exercise our will to expose ourselves to a peer group; the peer group is always right there in our pockets, staring back at us every time we pull out our smartphones. The barrier to entering a peer-pressure group is so reduced that we don't do it consciously anymore. We used to have to make an active decision to try to enter a behavior-modification program. Now we're signing up for powerful mind-control pressures without an active decision to do so, without even understanding that this is what we're doing when we sign up for the latest social fad.

At the same time, the volume and precision of data flowing back and forth between players and game masters allow for a complexity and frequency of rewards—badges, ribbons, achievements, points, coins—that would have been unimaginable prior to the advent of digital information. "Players" in one of these behavior-modification schemes are subject to a nearly unending and endlessly varied—yet personalized—flood of positive reinforcement so long as they continue playing the game. Computer algorithms dole out virtual treats to push you along, while the social networks keep you embedded. Pretty soon you lose perspective—you don't realize how much you've given up to keep playing this game seven days a week.

That's one common denominator in all of these Skinnerian social games: you're forced to give something up in order to belong. Sometimes you're giving up something as obvious as money; by paying a few dollars to the *FarmVille* team, you boost your efficiency and social status so that you're ahead of other, more casual players. But more often, you're giving up something more abstract. Sometimes you're merely giving up your time. Other times you're giving up information—your location, your spending habits, even your weight— that allows companies to understand (and control) you better. Outside of the context of a social application, you wouldn't casually give out this information to a stranger; you'd only reveal it for a good reason— say, to a doctor or a credit counselor. But nowadays we are willing to share almost everything reflexively, even to the point that it could be considered *anti*social.

A decade ago, if a corporation asked for the e-mail addresses of all of your friends and family members, you'd almost certainly have refused. From the advent of the internet, everyone knew that e-mail addresses needed to be protected, to some extent, from outsiders who were constantly on the lookout for new people to spam. If you gave out people's e-mail addresses willy-nilly, you'd probably piss off quite a few of them. But nowadays, people are happy to hand their entire e-mail contact list over to LinkedIn or Facebook or Google or Pinterest or any other site that convinces people to sell out their closest acquaintances in hopes of increasing their own social status. Our social norms are changing as a result of these commercial enterprises.

There's no telling how far this trend will go. As powerful as Skinnerian conditioning with social pressure might be, we humans have a fairly potent defense against such manipulation: boredom. It may be that our short attention spans—our constant need for novelty—will limit the effect that these gamified behavior-modifying programs can have upon us. Perhaps with overuse of the technique we will become less susceptible. Zynga, the maker of *FarmVille,* is already seeing its revenue flatten out after its initial booming growth. Foursquare is even beginning to drop in popularity. Even so, there's no question that, right now, the behavior-modification business, which uses digital technology to try to put us all in socially connected Skinner boxes, is a multi-billion-dollar enterprise. And this is because it works.

Seldom do we really question why we're taking a particular action. We, as autonomous, intelligent beings, find it hard to imagine that our minds are being manipulated by unseen forces. Yet if you take a step back and look carefully at how you spend your time on the internet, on your computer, or on your smartphone, you might well discover that you might have been sacrificing your own self-interest—in almost imperceptible ways—to benefit a commercial enterprise. And it is through self-awareness that we can once again take control of our own brains, despite the parasites that are trying to use us for their own purposes.

CHAPTER 11
LIVING IN THE RAW

You shall no longer take things at second or third hand, nor
     look through the eyes of the dead, nor feed on the spectres
     in books,
You shall not look through my eyes either, nor take things
     from me,
You shall listen to all sides and filter them from your self.

—WALT WHITMAN, "SONG OF MYSELF"

Like television, the internet is immediate. It can bounce from one
end of the world to a satellite and back down to the other end of
the world in a fraction of a second. It's typically highly visual and
very busy, with multiple stimuli competing for attention. But digital
information is also like a book; it can be densely packed with layer
upon layer of information, and can be skimmed or read deeply, ac-
cessed from beginning to end or in random order. Like a TV or radio
broadcast, digital information can be evanescent, gone almost as fast
as it's consumed. But like the written word, it can be extremely stable,
lasting for years even without anybody's intervention. Digital information is a bundle of contradictions, and these contradictions are

what give it its peculiar properties—and make it so wonderful and so frustrating at the same time.

The transmissibility of digital information makes it unlike any other information that we've yet encountered. It can be moved from place to place at the speed of light with perfect fidelity, and it is accessible to anyone who's hooked in to the internet with a computer or a mobile device. At the same time, the very flood of information that we're creating is making it harder to access any single item that we're interested in. Noise is swamping signal. The persistence of digital information is likely to surpass everything else. The sheer number of copies made possible by digital technology can give even the most mundane information a nearly eternal lifespan.* However, anyone who's attempted to search through archives on the internet knows how links and documents disappear without a trace, how old pages get clobbered and replaced by new ones, and how data can become unreadable over time. The internet has connected us all in ways that we could never have imagined just a few decades ago—yet, at the same time, it has isolated each of us more and more. Even communal activities that have survived for millennia, such as shopping in public and going to the theater, are being replaced by a virtual person in an electronic community that you can hold in the palm of your hand.

All of these contradictions are as wonderful as they are terrifying. The democratization of publishing means that everybody has the ability to be heard; the elimination of physical and economic barriers to communication means that our society is interconnected in a way that it has never been before. With those benefits we also see the destabilizing—and outright negative—effects that have been described

----

* A random example: On February 1, 1999, Chris Metzler, a graduate student in physics at the University of Illinois at Urbana-Champaign, had a three-piece KFC meal (original recipe) for dinner, along with a side of mashed potatoes and a side of macaroni and cheese. We know this because he happened to post it to the internet. I wager that this bit of information will be just as accessible in the year 2099 as it is today.

in this book. But we're not powerless against those effects. Once we recognize them, we can fight them.

On April 15, 2013, two bombs exploded at the finish line of the Boston Marathon, killing three people and wounding more than two hundred others. The most important question in the nation suddenly became: Who did it? Until we figured out who the perpetrators were, we wouldn't be able to understand whether they were acting alone or were part of a larger plot, why the bombs had been planted, and whether we could expect more terror in the next few hours or weeks.

In America—and around the world—we logged into our computers and looked for answers on the internet. We replayed the videos of the bombings over and over, hoping for clues. We listened, live, to the Boston Police Department's scanners as emergency services tried to get control of the situation. And we tried to take those fragments of information and turn them into knowledge, into something that we could use to understand the situation a little better.

The website Reddit has a reputation for, well, a lot of things. It's an anarchic site that reflects the desires and interests of its users, be they politics or be they episodes of *My Little Pony* cartoons. But Reddit has justly acquired a reputation for revealing hoaxes and untangling mysteries, thanks to a diverse, distributed, and relatively intelligent user base.* Reddit often becomes a spot where people can join forces and collectively piece together bits of information that Reddit-connected people gather and publish on the website. And soon after the bombing, Redditors were on the case: they created a "Find Boston Bombers" thread where people could share their photos of the event and other information.

Working with what little they had from officials—that the bombs were made from pressure cookers, that there were two suspects, and that there were images of a blown-up backpack—Reddit denizens quickly spotted several photos in which people were carrying

----

* Reddit managed to unmask the fake-pirate hoax described in chapter 2.

suspicious backpacks. One photo became a leading candidate, not just because the backpack was apparently carrying an oddly shaped object, but also because the person carrying it was swarthy-looking. It quickly circulated around the internet, and on Thursday, April 18, the photo became the front page of the *New York Post*. "Bag Men," the headline trumpeted. "Feds seek these two pictured at Boston Marathon." The problem was that it wasn't true. There were, indeed, two suspects, but Reddit—and the *Post*—had fingered the wrong guys.

After the *Post* story, the FBI felt obliged to publish their photographs of the real suspects—not because it would help with the investigation, but because the swirling rumors on the internet (which had begun to leak into the less responsible corners of the mainstream press) were harming innocent bystanders. As *The Washington Post* reported:

> In addition to being almost universally wrong, the theories developed via social media complicated the official investigation, according to law enforcement officials. Those officials said . . . that the decision on Thursday to release photos of the two men in baseball caps was meant in part to limit the damage being done to people who were wrongly being targeted as suspects in the news media and on the Internet.

In fact, the FBI hadn't wanted to release the photos to the public, fearing that the manhunt would become a "chaotic free-for-all," with news media and internet vigilantes muddying the waters with their "freelance sleuthing." But their hand was forced by those very same vigilantes, and the Bureau relented, hoping to squelch the rumors.

It did anything but. The suspects still needed to be identified, and soon the Reddit board was swarming with activity. They thought they had ID'd one of the two men as Sunil Tripathi, a Brown University student who had gone missing about a month earlier. (Tripathi's body turned up several weeks later, an apparent suicide.) Early the next morning, a cryptic announcement on the Boston Police Department's radio reading out the spelling of a name—Mike Mulugeta—triggered another avalanche. A tweet revealed that Mulugeta's name had been mentioned on the scanner, and within about half an hour, people on Reddit and Twitter had somehow turned that fragment of information into a full-blown confirmation that the bombing suspects were Mulugeta and Tripathi. From there the information spread like a virus: to a local CBS station, to *BuzzFeed*, to *Politico*, to *Newsweek*. The rumor died only when NBC anchor Brian Willams announced the correct names of the suspects a few hours later: Dzhokhar and Tamerlan Tzarnaev.

This isn't fundamentally an internet-versus-traditional-media story; the *New York Post*, *Newsweek*, and other brick-and-mortar newsrooms played a role in the misinformation cascade just as did Reddit and Twitter. It's a story of fast versus slow, of twitchiness versus reflection, of raw data versus knowledge.

The speed and ubiquity of our digital sensorium is feeding us an unprecedented amount of information—far too much and far too quickly for us to digest or understand. We are getting used to (and are demanding) an increasing stream of raw data; without it, without the ceaseless updates, we feel as if we're in the dark, unplugged from the reality that's unfolding around us.* We rely on automated tools such as search engines, news aggregators, and our social networks to do the selection for us. There's no time for our information suppliers to analyze the data, to winnow the signal from the noise, and to synthesize a succinct and accurate summary of what's going on. We're addicted to getting our information in fragments.

It used to be that there were curators of information, people who specialized in trying to turn a jumble of self-contradictory information and half-truths into something reliable, people who helped us cut through the clutter of noise and extract knowledge that we could use.

----

* This is why we seem to be addicted to news reports marked "Live," even when there's no conceivable reason why a live report would be an improvement over one that was recorded and edited a few hours earlier.

They were far from perfect, but these people—seasoned librarians, journalists, editors, authors—were essential to our information-gathering process. And these are the people who are getting hit the hardest by the internet revolution. The work they do is slow and expensive, in a world where information is quick and all but free.

This isn't meant to be a lament for a bygone time or a threnody for professions that are passing away. There will always be reliable journalists and authors and librarians (just as there will always be bad ones). Rather, it's meant to be a warning. The people we once relied upon to take raw information and analyze it for us, to help us tell fact from fiction and real from fake, are no longer able to keep up with the demands of our society. The relatively slow and labor-intensive process is becoming rarer, even as the very nature of digital information makes it more important than ever. As individuals and corporations create phony facts and people try to lead you astray, you are increasingly forced to rely upon your own devices to realize when you're being had.

If we want to be able to tell what's real and what's not, we must learn to see through the haze of virtual unreality that's settling around us. As the professions built on information curation decline in influence, we can't allow self-interested people and corporations—and their algorithms—to fill the void, lest we be at their mercy. They will try to shape our view of the world around us, whether we're aware of it or not. Instead we must change our relationship with information, becoming more skeptical and more cynical, and arm ourselves with powerful tools to allow us to interrogate dubious facts. And we have to be willing to spend the time to do it.

As the world moves ever faster, this means sacrificing immediacy in favor of reflection. As our information sources tailor themselves to our prejudices, this means eschewing the chatter that reinforces our preexisting beliefs and seeking out ones that challenge us. And above all, it means that we must accept that the rules are changing, and learn how to see the world differently than we did just a few years ago.

ACKNOWLEDGMENTS

I've been lucky enough to have written six books under the guidance of the very same editor, Wendy Wolf, who gets my most heartfelt gratitude. My agents, Katinka Matson and John Brockman, have been with me for five of those six books, and I am in their debt as well. I am also grateful for the assistance of Melanie Tortoroli, whose comments were very helpful.

My colleagues at New York University have been wonderful, as have the deans who give us an incredible amount of freedom and support. My thanks go to them, too.

Most of all, though, I am grateful for the love and support of my family. My mother and father and brother, Mark, all have earned my gratitude, but above all, my wife, Meridith, has been a pillar for me. And last but not least, I must thank my daughter, Eliza, as well as my new son, Daniel Morris—the best reason ever to miss a deadline (if only by a month).

APPENDIX:
THE TOP TEN DICTA OF
THE INTERNET SKEPTIC

----

1) WIKIPEDIA IS LIKE AN OLD AND ECCENTRIC UNCLE.

He can be a lot of fun—over the years he's seen a lot, and he can tell a great story. He's also no dummy; he's accumulated a lot of information and has some strong opinions about what he's gathered. You can learn quite a bit from him. But take everything he says with a grain of salt. A lot of the things he thinks he knows for sure aren't quite right, or are taken out of context. And when it comes down to it, sometimes he believes things that are a little bit, well, nuts.

If it ever matters to you whether something he said is real or fictional, it's crucial to check it out with a more reliable source.

2) EVERYBODY'S A FAKE. AT LEAST THAT'S WHAT YOU SHOULD ASSUME.

Nowadays, it's easy for people to create multiple personae online and just as easy to discard them at will. Unless someone's known to you personally, assume that an online personality isn't telling the truth about himself. If someone's true identity is important to you in some manner, you should be on your guard.

It's not easy to figure out whether someone online is real or fake. The best way is to search the person's online footprints for any scraps of personal information that might give a small clue about his real identity. The region in which a person lives, a telephone number, a school where he got a degree—all of these can be used to piece together a mosaic of who the person really is. Photographs are a great way of figuring out whether someone's real or fake; pop a photo into a reverse image search, like Google Images or TinEye, and you might be surprised at what comes up.

Just as valuable is an electronic signature known as an IP address, which can be found in every e-mail exchange (and in some online postings). An IP address is an electronic address that tells you where the message is being sent from. For example, when someone claiming to be in England sent me an e-mail not so long ago, his IP address, 41.66.6.175, revealed that he was really in the Ivory Coast. No, I wouldn't be sending him any money.

3) YOU DON'T HAVE TO FOOL ALL OF THE PEOPLE SOME OF THE TIME OR SOME OF THE PEOPLE ALL OF THE TIME. . . .ALL YOU NEED IS TO FOOL JUST A TINY FRACTION OF THE PEOPLE ONCE IN A WHILE.

Life as a scammer has never been easier. Because the internet allows you to contact tens or hundreds of thousands of people with the click of a button, you don't have to have a sophisticated scam to make money. Come up with something just barely good enough to fool one out of ten thousand or fifty thousand people and you'll still be able to make scads of money if you reach enough potential suckers. There are plenty of them out there.

4) THE EARLY BIRD GETS THE WORM. THE LATE BIRD GETS THE EARLY BIRD.

It used to be that there was a premium on finding information first. A newspaper journalist who got a scoop, for example, would be guaranteed exclusivity for a news cycle—that he'd be the only one with the story, at least until the news broadcasts came on early that evening. He was the only game in town, so if you wanted to learn about the story, you went to him. Nowadays, a juicy scoop will last only minutes before other outlets begin repackaging it in order to steal readers away. And some of those other outlets, like *The Huffington Post,* are wildly successful at stealing those readers.

There's now little advantage to being first to the story—just the opposite. If you're first out of the gate, there's a chance that nobody will follow you, that nobody will care about what you're offering. If you wait to see where the crowd is headed, then you're guaranteed to find a story that people are interested in. And if you're smart about it, despite being a latecomer you can steal the lion's share of the audience away from the ones who were there first.

If you're interested in getting the most accurate, most direct version of the story, you're going to have to fight against the crowd. Often, the most popular links aren't the most informative.

5) IN THE MEDIA WORLD, LAZINESS IS INCREASINGLY A VIRTUE.

A corollary to dictum number 4 is that it pays to be lazy. Let the others fight to break news; let your competitors spend their time, effort, and money finding stories, interviewing sources, and doing the reporting. That's the expensive part of the media equation. The less you do on that front, the more resources you'll have for optimizing your website to grab big audiences. Cut, paste, add a bit of snark, and link out— that's all you really need to do.

This sets up an echo chamber; the same tiny bits of information get repeated, amplified, and distorted. The best way to fight this as a media consumer is to expend extra effort to figure out the original, primary source of any piece of information.

6) NOT EVERYTHING IS ONLINE.

As the digital world expands, it's increasingly difficult to remember that there are broad segments of human knowledge that haven't been digitized. This means that you're unable to use them if you don't get off your duff and actively seek them out. For example, no government agency is going to put the bulk of its internal documents on the web, as a matter of course—so if you're trying to figure out, say, whether your local school board is accounting for funds properly, you'll never find out by Google alone.

There's the old story of the drunk crawling around under a lamppost, late one evening. "I'm looking for my keys," he tells a passerby. "I dropped them in the alley over there."

"If you dropped your keys over there, why are you searching for them over here?"

"Because the light's so much better near the lamp."

The internet is a powerful lamp. But for lots of things worth finding, you'll have to venture out of its glare.

7) A SOCIAL MEDIA SITE'S PURPOSE IS TO SERVE ITS USERS—IN THE SAME SENSE AS A ZOO'S PURPOSE IS TO SERVE ITS ANIMALS.

No zoo can succeed without a large and varied collection of animals. So any decent zookeeper will try to keep a zoo's animals happy and healthy—that way, the animals will stick around a long time without causing any problems. If keepers do their job well, the animals might even convince themselves that the whole point of the zoo is to give exotic animals great food, a pleasant living space, and plenty of leisure time. All those people wandering around and gawking, well, they must just be part of the scenery.

With a typical social media company, you don't have to delve too deeply to see the real aim of the company. Facebook, for example, tells you that its purpose is to enable you "to express yourself and connect with the world around you instantly and freely." How does it do that? "We build products that support our mission by creating utility for users, developers, and marketers." Funny . . . one wouldn't think that marketers play a big role in helping you express yourself. But they—and the developers (such as *FarmVille* creator Zynga)—certainly help Facebook: "We generate substantially all of our revenue from advertising and from fees associated with our Payments infrastructure that enables users to purchase virtual and digital goods from our Platform developers." That's some $1.6 billion in revenue in 2012 alone. And that number tells you whom Facebook really serves. Which is going to cause more concern in the corporate ranks of Facebook: an angry user or an angry advertiser?

Here's a hint: to figure out whom a zoo is really meant to serve, just look at who's paying for admission.

It's not just social media companies that are putting us in cages and displaying us like zoo animals. Google makes its money by collecting as much of your behavior online as possible and using that data to target advertising to you more effectively. LinkedIn makes money by collecting information about you and your network and selling it to talent scouts and marketing firms. This isn't inherently a bad thing; if you feel that you get more from these companies than you lose in privacy, then everybody wins. But you should at least be aware of what you're giving up to use these "free" services.

8) THE INTERNET DOESN'T REPRESENT A REVOLUTION FOR FREE SPEECH AS MUCH AS A REVOLUTION IN FREE AUDIENCES.

If you're living in the United States, chances are you've never encountered any real threat to your right of free speech—before the internet or after it. In other countries, digital information has made it harder for governments to control communication between its citizens, though if you've ever used a search engine in China, you'll know that the internet is no panacea for freedom of expression.

On the other hand, digital information has completely transformed our ability to reach a sizable audience without a lot of money. It used to be a struggle to reach an audience of a decent size. Unless you had the advantage of great wealth or power, you had to be very eloquent or incredibly lucky if you were to get more than a handful of people to listen to what you had to say or read a tract that you wrote. Unless you had a pulpit from which you could make people pay attention to you, all the free speech in the world didn't make a whit's worth of difference, because your speech wouldn't be heard by a great enough number of people to matter.

No longer. Everybody connected to the internet can instantly reach everyone else. Your random mumblings, posted on your own little blog in a forgotten corner of cyberspace, can theoretically be read by billions of people on every continent. Your tiniest whisper can be heard halfway around the world, by an audience vaster than ever before.

For the price of your internet connection, you've now got an audience of billions. They can all hear you. You just have to say something that they want to listen to.

9) PEOPLE ARE USING DIGITAL TECHNOLOGY TO MAKE YOU ACT AGAINST YOUR OWN SELF-INTEREST—AND YOU'RE MORE THAN HAPPY TO GO ALONG.

Digital technology has allowed marketers to combine two very powerful behavior-modification techniques and use them to exert subtle control over what you do. You don't have to click hundreds of cows on *FarmVille* or report your location to Foursquare every thirty minutes to have had your behavior altered in mildly self-destructive ways. Do you have a badge that says you're a valuable contributor to an online forum? Have you ever played a video game just a bit longer so you could unlock that final achievement? Ever felt compelled to take a photograph of your dinner at a nice restaurant so you'll have something to upload to a website? Congratulations. Your brain has been rewired.

10) TOP TEN LISTS ARE JUST MARKETING GIMMICKS INTENDED FOR SUCKERS.

People seem drawn to anything that says "Top 10" or "Top 20" or "33 Best" or whatever. Women's magazines figured this out long ago; it's nigh impossible to find one that doesn't have a list of the hundred best sex positions, fat-burning foods, or must-have accessories for the coming season. Online media have caught the bug. Even the most serious news outlets now seem set on matching *Elle* and *Cosmopolitan*, top-ten list for top-ten list.* These lists are like catnip to readers, and they're everywhere. As an added bonus, anything that ranks things in an order will automatically be contentious, generating lots of online discussion by people who have a different idea of what should be number one.

In truth, most of these lists are cobbled together with no real method behind them—or, at best, with a very flawed method that breaks down under closer scrutiny. And readers tend not to notice that they're a way of writing about a subject without having to do any in-depth reporting or analysis. They're meant to draw an audience as cheaply and as easily as possible.

So all these "Top 10" and "Top 20" lists that have proliferated on the web are a by-product of the media's increasing reflex to grab audiences with as little effort, expenditure, and reporting as possible. Either that or you can believe Ben Smith, the editor in chief of *BuzzFeed*, who told *The New York Times*, "'Thirty-three Animals Who Are Disappointed in You' is a work of literature. . . . I'm totally not joking."

----

* I recently did some investigative reporting for a major high-quality organization and saw one of the pieces I co-wrote get a "top five"–type headline. "Heds [newspaper-speak for 'headlines'] that start with numbers pull better than any others," I was told by one of the web-guru types.

NOTES

INTRODUCTION: VIRTUAL UNREALITY

1 **He was first spotted in Bangladesh:** Associated Press, "Sesame Street Character Depicted with bin Laden on Protest Poster," October 11, 2001.

2 **"Do the global terror links reach even as far as Sesame Street?":** FoxNews.com, "Bin Laden's Felt-Skinned Henchman?" October 14, 2001, http://www.foxnews.com/story/2001/10/14/bin-laden-felt-skinned-henchman.

2 **"This is a legitimate photograph":** Josh Grossberg, "The Bert-Bin Laden Connection?" EOnline.com, October 10, 2001, http://www.eon line.com/news/42292/the-bert-bin-laden-connection.

2 **"We haven't changed the photo at all":** FoxNews.com, "Felt-Skinned Henchman."

2 **"Sesame Street has always stood for mutual respect and understanding":** "'Muppet' producers miffed over Bert-bin Laden image," CNN.com, October 11, 2001, http://edition.cnn.com/2001/US/10/11/muppets.binladen/.

3 **when a Bangladeshi print shop sought bin Laden photos:** Associated Press, "Sesame Street Character Depicted."

3 **"Yesterday a lot of you alerted me":** Declan McCullagh, "Osama Has a New Friend," Wired.com, October 10, 2011, http://www.wired.com /politics/law/news/2001/10/47450.

3 **"I am doing this because I feel this has gotten too close to reality":** Dino Ignacio, Bert Is Evil, FractalCow.com/bert, captured December 11, 2001, by archive.org.

7 **To SEAL Team Six, their target was "Bert":** Christina Lamb, "Seals tell of killing 'Bert' Laden," *Sunday Times* (UK), November 6, 2011.

CHAPTER 1: CATCHING THE STUPID BUG

9 **"turning the capital cities into death traps":** Eric Lofgren and Nina Fefferman, "The untapped potential of virtual game worlds to shed light on real world epidemics," *The Lancet Infectious Diseases* 7, no. 9 (September 2007), 626.

9 **people run willy-nilly:** See, e.g., Brian Howell, "WoW Plague Video," YouTube.com, August 23, 2007, http://www.youtube.com/watch?v= sAEhyHiNdrA.

10 **In other words, reboot:** Lofgren and Fefferman, "Untapped," 627.

13 **Scientists estimate that it has an R_0 of 12 or more:** Paul E. M. Fine, "Herd Immunity: History, Theory, Practice," *Epidemiologic Reviews* 15, no. 2 (1993), 268.

14 **"In an effort to control the outbreak":** Lofgren and Fefferman, "Untapped," 627.

20 **"HAVE STRONG SUSPICION THAT CRIPPEN":** Henry George Kendall's witness statement, www.drcrippen.co.uk/sources/kendall _statement.html.

22 **At noon on May 16, 2007, the technology website Engadget posted a scoop about Apple:** Tom Krazit, "Engadget sends Apple stock plunging on iPhone rumor," CNET.com, May 16, 2007, http://news.cnet .com/8301-17938_105-9719952-1.html.

CHAPTER 2: APPEAL TO AUTHORITY

24 **the fans wear hats made out of shoes:** David Anderson, "New-look Manchester City side begin their UEFA Cup campaign in earnest," *Daily Mirror* (UK), September 18, 2008.

24 **The Zany Ones often sing a song:** "AC Omonia," Wikipedia.org, edit of September 18, 2008, 4:51 p.m. Note that Wikipedia entries are regu-

larly edited and can change content—often in significant ways—from minute to minute. (Most change more slowly than that.)

24 **The team's Wikipedia page had been "enhanced":** See www.b3ta.com/links/Lazy_Journalist.

25 **"What we're doing is bringing democracy to knowledge":** Stephen Colbert, *The Colbert Report*, July 31, 2006.

25 **Wikipedia contributors such as "EvilBrak":** "Elephant," Wikipedia.org. EvilBrak's contribution was on August 1, 2006, 3:40 a.m.; Wiki Wikardo's was at 8:41 a.m.; and Spockguy's was at 9:22 a.m.

26 **"make up our own hoaxes and turn them loose on the Internet":** T. Mills Kelly, "Lying About the Past," syllabus for History 389-009, George Mason University, spring 2012.

26 **The first time he ran the course, he and his students fabricated the tale:** Yoni Applebaum, "How the Professor Who Fooled Wikipedia Got Caught by Reddit," TheAtlantic.com, May 15, 2012, http://www.theatlantic.com/technology/archive/2012/05/how-the-professor-who-fooled-wikipedia-got-caught-by-reddit/257134/.

27 **"I am 100 percent convinced that if I hadn't come forward":** Shawn Pogatchnik/Associated Press, "Student hoaxes world's media on Wikipedia," May 12, 2009.

27 **Editors at Wikipedia became suspicious:** "Wikipedia:Admini-strators' Noticeboard, November 19, 2012, en.wikipedia.org/wiki/Wikipedia:Administrators%27_noticeboard/Archive241#Fictional_entry.3F.

27 **On June 28, 2012, an anonymous Wikipedia contributor:** "Mike Trout," Wikipedia.org, edit of June 28, 2012, 3:42 a.m.

28 **"Trout was nicknamed the Millville Meteor":** Mike Gavin, "Phenom Trout brings his talents to Yankee Stadium," *Newsday*, July 14, 2012.

28 **"I don't know where they got that":** Sam Miller, "The Phenom," *ESPN The Magazine*, September 20, 2012.

30 **Perhaps the clearest illustration of just how radical that idea is:** "*The Human Stain,*" Wikipedia.org. Edits referred to in text are on October 17, 2004, 6:45 a.m. (the original addition of Broyard); January 23, 2008, 8:34 p.m. (the disappearance of Broyard); March 24, 2008, 6:21 a.m. (the reappearance of Broyard); August 20, 2012, 3:47 and 3:48 p.m. (Bailey's first edit and its reversion by Jprg1966); and August 20, 2012, 4:07 p.m. and 4:13 p.m. through 6:30 p.m. (Bailey's second edit, its reversion, and the doubling down by Parkwells).

31 **"[M]y interlocutor [Bailey] was told":** Philip Roth, "An Open Letter to Wikipedia," NewYorker.com, September 7, 2012, http://www.newyorker.com/online/blogs/books/2012/09/an-open-letter-to-wikipedia.html.

32 **In March, 2006, a minor "edit war" about orcas erupted:** "SeaWorld," Wikipedia.org. Edits referred to in text are on March 20, 2006, 6:48 p.m. (change from "orca" to "killer whale") and on January 13, 2011, 10:13 p.m. (JNemo412's edit). See also Katie Hafner, "Corporate Editing of Wikipedia Revealed," *New York Times*, August 19, 2007.

33 **the anonymous Wikipedian admitted that he was the communications director:** "SeaWorld," Wikipedia.org. Talk page, entry of April 3, 2006.

33 **There were oodles of examples:** John Borland, "See Who's Editing Wikipedia," Wired.com, August 14, 2007, http://www.wired.com/politics/onlinerights/news/2007/08/wiki_tracker?currentPage=all.

34 **"wiped out references to his broken term-limits pledge":** Evan Lehmann, "Rewriting history under the dome," *Lowell Sun*, January 27, 2006.

35 **"holds a Ph.D. in theology and a degree in canon law":** Stacy Schiff, "Know It All," *New Yorker*, July 31, 2008.

36 **"it was important that the general public not think":** Noam Cohen, "After False Claim, Wikipedia to Check Degrees," *New York Times*, March 12, 2007.

36 **"a pseudonym and I don't really have a problem with it":** Editor's note appended to Schiff, "Know It All."

36 **"I care deeply about the integrity of Wikipedia":** Cade Metz, "Jimbo Wales dumps lover on Wikipedia," *Register*, March 3, 2008. See also the Canadian Press, "Canadian pundit, Wikipedia founder in messy breakup," CBC.ca, March 2, 2008, http://www.cbc.ca/news/canada/canadian-pundit-wikipedia-founder-in-messy-breakup-1.729627; and Owen Thomas, "The dirtiest Wikipedia sex chat you can imagine," Gawker.com, March 3, 2008, http://gawker.com/363153/the-dirtiest-wikipedia-sex-chat-you-can-imagine.

36 **According to the BBC, Wales called the claim "nonsense":** BBC News, "Wiki boss 'edited for donation,'" BBC.co.uk, March 12, 2008, http://news.bbc.co.uk/2/hi/technology/7291382.stm.

37 **Wales said that, if true, such activities were "wildly inappropriate":** Violet Blue, "Corruption in Wikiland?" CNET.com, September 18,

2012, http://news.cnet.com/8301-1023_3-57514677-93/corruption-in
-wikiland-paid-pr-scandal-erupts-at-wikipedia/.

38 **"Some said that Benedict's decision to step down was one of the
most dramatic acts"**: Rachel Donadio and Nicholas Kulish, "A Statement Rocks Rome, Then Sends Shockwaves Around the World," *New
York Times*, February 11, 2013.

CHAPTER 3: AN ARMY OF ONE

43 **"an unlikely hero of revolt in a conservative country"**: Katherine
Marsh, "A Gay Girl in Damascus becomes a heroine of the Syrian
revolt," *Guardian,* May 6, 2011.

43 **In the early evening of Monday, June 6, 2011**: David Harris, "Syria:
Gay blogger Amina Araf seized by 3 men and now missing," Veloci-
raptorOnZebra.BlogSpot.com, June 6, 2011, http://velociraptoronze-
bra.blogspot.com/2011/06/syria-gay-blogger-amina-arraf-seized-by
.html.

44 **The *International Business Times* asked**: Ellen Killoran, "Gay Girl in
Damascus Kidnapped: How Should U.S. Respond?" IBTimes.com,
June 7, 2011, http://www.ibtimes.com/gay-girl-damascus-kidnapped
-how-should-us-respond-289111.

44 **"It's just odd that I can't find anyone"**: Andy Carvin, Twitter post,
June 7, 2011, 4:12 p.m., http://twitter.com/acarvin.

44 **Shortly thereafter, a website in communication with Arraf**: Linda
Carbonell, "An apology to our readers about Amina Araf," Lez-
GetReal.com, June 10, 2011, as captured by Google Cache on June 14,
2010.

44 **"I was involved with numerous online science-fiction/alternate-
history discussion lists"**: Tom MacMaster (writing as "Amina A."),
DamascusGayGirl.BlogSpot.com, June 13, 2011.

45 **"I have begun to calculate from the time that the sun enters into
Aries"**: Jonathan Swift (writing as "Isaac Bickerstaff"), "Predictions for
the Year 1708."

46 **"After half an hour's conversation I took my leave"**: Jonathan Swift
(writing anonymously), "The Accomplishment of the First of Mr Bickerstaff's Predictions."

46 **"Here, five Foot deep, lies on his Back"**: Jonathan Swift (writing
anonymously), "An Epitaph on Partridge."

47 **"My nameless old persecutor had provided me a monument":** John Partridge, "Squire Bickerstaff detected; or, the astrological impostor convicted."

49 **One infamous example:** Stephen Beachy. "Who is the Real JT LeRoy?" *New York* magazine, October 10, 2005. http://nymag.com/nymetro /news/people/features/14718/.

50 **Debbie Swenson, it appears:** Dianne Lynch, "Beautiful Cancer Victim a Hoax," ABCNews.com, May 30, 2001, http://abcnews.go.com/Tech -nology/story?id=98503.

50 **"Rest in peace, kind, bright, wonderful soul":** "y6y6y6," on MetaFil ter.com, May 15, 2001, 5:29 p.m., http://www.metafilter.com/7704 /Godspeed-Kaycee-Nicole.

50 **"My mind is kinda blurry now":** "halcyon," on MetaFilter.com, May 15, 2001, 7:47 p.m., http://www.metafilter.com/7704/Godspeed-Kaycee -Nicole.

50 **"Is it possible that Kaycee did not exist?":** "acridrabbit," on MetaFilter .com, May 19, 2001, 1:00 a.m., http://www.metafilter.com/7819/Is-it -possible-that-Kaycee-did-not-exist.

50 **"STOP! STOP!! STOP!!! this is deplorable":** "bwg," on MetaFilter .com, May 19, 2001, 2:30 a.m, http://www.metafilter.com/7819/Is-it -possible-that-Kaycee-did-not-exist.

51 **a syndrome that's now called "virtual factitious disorder":** M. D. Feldman et al., "'Virtual' factitious disorders and Munchausen by proxy," *Western Journal of Medicine* 168, no. 6 (June 1998), 537.

51 **"Munchausen by internet":** Jenny Kleeman, "Sick note: Faking illness online," *Guardian*, February 25, 2011.

51 **"Online, one can quickly acquire an education":** Jenn Shreve, "They Think They Feel Your Pain," Wired.com, June 6, 2001, http://www .wired.com/medtech/health/news/2001/06/44245.

52 **John Lott, a gun researcher, created a fake student:** Julian Sanchez, "The Mystery of Mary Rosh," *Reason*, May 2003. See also Chris Mooney, "Double-Barreled Double Standards," MotherJones.com, October 13, 2003, http://www.motherjones.com/politics/2003/10/double -barreled-double-standards, and Tim Lambert, "Mary Rosh's Blog," Scienceblogs.com, January 21, 2003, http://scienceblogs.com/deltoid /2003/01/21/maryrosh/.

52 **Amazon reviews are a common leitmotif:** David Streitfelt, "Giving Mom's Book Five Stars? Amazon May Cull Your Review," *New York Times*, December 22, 2012.

52 **Bing Liu, a computer scientist at the University of Illinois:** David Streitfelt, "The Best Book Reviews Money Can Buy," *New York Times*, August 25, 2012.

52 **R. J. Ellory used a brigade of sockpuppets:** Andrew Hough, "RJ Ellory: detected, crime writer who faked his own glowing reviews," *The Telegraph* (UK), September 2, 2012.

52 **Professor Orlando Figes, an esteemed British historian:** Alexandra Topping, "Historian Orlando Figes agrees to pay damages for fake reviews," *Guardian*, July 16, 2010.

52 **"he has a certified genius I.Q.":** Scott Adams (writing as "planned-chaos"), on MetaFilter.com, April 14, 2011, 4:06 p.m., http://www.metafilter.com/102472/How-to-Get-a-Real-Education-by-Scott-Adams

52 **"Welcome to Metafilter, Scott!":** "StrikeTheViol," on MetaFilter.com, April 14, 2011, 4:38 p.m. http://www.metafilter.com/102472/How-to-Get-a-Real-Education-by-Scott-Adams

52 **Journalists like *The New Republic*'s Lee Siegel and the *Los Angeles Times*'s Michael Hiltzik were disciplined:** Maria Aspan, "New Republic Suspends Editor for Attack on Blog." *New York Times*, September 4, 2006. http://www.nytimes.com/2006/09/04/technology/04republic.html.

53 **"one or more people created two false identities":** Jennifer Preston, "Fake Identities Were Used on Twitter in Effort to Get Information on Weiner," *New York Times*, June 17, 2011.

54 **In 2012, Raymond Kelly, commissioner of the New York City Police Department:** Rocco Parascandola, "New York Police Dept. issues first rules for use of social media during investigations," *New York Daily News*, September 11, 2012.

54 **In a few years, she managed to become the online friend:** Henry Copeland, "Are you exposing your private parts to strangers on Facebook?" BlogAds.com, June 8, 2011, http://web.blogads.com/blog/2011/06/08/are-you-also-exposing-your-private-parts-to-strangers-on-facebook/#axzz2htwkHFCe.

54 **"it seems likely that our conversations are being spied on"**: Copeland, "Are you exposing."

55 **In March 2012, unknown parties:** Nick Hopkins, "China suspected of Facebook attack on Nato's supreme allied commander," *Guardian*, March 10, 2012.

55 **signed a $2.76 million contract:** Nick Fielding and Ian Cobain, "Revealed: US spy operation that manipulates social media," *Guardian*, March 17, 2011.

55 **"replete with background, history, supporting details":** Department of the Air Force, "Persona Management Software," Solicitation Number RTB220610.

CHAPTER 4: THE LONELINESS OF THE INTERCONNECTED

64 **"It is unlikely that one isolated believer":** Leon Festinger and Henry W. Riecken, *When Prophecy Fails* (London: Pinter & Martin, 2008; first published 1956 by University of Minnesota Press), 4.

67 **As of 2013, the video had been viewed:** "raze7ds," "Star Wars Kid," YouTube.com, January 15, 2006, http://www.youtube.com/watch?v= HPPj6viIBmU.

68 **The name Morgellons was coined by Mary Leitao:** Elizabeth Devita-Raeburn, "The Morgellons Mystery," *Psychology Today*, March 1, 2007.

68 **the CDC received about twelve hundred reports of Morgellons:** Centers for Disease Control and Prevention, "Press Briefing Transcripts: CDC to Launch Study on Unexplained Illness," January 16, 2008, http://www.cdc.gov/media/transcripts/2008/t080116.htm.

68 **"shares a number of clinical and epidemiologic features":** Michele L. Pearson et al., "Clinical, Epidemiologic, Histopathologic, and Molecular Features of an Unexplained Dermopathy," *PLOS One* 7, no. 1 (January 2012), e29908, doi:10.1371/journal.pone.0029908.

69 **"a belief is not considered delusional":** Fidel Vila-Rodriguez and Bill MacEwen, "Delusional Parasitosis Facilitated by Web-Based Dissemination," *American Journal of Psychiatry* 165, no. 12 (December 2008), 1612, doi:10.1176/appi.ajp.2008.08081283.

71 **In 1980, roughly 90 percent of prime-time television watchers:** Douglas Blanks Hindman and Kenneth Wiegand, "The Big Three's Prime-Time Decline: A Technological and Social Context," *Journal of*

Broadcasting and Electronic Media 52, no. 1 (March 2008), 119, doi: 10 .1080/08838150701820924.

71 **the Big Three's evening news programs have lost 55 percent:** Emily Guskin et al., "Network News: Durability and Decline," in Pew Research Center, *The State of the News Media 2011,* http://stateofthemedia .org/2011/network-essay.

74 **soundly rejected by the scientific community:** See, for example, Richard Horton, "Will Duesberg Now Concede Defeat?" *The Lancet,* September 9, 1995, p. 656.

75 **"Many in our country have called":** Thabo Mbeki, Address to the National Council of Provinces, Cape Town, October 28, 1999, http:// www.dfa.gov.za/docs/speeches/1999/mbek1028.htm.

75 **almost 13 percent of the population:** UNAIDS, *Report on the Global HIV/AIDS Epidemic,* June 1998, http://www.unaids.org/en/media /unaids/contentassets/dataimport/pub/report/1998/19981125_global _epidemic_report_en.pdf.

75 **"To understand this matter better":** Mbeki, Address to the National Council.

75 **"Mark Lurie . . . was 'flabbergasted'":** Adele Sulcas and Estelle Randall, "Mbeki sparks row over AIDS drug," *Sunday Independent,* October 30, 1999, http://www.iol.co.za/news/south-africa/mbeki-sparks-row -over-aids-drug-1.17874?ot=inmsa.ArticlePrintPageLayout.ot.

76 **A 2008 study in the *Journal of*:** Pride Chigwedere et al., "Estimating the lost benefits of antiretroviral drug use in South Africa," *Journal of Acquired Immune Deficiency Syndromes,* 49, no. 4 (December 1, 2008), 410–415.

CHAPTER 5: COPY, RIGHT?

78 **The writer set up a famous unsolved problem:** John L. Casti, *Mathematical Mountaintops* (New York: Oxford University Press, 2001), 165.

79 **A year earlier, I had written:** Charles Seife, "Is that your final equation?" *Science,* May 26, 2000, 1328.

79 **the Oxford book was chock-full:** Edward Rothstein, "Plagiarism That Doesn't Add Up," *New York Times,* March 9, 2002.

85 **an internal memo at *The Washington Post*:** Andrew Beaujon, "Washington Post seeks blogger for Style section," Poynter.org, March

20, 2013, http://www.poynter.org/latest-news/mediawire/207858/washington
-post-seeks-blogger-to-post-at-least-12-times-per-day/.

85 **"At its best, aggregation can mean collecting stories":** Patrick B. Pexton, "The Post fails a young blogger," WashingtonPost.com, April 20, 2012, http://articles.washingtonpost.com/2012-04-20/opinions/35454516 _1_aggregation-web-links-international-stories.

85 **"[Flock] did a roundup on Republican presidential candidate Mitt Romney":** Pexton, "The Post fails a young blogger."

87 **an article in the *Proceedings of the National Academy of Sciences*:** Darby Proctor et al., "Chimpanzees play the ultimatum game," PNAS .org, January 14, 2013, doi: 10.1073/pnas.1220806110.

87 **The *Daily Mail* quoted one of the researchers:** Nick McDermott, "Fair play: Scientists find chimpanzees have a similar sense of fairness to humans," *Daily Mail*, January 14, 2013.

87 **The *Telegraph* also got a quotation:** Telegraph reporters, "Chimpanzees have 'sense of fairness,'" *The Telegraph*, January 15, 2013.

87 **"commentary and opinion are far more prevalent":** Mark Jurkowitz et al. for the Pew Research Center, "The State of the News Media 2013— The Changing TV News Landscape." http://stateofthemedia.org/2013 /the-changing-tv-news-landscape/

88 **Agence France-Presse quoted Frans de Waal:** "Chimps possess a sense of 'fairness,'" Agence France-Presse, January 15, 2013.

88 **cut and pasted from a press release issued by Emory:** Lisa Newbern, "Chimpanzees successfully play the Ultimatum Game," press release, Emory University, January 14, 2013.

88 **Of the fourteen distinct versions:** In addition to the *Daily Mail*, *Telegraph*, and Agence France-Presse versions cited above, I found: Victoria Gill, "Sharing: Chimp study reveals origin of human fair play," BBC.co.uk, January 14, 2013, http://www.bbc.co.uk/news /science-environment-20973753; Tia Ghose, "Chimpanzees have a sense of fairness," CBSNews.com/LiveScience.com, January 15, 2013, http:// www.livescience.com/26245-chimps-value-fairness.html; Press Association, "Chimpanzees Have Sense of Fair Play Similar to That of Humans Say Researchers," HuffingtonPost.co.uk; January 14, 2013, http:// www.huffingtonpost.co.uk/2013/01/14/chimps-fair-play_n_2472799 .html; Amina Khan, "Hunger Games: Chimps play fair—when it suits them," LATimes.com, January 15, 2013, http://articles.latimes.com

/2013/jan/15/science/la-sci-sn-hunger-games-chimpanzees-play-fair -study-pnas-20130114; Ed Yong, "Do chimpanzees care about fairness? The jury's out," NationalGeographic.com, January 14, 2013, http://phe nomena.nationalgeographic.com/2013/01/14/do-chimpanzees -care-about-fairness-the-jurys-out/; Alan Boyle, "Do chimps have a sense of fair play? Study adds to an evolutionary debate," NBCNews .com, January 14, 2013, http://www.nbcnews.com/science/do-chimps -have-sense-fair-play-study-adds-evolutionary-debate-1B7968843; Bruce Bower, "Claims of fairness in apes have critics crying foul," *Sci enceNews.org*, January 14, 2013, https://www.sciencenews.org/article /claims-fairness-apes-have-critics-crying-foul; "Chimps and humans share sense of fair play," News.Sky.com, January 15, 2013, http://news .sky.com/story/1038020/chimps-and-humans-share-sense-of-fair-play; Nolan Feeney, "Chimps can play fair, too," Healthland.Time.com, January 14, 2013, http://healthland.time.com/2013/01/14/chimps-can-play-fair -too/; "Chimpanzees, Like Humans, Seem to Have Sense of Fairness." *U.S.News/HealthDay*, January 14, 2013; and Michael Balter, "Chimps might have a sense of fair play," Wired.com/ScienceNOW, January 15, 2013, http://www.wired.com/wiredscience/2013/01/chimp-fairness/.

88 **only six would have lived up to the standards of minimally competent:** BBC News, CBS, *National Geographic*, NBC, *Science News*, and *Wired* were the six that bothered to speak to an outside source, meeting (and in some cases far exceeding) the minimum standard. *Time* apparently interviewed one of the authors but not any outsiders. The remaining seven appear not to have performed any interviews at all.

89 **"lifted material from press releases verbatim":** "Star dismisses columnist Steve Penn," *Kansas City Star*, July 12, 2011.

89 **"training (and the widespread practice at the *Star*)":** *Steve Penn v. McClatchy Newspapers, Inc. d/b/a The Kansas City Star*, Circuit Court of Jackson County, Kansas.

89 **"I had no intention of replicating someone else's work":** Julie Moos, "WUSA removes story from website after discovering parts of it came from the Washington Post," Poynter.org, December 23, 2011, http:// www.poynter.org/latest-news/mediawire/157246/wusa-removing -story-from-website-after-plagiarism-inquiries/.

89 **illegal "covert propaganda" campaigns:** Government Accountability Office, "Video News Releases: Unattributed Prepackaged News Stories

Violate Publicity or Propaganda Prohibition," Testimony before the
Committee on Commerce, Science, and Transportation, May 12, 2005.
GAO-05-643T, http:// www.gao.gov/new.items/d05643t.pdf.

90 **First came accusations:** Ed Champion, "How Jonah Lehrer Recycled
His Own Material for *Imagine*," EdRants.com, June 20, 2012, http://www
.edrants.com/how-jonah-lehrer-recycled-his-own-material-for-imagine/.

91 **Lehrer recycled so much of his prose so often:** Charles Seife, "Jonah
Lehrer's Journalistic Misdeeds at Wired.com," Slate.com, August 31,
2012, http://www.slate.com/articles/health_and_science/science/2012
/08/jonah_lehrer_plagiarism_in_wired_com_an_investigation
_into_plagiarism_quotes_and_factual_inaccuracies_.html.

91 **Then he got caught making up Bob Dylan quotations:** Michael Moynihan,
"Jonah Lehrer's Deceptions," TabletMag.com, July 30, 2012, http://www.tab
letmag.com/jewish-news-and-politics/107779/jonah-lehrers-deceptions.

91 **Why, yes. There were:** Seife, "Jonah Lehrer's Journalistic Misdeeds."

91 **Lehrer had written on Wired.com:** Jonah Lehrer, "The Difficulty of
Loving Strangers," Wired.com, January 12, 2011, http://www.wired
.com/wiredscience/2011/01/the-difficulty-of-loving-strangers/.

92 **Lehrer had described the same case:** Jonah Lehrer, "Ritalin in the
Water," Wired.com, August 6, 2010, http://www.wired.com/wired
-science/2010/08/ritalin-in-the-water/.

92 **Lehrer also got some substantial details of this anecdote wrong:**
Daniel Bor, "What Jonah Lehrer reveals about popular science writing," DanielBor.com, August 1, 2012.

92 **He's apparently writing a new book:** Daniel Engber, "Update: Jonah
Lehrer Sold His New Book." Slate.com, June 4, 2013.

93 **In 1980, there were 1.25 flacks for every journalist:** John Sullivan, "PR
Industry Fills Vacuum Left by Shrinking Newsrooms," ProPublica.org,
May 1, 2011, http://www.propublica.org/article/pr-industry-fills-vacuum
-left-by-shrinking-newsrooms. See also "Slime Slinging: Flacks vastly
outnumber hacks these days. Caveat lector," *The Economist*, May 19, 2011.

CHAPTER 5½: SCARCITY

94 **Some fourteen billion shells:** Jan Hogendorn and Marion Johnson,
The Shell Money of the Slave Trade, 139.

95 **"It is our misfortune to live through":** Clay Shirky, "The Shock of Inclu-
sion," Edge.org, January 2010. http://www.edge.org/response-detail/11609.

CHAPTER 6: ALL HAT, NO CATTLE

99 **"the media arm of the Iranian Revolutionary Guards":** Mike Nizza and Patrick Lyons, "In an Iranian Image, a Missile Too Many," NY Times.com, July 10, 2008, http://thelede.blogs.nytimes.com/2008/07/10/in-an-iranian-image-a-missile-too-many/.

100 **an undoctored photo:** Nizza and Lyons, "In an Iranian Image."

100 **"Iran: You Suck at Photoshop":** Xeni Jardin, "Iran: You Suck at Photoshop," BoingBoing.net, July 10, 2008, http://boingboing.net/2008/07/10/iran-you-suck-at-pho.html.

103 **"It's all so easy with Photoshop":** Mike Rossner and Kenneth Yamada, "What's in a picture? The temptation of image manipulation," *Journal of Cell Biology* 166, no. 1 (July 6, 2004), 11.

104 **image-manipulation cases made up less than 3 percent:** John Krueger, "Incidences of ORI Cases Involving Falsified Images," *Office of Research Integrity Newsletter,* September 2009, 3. Also John Krueger, "Confronting Manipulation of Digital Images in Science," *Office of Research Integrity Newsletter,* June 2005, 8.

104 **four of seven figures had been manipulated:** The University of Minnesota, "Statement from the University of Minnesota: University Misconduct Panel Concludes that Certain Data in Stem Cell Paper Were Falsified," https://www.google.com/url?q=http://www.mndaily.com/sites/default/files/U%2520of%2520MN%2520Investigation%2520Statement.doc. See also Peter Aldhous, "Stem-cell researcher guilty of falsifying data," *New Scientist,* October 7, 2008.

105 **I want to lessen my exposure:** Bob Grant, "Editors quit after fake paper flap," *Scientist,* June 11, 2009.

105 **"I received solicitations for journals":** Peter Aldhous, "CRAP paper accepted by journal," *New Scientist,* September 28, 2008.

106 **classified as a . . . "predatory . . . publisher":** Jeffrey Beall, "Beall's List," Scholarly Open Access, http://scholarlyoa.com/publishers.

107 **"[New Word City's] ebooks appear regularly":** "About New Word City," http://www.newwordcity.com/about.

107 **"Churchill struggled to overcome a speech impediment":** The editors of New Word City, *Winston Churchill: A Life* (New Word City, Inc., 2012), Kindle edition.

108 **claims he can write one in about twenty minutes:** Marc Abrahams, "Speed writing," *Guardian*, January 28, 2008. See also Marc Abrahams, "Automatic writing," *Guardian*, February 4, 2008.

109 **"[Kindle Direct Publishing] gives you everything":** Amazon.com, "Self-Publish With Us," http://www.amazon.com/gp/seller-account /mm-summary-page.html?topic=200260520.

110 **The book consisted of one word:** Catherine Eccles, "The Kindle Basics," posted by Nicholas Clee, BookBrunch.co.uk, July 28, 2011, http:// www.bookbrunch.co.uk/bbrunch/pid/article_free/the_kindle_basics.

110 **Once her minimum opus was mentioned in the *Evening Standard*:** Catherine Eccles, *The Kindle Basics.*

111 **Penguin . . . acquired Author Solutions:** Julie Bosman, "Penguin Acquires Self-Publishing Company," NYTimes.com, July 19, 2012, http:// mediadecoder.blogs.nytimes.com/2012/07/19/penguin-acquires-self -publishing-company/.

112 **some deceptive editing:** Scott Baker, "Does Raw Video of NPR Exposé Reveal Questionable Editing & Tactics?" TheBlaze.com, March 10, 2011, http://www.theblaze.com/stories/2011/03/10/does-raw-video-of -npr-expose-reveal-questionable-editing-tactics/.

CHAPTER 7: WHITE NOISE AND THE RED QUEEN

114 **We are at the beginning of an information famine:** This passage is modeled in part after my 2009 essay "Malthusian Information Famine," http://www.edge.org/q2009/q09_6.html#seife.

115 **current estimates run around 75 percent:** Kaspersky Lab, "Spam report: April 2012," SecureList.com, May 17, 2012, http://www.securelist .com/en/analysis/204792230/.

115 **There are roughly two hundred million blogs:** The Nielsen Company, "Buzz in the Blogosphere: Millions More Bloggers and Blog Readers," Nielsen.com, March 8, 2012, http://www.nielsen.com/us/en/newswire /2012/buzz-in-the-blogosphere-millions-more-bloggers-and-blog -readers.html.

116 **According to internet legend:** Andrea Seabrook, "At 30, Spam Going Nowhere Soon," *All Things Considered*, National Public Radio, May 3, 2008.

116 **"Digital will be giving a product presentation":** Brad Templeton, "Reaction to the DEC Spam of 1978," http://www.templetons.com /brad/spamreact.html#msg.

118 **"Furthermore, recliner near gets stinking drunk":** This particular gem can be found at http://anendeavorinideas.wordpress.com/2004 /02/06/surreal-spam-poetry.

120 **to enslave more than half a million computers:** Criminal complaint in *United States of America v. Oleg Y. Nikolaenko*, 2:10-MJ-00093, United States District Court, Eastern District of Wisconsin. As part of a plea deal in early 2013, Nikolaenko admitted breaking antispam laws.

124 **roughly a third of all internet traffic to news sites:** Kenny Olmstead et al., "Navigating News Online," Pew Research Center, Journalism .org, May 9, 2011, http://www.journalism.org/2011/05/09/navigating -news-online/.

126 **"Better Never Than Late":** Gene Weingarten, "Gene Weingarten Column Mentions Lady Gaga," *Washington Post*, July 18, 2010.

127 **started gaming the system:** John Andrews, "The *New York Times* flexes its SEO Muscle," JohnOn.com, May 7, 2007, http://www.johnon .com/303/nytimescom.html.

127 **"A business strategy of *The New York Times* to get its articles":** Clark Hoyt, "When Bad News Follows You," *New York Times*, August 26, 2007.

128 **In 2011, J.C. Penney got caught doing just that:** David Segal, "The Dirty Little Secrets of Search," *New York Times*, February 12, 2011.

128 **the number-three hit:** Danny Sullivan, "Newspapers Amok! *New York Times* Spamming Google? *LA Times* Hijacking Cars.com?" Search EngineLand.com, May 8, 2007, http://searchengineland.com/newspapers -amok-new-york-times-spamming-google-la-times-hijacking -carscom-11169.

129 **a long original story:** Laura June, "For Amusement Only: the life and death of the American arcade," TheVerge.com, January 16, 2013, http:// www.theverge.com/2013/1/16/3740422/the-life-and-death-of-the -american-arcade-for-amusement-only.

129 ***The Huffington Post* promptly published:** John Herman, "Why Does Google Still Reward Content Scraping?" BuzzFeed.com, January 24, 2013, http://www.buzzfeed.com/jwherrman/why-does-google -still-reward-content-scraping.

129 ***The Huffington Post* used this feature to flag its own version:** Herman, "Why Does Google."

130 **sometimes crossing it:** Whet Moser, "Grand Theft HuffPo," Chicago Reader.com, December 18, 2008, http://www.chicagoreader.com/Bleader /archives/2008/12/18/grand-theft-huffpo.

130 **"as close to the front [of the article] as possible":** Seed Academy editors, "SEO and SEO Copywriting," Seed.com, November 12, 2009, http://academy.seed.com/2009/11/12/seo-and-seo-copywriting/.

131 **"carefully craft headlines to grab users' interest":** Nicholas Carlson, "Leaked: AOL's Master Plan," quoting America Online, "The AOL Way," BusinessInsider.com, February 1, 2011, http://www.businessin sider.com/the-aol-way.

131 **"identify in-demand topics":** Carlson, "Leaked."

133 **"My 'ideal' turn-around time":** Oliver Miller, "AOL Hell," *Faster Times*, June 16, 2011.

134 **"Newt Gingrich Gains Attention":** As quoted in Peter Kafka, "Twitter + Robots = Instant Stories, No Humans Required," AllThingsD.com, February 16, 2012, http://allthingsd.com/20120216/twitter-robots-instant -stories-no-humans-required/.

135 **an exposé on NPR's radio show:** Sarah Koenig, "Forgive us our press passes," *This American Life*, WBEZ, June 29, 2012.

135 **fired roughly twenty people:** Robert Channick, "Journatic to provide TribLocal suburban content," *Chicago Tribune*, April 23, 2012.

135 **articles that were plagiarized:** Vince Casanova, "*Chicago Tribune* suspends use of Journatic," *Chicago Tribune*, July 13, 2012.

135 **the *Trib* dropped Journatic in July 2012:** Casanova, "*Chicago Tribune* suspends."

135 **picked it back up in December:** Julie Moos, "*Chicago Tribune* resumes work with Journatic after 5-month suspension," Poynter.org, December 7, 2012, http://www.poynter.org/latest-news/mediawire /197429/chicago-tribune-resumes-work-with-journatic-after-5-month -suspension/.

136 **significant damage to the rankings of certain content farms:** Tim Chen, "Demand Media's eHow Slammed Again by Google's Panda 2," SeekingAlpha.com, June 22, 2011, http://seekingalpha.com/article/276218 -demand-medias-ehow-slammed-again-by-googles-panda-2. See also Matt McGee, "*New York Times*: Yes, Google's Panda Update Hit NYT-Owned About.com," SearchEngineLand.com, April 29, 2011, http:// searchengineland.com/googles-panda-update-hit-about-com-75145.

CHAPTER 8: ARTIFICIAL UNINTELLIGENCE

139 **"her photos were so attractive and her e-mails so warm"**: Robert Epstein, "From Russia with Love," *Scientific American Mind*, October/November 2007.

139 **"I have told to mine close friends about you"**: Epstein, "From Russia with Love."

140 **"asdf;kj as;kj l;jkj;j ;kasdkljk ;klkj 'klasdfk; asjdfkj"**: Epstein, "From Russia with Love."

140 **"I had been interacting for nearly four months with a computer program"**: Epstein, "From Russia with Love."

141 **Here's an online chat I had with an ELIZA clone**: This version is available at http://www.masswerk.at/elizabot/eliza.html.

143 **"IRC is a network full of chat rooms"**: Jake Kaufman (writing as "Virt"), "Jenny18—A Cybersex Bot Implemented in Eliza," http://virt.vgmix.com/jenny18.

143 **"3,800 responses on all sorts of topics"**: Kaufman, "Jenny18."

144 **"Scorpion832: do you have and nude pics"**: Jake Kaufman (writing as "Virt"), Scorpion832.txt chat log, http://virt.vgmix.com/jenny18/logs/Scorpion832.txt.

147 **"inactive, fake or fraudulent members"**: *David Robinson et al. v. Match.com LLC*, 3:10-CV-2651, United States District Court, Northern District of Texas.

147 **"These online dating sites allow you"**: "Online Dating Alert," Scambook TV, http://blip.tv/scambook/online-dating-alert-the-truth-about-singles-sites-like-xdating-christianmingle-and-seniorpeoplemeet-6395654.

149 **"I know we just met but these feelings"**: Chris Fuller, "Vanessa Bauer," http://scamwarners.com/forum/viewtopic.php?f=13&t=18327.

149 **"the best he could offer us"**: Fuller, "Vanessa Bauer."

150 **In 2007, Russia's "CyberLover"**: Ina Fried, "Warning sounded over 'flirting robots,'" CNET.com, December 7, 2007, http://news.cnet.com/8301-13860_3-9831133-56.html.

151 **Turing himself eschewed the word**: A. M. Turing, "Computing Machinery and Intelligence," *Mind*, October 1950, 433.

152 **"The development of congestion control"**: Rohollah Mosallahnezhad, "Cooperative, Compact Algorithms for Randomized Algorithms,"

Applied Mathematics and Computation (2007), doi:10.1016/j.amc.2007 .03.011 (since retracted by the editor of the journal).

154 **Facebook announced that 83 million profiles:** Mark Sweney, "Facebook quarterly report reveals 83m profiles are fake," *Guardian*, August 2, 2012. See also Facebook Inc. 10-Q, filed 7/31/2012, p. 47, which states that 8.7 percent of user accounts are duplicate, fake, misclassified, or undesirable.

156 **Danny Sheridan, a sports analyst, was accused of buying thousands of Twitter users:** John Koblin, "Is *USA Today*'s Veteran Gambling Guy Buying Twitter Followers?" Deadspin.com, June 29, 2012, http://dead -spin.com/5921915/is-usa-todays-veteran-gambling-guy-buying -twitter-followers.

156 **[Sheridan] denied the charge:** Bob Velin, "Sports analyst Sheridan denies buying Twitter followers." USAToday.com, June 27, 2012, http:// content.usatoday.com/communities/gameon/post/2012/06/sports -analyst-sheridan-denies-buying-twitter-followers/1.

156 **James O'Keefe had his twenty-thousand-odd followers:** "Anomaly," "Just James 'the pimp' O'Keefe buying Twitter followers by the thousands," FreakOutNation.com, August 31, 2012, http://freakoutnation .com/2012/08/31/just-james-the-pimp-okeefe-buying-twitter -followers-by-the-thousands/.

156 **"Clever tactic of whoever considers me an enemy":** James O'Keefe, Twitter post, August 31, 2012, 3:46 p.m., twitter.com/jameso keefeiii.

156 **first major presidential hopeful to announce his candidacy:** Arlette Saenz, "Newt Gingrich Campaign Pushes Back on Fake Twitter Followers' Accusation," ABCNews.go.com, August 2, 2011, http://abcnews .go.com/blogs/politics/2011/08/newt-gingrich-campaign-pushes -back-on-fake-twitter-followers-accusation/.

156 **"I have six times as many Twitter followers":** Jon Gillooly, "Gingrich: I'm not giving up," MDJOnline.com, July 31, 2011, http://www.mdjon line.com/view/full_story/14902000/article-Gingrich--I-m-not -giving-up.

157 **"Newt Gingrich's [8 percent] was the lowest we had ever seen":** "Follower Gate: PeekYou Analysis Supports ex-Gingrich Staffer Claims of Twitter Follower Fraud," PeekYou.com, August 2, 2011, http://blog.peek you.com/follower-gate-peekyou-analysis-supports-ex-gingrich

-staffer-claims-of-follower-fraud/. [Defunct link, but presently available through www.archive.org.]

157 **spambots attempted to drown out anti-PRI voices:** Manuel Rueda, "Mexico: Twitterbots sabotage anti-PRI protest," *Univision News*, May 21, 2012.

CHAPTER 9: MAKE MONEY FAST

160 **"Nobody knows how many people have been cheated":** "An Old Swindle Revived," *New York Times*, March 20, 1898.

160 **hundreds of millions of dollars:** U.S. Department of State, "Nigerian Advance Fee Fraud," Department of State Publication 10465, April 1997.

160 **"thin, blue, cross-lined paper":** "An Old Swindle Revived," *New York Times*.

163 **Thomas Katona, the treasurer of Alcona County:** Michigan Attorney General's Office, "Former Alcona County Treasurer Charged with Embezzling Public Monies," press release, January 17, 2007.

163 **"not far removed from the classic, laughable Nigerian scams":** Mike Kilen, "Whirlpool of lies swallows Mezvinsky," *Des Moines Register*, August 3, 2003.

163 **In 1957, an episode of *Alfred Hitchcock Presents*:** The episode is "Mail Order Prophet," which first aired on October 13, 1957.

164 **In 2006, scholars estimated:** Laura Frieder and Jonathan Zitrain, "Spam Works: Evidence from Stock Touts and Corresponding Market Activity," Berkman Center Research Publication No. 2006-11, March 14, 2007.

165 **CR Intrinsic, a hedge fund, agreed to pay:** United States Securities and Exchange Commission, "CR Intrinsic agrees to pay more than $600 million in largest-ever settlement for insider trading case," press release, March 15, 2013. See also *Securities and Exchange Commission v. CR Intrinsic Investors, LLC, et al.*, Civil Action No. 12 CIV 8466, Southern District of New York, March 15, 2013.

166 **A classic case occurred in 1963:** *Securities and Exchange Commission v. Texas Gulf Sulphur Company*, No. 65, CIV 1182, Southern District of New York, August 19, 1966.

166 **"During the past few days, the exploration activities":** *Securities and Exchange Commission v. Texas Gulf Sulphur Company*.

167 **In late 1983, Winans struck a deal:** *United States of America v. R. Foster Winans, et al.*, No. 84 CR 605, Southern District of New York, June 24, 1985.

168 **typically over the space of a week:** Guolin Jiang et al., "Market Manipulation: A Comprehensive Study of Stock Pools," *Journal of Financial Economics*, forthcoming, available at http://ssrn.com/abstract=663513.

171 **executing some twenty-seven thousand trades in fourteen seconds:** United States Commodity Futures Trading Commission and United States Securities and Exchange Commission, "Findings regarding the market events of May 26, 2010," September 30, 2010.

171 **nearly 80 percent of all trades on the U.S. stock market:** Frank Zhang, "High-Frequency Trading, Stock Volatility, and Price Discovery," December 2010, http://dx.doi.org/10.2139/ssrn.1691679.

CHAPTER 10: THIS IS YOUR BRAIN...

176 **luckily for the liver fluke:** See David Hughes et al., *Host Manipulation by Parasites* (Oxford, UK: Oxford University Press, 2012), e.g., 2–6.

177 **it appears to make the fish bolder:** N. Giles, "Behavioural effects of the parasite Schistocephalus solidus (Cestoda) on an intermediate host, the three-spined stickleback, Gasterosteus aculeatus L," *Animal Behavior*, November 1983, 1193.

177 **"surfacing, flashing, contorting":** Kevin D. Lafferty and A. Kimo Morris, "Altered Behavior of Parasitized Killifish Increases Susceptibility to Predation by Bird Final Hosts," *Ecology* 77, no. 5 (July 1996), 1391.

178 *Toxoplasma gondii:* See Carl Zimmer, "The Return of the Puppet Masters," Discover.com, January 17, 2006, http://blogs.discovermagazine.com/loom/2006/01/17/the-return-of-the-puppet-masters/.

178 **played by more than sixty million users:** Jack Arnott, "FarmVille: Who knew boredom could be a cash crop?" *Guardian*, November 11, 2009.

179 **"hardly even a game":** Dan Fletcher, "The 50 Worst Inventions: FarmVille," *Time*, May 27, 2010.

179 **"fun pain":** Betable Blog, "Roger Dickey's Tactics for Game Monetization," Gamasutra.com, November 29, 2011, http://www.gamasutra.com/blogs/TylerYork/20111129/9000/.

180 **on track to earn roughly a billion dollars:** Zynga, prospectus filed pursuant to rule 424(b)(4), December 15, 2011.

180 **"But then when you look at the design process":** Simon Parkin, "Catching up with Jonathan Blow," Gamasutra.com, December 6, 2010, http://www.gamasutra.com/view/feature/134595/catching_up _with_jonathan_blow.php?print=1.

182 **"*Cow Clicker* developed an active player base":** Leigh Alexander, "The Life-Changing $20 Rightward-Facing Cow," Kotaku.com, October 3, 2011, http://kotaku.com/5846080/the-life+changing-20-rightward +facing-cow.

183 **"It wasn't very fun before.":** Alexander, "Rightward-Facing Cow."

183 **"amazing" and "life changing":** David Lynch, "Peter Molyneux: Life During and After Curiosity," NowGamer.com, November 13, 2012, http://www.nowgamer.com/features/1677386/peter_molyneux_life _during_and_after_curiosity.html.

184 **the pigeons had become superstitious:** See B. F. Skinner, "'Superstition' in the pigeon," *Journal of Experimental Psychology* 38, no. 2 (April 1948), 168–72.

185 **"We're capturing all the analytical data":** Keith Andrew, "Molyneux: Curiosity's monetization will be 'part of the experiment,'" PocketGamer.biz, August 11, 2012, http://www.pocketgamer.biz/r/PG.Biz /22Cans+news/news.asp?c=46449.

188 **"[help] you and your friends make the most of where you are":** "About Foursquare," Foursquare.com, https://foursquare.com/about.

188 **"Happiness Quest":** Victor Luckerson, "Let the Gamification Begin," *Time*, November 14, 2012.

CHAPTER 11: LIVING IN THE RAW

193 **"On February 1, 1999, Chris Metzler":** "My dinner last night." Posted by Chris Metzler on rec.sport.football.college, February 9, 1999.

195 **"In addition to being almost universally wrong":** David Montgomery et al., "Police, citizens, and technology factor into Boston bombing probe," *Washington Post*, April 29, 2013.

195 **"chaotic free-for-all":** Montgomery et al., "Police, citizens."

196 **A tweet revealed:** Alexis Madrigal, "It wasn't Sunil Tripathi: The Anatomy of a Misinformation Disaster," TheAtlantic.com, April 19, 2013,

http://www.theatlantic.com/technology/archive/2013/04/it-wasnt
-sunil-tripathi-the-anatomy-of-a-misinformation-disaster/275155/.

APPENDIX: THE TOP TEN DICTA OF THE INTERNET SKEPTIC

204 **"to express yourself and connect with the world around you"**: Facebook, 10-K filing for the fiscal year ended December 31, 2012.

BIBLIOGRAPHY

Abrahams, Marc. "Automatic writing." *The Guardian,* February 4, 2008.

———. "Speed writing." *Guardian,* January 28, 2008.

Aldhous, Peter. "CRAP paper accepted by journal." *New Scientist,* September 28, 2008.

———. "Stem-cell researcher guilty of falsifying data." *New Scientist,* October 7, 2008.

Alexander, Leigh. "The Life-Changing $20 Rightward-Facing Cow." Kotaku.com, October 3, 2011.

"An Old Swindle Revived." *New York Times,* March 20, 1898.

Anderson, David. "New-look Manchester City side begin their UEFA Cup campaign in earnest." *Daily Mirror* (UK), September 18, 2008.

Andrew, Keith. "Molyneux: Curiosity's monetization will be 'part of the experiment.'" PocketGamer.biz, August 11, 2012.

Applebaum, Yoni. "How the Professor Who Fooled Wikipedia Got Caught by Reddit." TheAtlantic.com, May 15, 2012.

Arnott, Jack. "FarmVille: Who knew boredom could be a cash crop?" *Guardian,* November 11, 2009.

Aspan, Maria. "New Republic Suspends Editor for Attack on Blog," *New York Times,* September 4, 2006.

Balicer, Ron D. "Modeling Infectious Diseases Dissemination Through Online Role-Playing Games." *Epidemiology,* March 2007, 260–61.

Beachy, Stephen. "Who is the Real JT LeRoy?" *New York*, October 10, 2005.

Beaujon, Andrew. "*Washington Post* seeks blogger for Style section." Poynter.org, March 20, 2013.

Betable Blog, "Roger Dickey's Tactics for Game Monetization." Gamasutra.com, November 29, 2011. www.gamasutra.com/blogs/TylerYork/20111129/9000.

"Bin Laden's Felt-Skinned Henchman." FoxNews.com, October 14, 2011.

Blue, Violet. "Corruption in Wikiland?" CNET.com, September 18, 2012.

Boehlert, Eric. "James O'Keefe and the myth of the ACORN pimp." MediaMatters.org, February 17, 2010.

Bor, Daniel. "What Jonah Lehrer reveals about popular science writing." DanielBor.com, August 1, 2012.

Borland, John. "See Who's Editing Wikipedia." Wired.com, August 14, 2007.

Bosman, Julie. "Penguin Acquires Self-Publishing Company." NYTimes.com, July 19, 2012.

"Canadian pundit, Wikipedia founder in messy breakup." CBC.ca, March 2, 2008.

Carbonell, Linda. "An apology to our readers about Amina Arraf." LezGet Real.com, June 10, 2011, as captured by Google Cache on June 14, 2010.

Carlson, Nicholas. "Leaked: AOL's Master Plan." BusinessInsider.com, February 1, 2011.

Casanova, Vince. "*Chicago Tribune* suspends use of Journatic." *Chicago Tribune*, July 13, 2012.

Casti, John L. *Mathematical Mountaintops*. New York: Oxford University Press, 2001.

Champion, Ed. "How Jonah Lehrer Recycled His Own Material for Imagine." EdRants.com, June 20, 2012.

Channick, Robert. "Journatic to provide TribLocal suburban content." *Chicago Tribune*, April 23, 2012.

Chen, Tim. "Demand Media's eHow Slammed Again by Google's Panda 2." SeekingAlpha.com, June 22, 2011.

Chigwedere, Pride, et al. "Estimating the lost benefits of antiretroviral drug use in South Africa." *Journal of Acquired Immune Deficiency Syndromes* 49, no. 4 (December 1, 2008), 410–15.

Cohen, Noam. "After False Claim, Wikipedia to Check Degrees." *New York Times*, March 12, 2007.

Colbert, Stephen. *The Colbert Report*, July 31, 2006.

Copeland, Henry. "Are you exposing your private parts to strangers on Facebook?" BlogAds.com, June 8, 2011.

Devita-Raeburn, Elizabeth. "The Morgellons Mystery." *Psychology Today*, March 1, 2007.

Donadio, Rachel, and Nicholas Kulish. "A Statement Rocks Rome, Then Sends Shockwaves Around the World." *New York Times*, February 11, 2013.

Eccles, Catherine. "The Kindle Basics." Posted by Nicholas Clee. Book Brunch.co.uk, July 28, 2011.

Engber, Daniel. "Update: Jonah Lehrer Sold His New Book." Slate.com, June 4, 2013.

Epstein, Robert. "From Russia with Love." *Scientific American Mind*, October/November 2007.

Feldman, M. D., et al. "'Virtual' factitious disorders and Munchausen by proxy." *Western Journal of Medicine* 168, no. 6 (June 1998), 537–39.

Festinger, Leon, and Henry W. Riecken. *When Prophecy Fails*. London: Pinter & Martin, 2008. First published 1956 by University of Minnesota Press.

Fielding, Nick, and Ian Cobain. "Revealed: US spy operation that manipulates social media." *Guardian*, March 17, 2011.

Fine, Paul E. M. "Herd Immunity: History, Theory, Practice." *Epidemiologic Reviews* 15, no. 2 (1993), 265–302.

Fried, Ina. "Warning sounded over 'flirting robots.'" CNET.com, December 7, 2007.

Frieder, Laura, and Jonathan Zitrain. "Spam Works: Evidence from Stock Touts and Corresponding Market Activity." Berkman Center Research Publication No. 2006-11, March 14, 2007.

Gavin, Mike. "Phenom Trout brings his talents to Yankee Stadium." *Newsday*, July 14, 2012.

Giles, Jim. "Internet encyclopaedias go head to head." *Nature*, December 15, 2005, 900–901.

Giles, N. "Behavioural effects of the parasite Schistocephalus solidus (Cestoda) on an intermediate host, the three-spined stickleback, Gasterosteus aculeatus L." *Animal Behavior*, November 1983, 1192–94.

Government Accountability Office. "Video News Releases: Unattributed Prepackaged News Stories Violate Publicity or Propaganda Prohibition."

Testimony before the Committee on Commerce, Science and Transportation, May 12, 2005. GAO-05-643T.

Graft, Kris. "GDC 2011: An Epidemiologist's View of *World of Warcraft*'s Corrupted Blood Plague." Gamasutra.com, February 28, 2011.

Grant, Bob. "Editors quit after fake paper flap." *The Scientist*, June 11, 2009.

Grossberg, Josh. "The Bert-Bin Laden Connection?" EOnline.com, October 10, 2011.

Guskin, Emily, et al. "Network News: Durability and Decline," in Pew Research Center, *The State of the News Media 2011*. http://stateofthemedia .org/2011/network-essay/

Hafner, Katie. "Corporate Editing of Wikipedia Revealed." *New York Times*, August 19, 2007.

Harris, David. "Syria: Gay blogger Amina Arraf seized by 3 men and now missing." VelociraptorOnZebra.blogspot.com, June 6, 2011.

Herman, John. "Why Does Google Still Reward Content Scraping?" BuzzFeed.com, January 24, 2013.

Hindman, Douglas Blanks, and Kenneth Wiegand. "The Big Three's Prime-Time Decline: A Technological and Social Context." *Journal of Broadcasting and Electronic Media*, March 2008, pp. 119–135.

Hopkins, Nick. "China suspected of Facebook attack on NATO's supreme allied commander." *Guardian*, March 10, 2012.

Horton, Richard. "Will Duesberg Now Concede Defeat?" *The Lancet*, September 9, 1995, 656.

Hough, Andrew. "RJ Ellory: detected, crime writer who faked his own glowing reviews." *The Telegraph* (UK), September 2, 2012.

Hoyt, Clark. "When Bad News Follows You." *New York Times*, August 26, 2007.

Hughes, David, et al. *Host Manipulation by Parasites*. Oxford: Oxford University Press, 2012.

Ignacio, Dino. "Bert Is Evil." FractalCow.com/bert, captured on December 11, 2001, by Archive.org.

Jiang, Guolin, et al. "Market Manipulation: A Comprehensive Study of Stock Pools." *Journal of Financial Economics*, forthcoming. http://ssrn .com/abstract=663513.

Jurkowitz, Mark, et al., "The Changing TV News Landscape," in Pew Research Center, *The State of the News Media 2013*. http://stateofthemedia .org/2013/the-changing-tv-news-landscape.

Kafka, Peter. "Twitter + Robots = Instant Stories, No Humans Required." AllThingsD.com, February 16, 2012.

Keyes, Scott. "Documentary proof: James O'Keefe's latest video is a fraud." ThinkProgress.org, May 18, 2012.

Kilen, Mike. "Whirlpool of lies swallows Mezvinsky." *Des Moines Register*, August 3, 2003.

Killoran, Ellen. "Gay Girl in Damascus Kidnapped: How Should U.S. Respond?" IBTimes.com, June 7, 2011.

Kleeman, Jenny. "Sick note: Faking illness online." *Guardian*, February 25, 2011.

Koenig, Sarah. "Forgive us our press passes." *This American Life*, WBEZ, June 29, 2012.

Koblin, John. "Is *USA Today*'s Veteran Gambling Guy Buying Twitter Followers?" Deadspin.com, June 29, 2012.

Krazit, Tom. "Engadget sends Apple stock plunging on iPhone rumor." CNET.com, May 16, 2007.

Krueger, John. "Confronting Manipulation of Digital Images in Science." *Office of Research Integrity Newsletter*, June 2005, 8–9.

———. "Incidences of ORI Cases Involving Falsified Images." *Office of Research Integrity Newsletter*, September 2009, 2–3.

Kurtz, Howard. "Scoop of the year." TheDailyBeast.com, February 25, 2013.

Lafferty, Kevin D., and A. Kimo Morris. "Altered Behavior of Parasitized Killifish Increases Susceptibility to Predation by Bird Final Hosts." *Ecology* 77, no. 5 (July 1996), 1390–97.

Lamb, Christina. "Seals tell of killing 'Bert' Laden." *Sunday Times* (UK), November 6, 2011.

Lambert, Tim. "Mary Rosh's Blog." ScienceBlogs.com, January 21, 2003.

Lehmann, Evan. "Rewriting history under the dome." *Lowell Sun*, January 27, 2006.

Lehrer, Jonah. "The Difficulty of Loving Strangers." Wired.com, January 12, 2011.

———. "Ritalin in the Water." Wired.com, August 6, 2010.

Lofgren, Eric, and Nina Fefferman. "The Untapped potential of virtual game worlds to shed light on real world epidemics." *The Lancet Infectious Diseases*, September 2007, 625–29.

Luckerson, Victor. "Let the Gamification Begin." *Time*, November 14, 2012.

Lynch, David. "Peter Molyneux: Life During and After Curiosity." Now Gamer.com, November 13, 2012.

Lynch, Dianne. "Beautiful Cancer Victim a Hoax." ABCNews.com, May 30, 2001.

MacMaster, Tom (writing as "Amina A."). DamascusGayGirl.BlogSpot .com, June 13, 2011.

Madrigal, Alexis. "It wasn't Sunil Tripathi: The Anatomy of a Misinformation Disaster." TheAtlantic.com, April 19, 2013.

Marsh, Katherine. "A Gay Girl in Damascus becomes a heroine of the Syrian revolt." *Guardian*, May 6, 2011.

Mbeki, Thabo. Address to the National Council of Provinces, Cape Town, October 28, 1999. http://www.dfa.gov.za/docs/speeches/1999/mbek1028 .htm.

McCullagh, Declan. "Osama has a new friend." Wired.com, October 10, 2011.

McGee, Matt. "*New York Times*: Yes, Google's Panda Update Hit NYT-Owned About.com." SearchEngineLand.com, April 29, 2011.

Metz, Cade. "Jimbo Wales dumps lover on Wikipedia." *The Register*, March 3, 2008.

Miller, Oliver. "AOL Hell." *Faster Times*, June 16, 2011.

Miller, Sam. "The Phenom." *ESPN The Magazine*, September 20, 2012.

Montgomery, David, et al. "Police, citizens, and technology factor into Boston bombing probe." *Washington Post*, April 29, 2013.

Mooney, Chris. "Double-Barreled Double Standards." MotherJones.com, October 13, 2003.

Moos, Julie. "*Chicago Tribune* resumes work with Journatic after 5-month suspension." Poynter.org, December 7, 2012.

———. "WUSA removes story from website after discovering parts of it came from the *Washington Post*." Poynter.org, December 23, 2011.

Moynihan, Michael. "Jonah Lehrer's Deceptions." TabletMag.com, July 30, 2012.

"'Muppet' producers miffed over Bert–bin Laden image." CNN.com, October 11, 2011.

Nizza, Mike, and Patrick Lyons. "In an Iranian Image, a Missile Too Many." NYTimes.com, July 10, 2008.

Olmstead, Kenny, et al. "Navigating News Online." Pew Research Center. Journalism.org, May 9, 2011.

Parascandola, Rocco. "New York Police Dept. issues first rules for use of social media during investigations." *New York Daily News*, September 11, 2012.

Parkin, Simon. "Catching up with Jonathan Blow." Gamasutra.com, December 6, 2010.

Pearson, Michele L., et al. "Clinical, Epidemiologic, Histopathologic, and Molecular Features of an Unexplained Dermopathy." *PLOS One* 7, no. 1 (January 2012), e29908.

Pexton, Patrick B. "The Post fails a young blogger." WashingtonPost.com, April 20, 2012.

Pogatchnik, Shawn. "Student hoaxes world's media on Wikipedia." Associated Press, May 12, 2009.

Preston, Jennifer. "Fake Identities Were Used on Twitter in Effort to Get Information on Weiner." *New York Times*, June 17, 2011.

Rossner, Mike, and Kenneth Yamada. "What's in a picture? The temptation of image manipulation." *Journal of Cell Biology*, July 6, 2004, 11–15.

Roth, Philip. "An Open Letter to Wikipedia." NewYorker.com, September 7, 2012.

Rothstein, Edward. "Plagiarism That Doesn't Add Up." *New York Times*, March 9, 2002.

Rueda, Manuel. "Mexico: Twitterbots sabotage anti-PRI protest." *Univision News*, May 21, 2012.

Saenz, Arlette. "Newt Gingrich Campaign Pushes Back on Fake Twitter Followers Accusation." ABCNews.go.com, August 2, 2011.

Sanchez, Julian. "The Mystery of Mary Rosh." *Reason*, May 2003.

Schiff, Stacy. "Know It All." *New Yorker*, July 31, 2008.

Seabrook, Andrea. "At 30, Spam Going Nowhere Soon." *All Things Considered*, National Public Radio, May 3, 2008.

Securities and Exchange Commission v. Texas Gulf Sulphur Company, No. 65 CIV 1182, Southern District of New York, August 19, 1966.

Sulcas, Adele, and Estelle Randall. "Mbeki sparks row over AIDS drug," *Sunday Independent*, October 30, 1999. http://www.iol.co.za/news/south-africa/mbeki-sparks-row-over-aids-drug-1.17874?ot=inmsa.ArticlePrintPageLayout.ot.

Sullivan, Danny. "Newspapers Amok! *New York Times* Spamming Google? *LA Times* Hijacking Cars.com?" SearchEngineLand.com, May 8, 2007.

Segal, David. "The Dirty Little Secrets of Search." *New York Times*, February 12, 2011.

Seife, Charles. "Is that your final equation?" *Science,* May 26, 2000, 1328–29.

——. "Jonah Lehrer's Journalistic Misdeeds at Wired.Com." Slate.com, August 31, 2012.

"Sesame Street character depicted with bin Laden on protest poster." Associated Press, October 11, 2011.

Shirky, Clay. *Here Comes Everybody.* New York: Penguin, 2008.

Shreve, Jenn. "They Think They Feel Your Pain." Wired.com, June 6, 2001.

"Slime Slinging: Flacks vastly outnumber hacks these days. Caveat lector." *The Economist,* May 19, 2011.

Streitfelt, David. "The Best Book Reviews Money Can Buy." *New York Times,* August 25, 2012.

——." Giving Mom's Book Five Stars? Amazon May Cull Your Review." *New York Times,* December 22, 2012.

Sullivan, John. "PR Industry Fills Vacuum Left by Shrinking Newsrooms." ProPublica.org, May 1, 2011.

Templeton, Brad. "Reaction to the DEC Spam of 1978." http://www.temple tons.com/brad/spamreact.html#msg.

Thomas, Owen. "The dirtiest Wikipedia sex chat you can imagine." Gawker .com, March 3, 2008.

Topping, Alexandra. "Historian Orlando Figes agrees to pay damages for fake reviews." *Guardian,* July 16, 2010.

Turing, A. M. "Computing Machinery and Intelligence." *Mind,* October 1950, 433–60.

UNAIDS. *Report on the Global HIV/AIDS Epidemic.* June 1998. http:// www.unaids.org/en/media/unaids/contentassets/dataimport/pub /report/1998/19981125_global_epidemic_report_en.pdf.

United States Commodity Futures Trading Commission and United States Securities and Exchange Commission. "Findings regarding the market events of May 26, 2010." September 30, 2010.

United States Department of State. "Nigerian Advance Fee Fraud." Department of State Publication 10465, April 1997.

United States of America v. R. Foster Winans, et al. No. 84, CR 605, Southern District of New York, June 24, 1985.

Van Heuvelen, Ben. "The Internet Is Making Us Stupid." Salon.com, November 7, 2007.

Velin, Bob. "Sports analyst Sheridan denies buying Twitter followers." USA Today.com, June 27, 2012.

Vila-Rodriguez, Fidel, and Bill MacEwen. "Delusional Parasitosis Facilitated by Web-Based Dissemination." *American Journal of Psychiatry* 165, no. 12 (December 2008), 1612.

Warren, Jamin. "Outbreak!" KillScreenDaily.com, April 18, 2011.

"Wiki boss 'edited for donation.'" BBC.co.uk, March 12, 2008.

"Wikipedia: List of Hoaxes on Wikipedia." http://en.wikipedia.org/wiki /Wikipedia:List_of_hoaxes_on_Wikipedia. Last visited April 7, 2013.

Zhang, Frank. "High-Frequency Trading, Stock Volatility, and Price Discovery." December 2010. http://dx.doi.org/10.2139/ssrn.1691679.

Ziebart, Andrew. "WoW Archivist: The Corrupted Blood plague." Joystiq .com, July 26, 2011.

Zimmer, Carl. "The Return of the Puppet Masters." Discover.com, January 17, 2006.

INDEX